Understanding Political Variables

THIRD EDITION

Understanding Political Variables

THIRD EDITION

William Buchanan
Washington and Lee University

Charles Scribner's Sons / New York

To Lanny and Dave and Mary
Who Helped

Copyright © 1980, 1974, 1969 Charles Scribner's Sons

Library of Congress Cataloging in Publication Data

Buchanan, William 1918-
 Understanding political variables.

Includes bibliographical references.
 1. Political science—Mathematical models.
I. Title.
JA73.B78 1980 320'.01'51 80-23707
ISBN 0-684-16673-9

3 5 7 9 11 13 15 17 19 Q/P 20 18 16 14 12 10 6 4

Printed in the United States of America

Contents

9 / NEW APPROACHES TO RESEARCH   *135*

10 / AVERAGES AND LEVELS OF MEASUREMENT   *149*

Foreword to the Instructor

When students advance beyond the purely institutional treatment of government that is characteristic of the high school course and undertake to study elections firsthand, to compare the outputs of governmental bodies, national, state, or local, and to examine accounts of politics couched in behavioral terms, they discover that they cannot read essential portions of the literature of the social sciences. They do not understand the meaning of certain words (Guttman scaling, coefficient of determination, *beta* weight) and symbolic expressions ($\chi^2 = 10.82$, CR = 94.8, $p < .05$, $R_s = .81$, $d_{yx} = .12$, $Y_c = 13.3 - 74X$). Such hieroglyphs are not difficult to understand once someone bothers to explain them. But this requires more than a footnote to a work that is intelligible only to those who do not need to consult it.

Students react to such impediments to learning in several ways. Some will "read around" the unintelligible matter and thereby acquire the habits of not reading closely or critically and of not really understanding what they read. They may feel, quite inappropriately, that they ought to recall what these symbols mean from some vaguely remembered math course. Others may react in the opposite way and conclude that the writer is trying to confuse or bedazzle them with erudition and could well have chosen to convey the same information more straightforwardly. Either reaction to insecurity is dysfunctional to the study of government.

Unfortunately, these rationalizations are occasionally encouraged by anti-intellectual currents within the academic community. There are those who still believe that anything having to do with numbers or symbols involves drudgery, despite the presence of pocket calculators and computers on almost every campus, or that it is repelling, despite the popularity of the new math in every high school where it is well taught. There are counsellors who foster the idea that some students are innately incapable of comprehending anything quantitative, thereby confirming students' illusions of inadequacy.

Purposes and Limitations

This book is designed as a supplementary text for introductory courses in research methods, political science or political behavior. It is written for the student who does not remember much algebra. The exercises and examples are an integral part of the exposition, but most of them are easy. They are designed not to give students a grounding in technique, for which repeated practice would be necessary, but to allow them to take the role of the researcher as a pedagogical device. One learns better by doing than merely by reading.

It is a reasonable expectation that a junior or senior taking a political science course should be able to read a substantial part of the material in the *American Political Science Review.* Analysis of the contents of the *Review* for 1963–1965 showed that 18% of the articles used such "low-level quantitative techniques" as simple counting or percentages, compared with 12% in previous decades. This is the point at which our exercises start. An additional 22% of the articles used "more powerful quantitative techniques," meaning ordinal or interval assumptions or significance tests. Only 1% had used such techniques in the 1940s and 5% in the 1950s.[1] The techniques and measures used in political research are now so varied that we cannot expect undergraduates to understand every article in the social science journals. Few of us who teach them can do that. However, a grasp of the more frequently used measures and what they communicate to the reader should reduce students' difficulties.

This is not a statistics text, nor is it an adequate substitute for one. On the one hand, it skirts or ignores several of the fundamental ideas of probability and the theory of statistics. On the other hand, it treats some procedures that are not usually encountered until the second year of statistics, because these procedures are used by a number of political researchers. The emphasis

---

[1] Albert Somit and Joseph Tanenhaus, *The Development of American Political Science; From Burgess to Behavioralism* (Boston: Allyn and Bacon and Co., 1967), p. 192.

on application stems from a belief that if students see the utility of quantitative analysis they will then undertake the study of statistics with a more purposeful orientation toward the subject.

Thus it is designed (a) to acquaint readers with a little of the logic of "scientific method" as it is currently applied in the behavioral sciences, raising some of the more central and obvious issues as to when and where quantitative techniques are appropriate, (b) to enable them to read the behavioral journals with more comprehension and confidence, (c) to give them a few tools of analysis, so they may use survey or aggregate data in class papers and begin to study government by original, systematic observation as well as by reading books, and (d) to prepare them for a society in which the major policy decisions have an important research component.

It is striking how rapidly the study of political behavior has developed since the first edition of this text came out in 1969. The obvious change is technological—the availability to undergraduates of the pocket calculator and the computer stat-pack. The less obvious but more important change is the incorporation of academic research techniques into the practice of policy-making at all levels. I have attempted to update the text to alert the undergraduate to these developments.

In seeking these goals within the covers of a brief handbook, certain strategic decisions were made. Some measures that might well have been included were left out: Rice indices, ordinal measures of dispersion, and the contingency coefficient, for example. Some oversimplifications will horrify some statisticians. Some readers may feel they are being "talked down to." Some students will misuse the techniques because the qualifications, assumptions, and restrictions have not been covered, and they may draw some incorrect conclusions. Many political scientists will feel that the coverage is too narrowly quantitative and not representative of behavioralism in its broadest scope.

These objections are all justified. But to do research, one must begin somewhere. Teachers of languages have discovered that attention to the niceties of grammar at the beginning inhibits learning, and that one does better to plunge in and start talking.

Acknowledgments

I am now even more indebted than before to others. James F. Herndon (Virginia Polytechnic and State University) read a draft of this edition, and Bernard Lammers (St. Lawrence University) of the second edition, and I profited greatly from their suggestions. Others who have responded to my requests for help or written to suggest improvements or catch errors are Theodore S. Arrington (University of North Carolina, Charlotte), Rudolph Gomez (University of Denver), Kenneth D.

Grimm (Sweet Briar College), Arthur B. Gunlicks (University of Richmond), Gordon G. Henderson (Texas Technological College), William H. Hunt (Southwest State University, Minnesota), Elisabeth Krabisch (Scribners), Leonard G. Ritt (Northern Arizona University), James C. Strouse, (University of Maryland), and John F. DeVogt, Delos D. Hughes, Frederick J. Nowak, and Joseph B. Thompson (Washington and Lee University). Despite all their help, I am bound to have made some errors, and I would be grateful to users of this edition if they would call them to my attention.

I am indebted to the Literary Executor of the late Sir Ronald A. Fisher, F.R.S., to Dr. Frank Yates, F.R.S., and to Longman Group Ltd., London, for permission to reprint abbreviated versions of Tables III and IV from their book *Statistical Tables for Biological, Agricultural and Medical Research.*

The Interuniversity Consortium for Political and Social Research has provided the data for several of the exercises and examples, notably the material in Exercises 5 and 16. The consortium is not responsible for the use I have made of this material, particularly since I have made substantial transformations for the purpose at hand.

WILLIAM BUCHANAN

Understanding Political Variables

THIRD EDITION

1 / Introduction

*As between the secondary school, with its emphasis on primary
skills and factual data, and the graduate or professional school,
whose necessary concern is with specialization and technique,
the distinctive function of the college is to deal with the
grounds of knowledge: not* what *one knows but* how *one knows.*
DANIEL BELL

To the Student

Most of your experience with the social sciences, particularly the study of government, has involved the process of getting information out of a book or article into your head, and then, later,
out of your head onto a quiz or term paper. While you are working in this book you should read-
just your point of view. Here we shall be concerned with another process: how the material you
found in the books and articles got there in the first place. You will need to adopt the author's
or researcher's frame of mind and perceive his or her dilemmas, choices, and pitfalls and how
these problems are solved.

The Subject Matter of Politics

The universe of social behavior consists of all patterned action by persons, including action
within institutions for producing, trading, worshipping, learning, relaxing, and governing. Habits,

1

customs, laws, attitudes, and roles people play in their everyday life are the stuff of social behavior. Political behavior is the part of this complex of activity that has some relevance to the processes of government. There is no sharp dividing line; neither the citizen nor the professional politician separates political activities from the activities of making a living or caring for a family. Hence *any* social act, any attitude toward church or profession, any relationship to others of one's own ethnic or religious group, or one's circle of friends, or any reaction to an out-group *may* have some political relevance.

Thus the population from which we draw the activities we wish to study consists initially of *all* the acts performed by all the people of the nation. Some persons may perform only one or two acts of political relevance each day—perhaps a chance remark that all police officers are crooked, or a glance at the headlines that confirms an impression that our foreign policy seems to be working better in the last week or so. Others may be quite active, paying dues to an interest group that supports a lobbyist, attending political rallies, and cheering the candidate. Virtually everything an officeholder does has some impact on government, and the president spends most of his waking hours doing things of considerable political significance. Allowing for the many political acts of a few million persons in this country and the occasional political acts of tens of millions of the rest of us, it is probable that the number of individual political acts performed in the course of a twenty-four-hour period is of the order of 200,000,000. Discovering and observing, and then describing, *one day's* output of the raw facts about American government and politics would be a task that would keep all students of political science busy for an entire year.

Yet this is only part of the domain of the study of government. The political events generated in the Soviet Union, Britain, Indonesia, Chile, Ghana, and the rest of the world have at least potential relevance for us. Then add the history of past leaders and groups: Henry Clay, Caesar, Lincoln, Metternich, Hitler, Gandhi, the Bull Moosers, the Levellers, the Kuomintang, the Founding Fathers, the Bolsheviki, the Mau Mau. The sum total of all this is "the facts"—the raw material for the study of government and politics.

It is quite clear that "the facts" cannot "speak for themselves." Someone must arrange and order them into generalizations, seek out the needles in this factual haystack, and abstract, synthesize, and compare. This process has been going on for generations with the help of historians, legal scholars, philosophers, journalists, sociologists, politicians, pollsters, political scientists, and writers of memoirs. In a lifetime one could read only a fraction of what has *already* been written about government. Some scholars have devoted their lives to rearranging what has already been written about government, without seeking out a single new fact. Yet new facts are accumulating daily at an astronomical rate.

Torn between (a) the infinite combinations and interpretations possible with existing facts of politics and (b) the new political phenomena being generated faster than they may be observed, the researcher seeks reliable and revealing techniques of selection, summary, and generalization. Once you have determined that *some* strategy is necessary to guide you through the thicket of data and interpretation, then you inevitably become conscious of your choice of method, the standards you apply to what is acceptable evidence, and your criteria for appraising the observations of others.

To become accustomed to self-consciousness about observation and generalization, let us take a concept so familiar to American government that most students learn it long before they are aware of method—the concept of "separation of powers." Is "separation of powers" a *real* thing? Can you identify it by touch, taste, smell, hearing, or sight? By these standards, it certainly is not real in the way that the parchment of the Constitution, the person of the president, and the structure called the Pentagon are "real." It is an abstraction, a notion, a theory—the idea that the things that people in government do can be classified into one of three categories—legislation, execution, or adjudication. This notion was familiar to John Locke in 1690, but its first clear and complete exposition was the work of the Baron de Montesquieu in 1748. Via the Founding Fathers, who thought highly of it, the concept has been incorporated into our government and our history textbooks and has been transmitted to you. You can recognize the act of "judging" when you see it or read about it—whether it is done by parliament, the Supreme Court, the mayor in traffic court, or Pontius Pilate. You can recognize legislation—"law-making"—whether it is done by the City Council or the Interstate Commerce Commission. You can recognize "execution" whether it is done by a Roman soldier, a welfare worker, or a janitor. But the three concepts also are abstractions. What you observe are the actions of persons in government upon other persons, which you appraise against your understanding of the three "powers" and classify as falling into one of the three categories. If, in the role of a historian, you were to examine the ancient records of a feudal duchy, you might classify each event recorded as falling under one of the three powers, and, according to whether they were performed by different persons, you would conclude that the government was or was not distinguished by "separation of powers." Your observation would be accurate and insightful even though the events you studied dated back to the fifteenth century, before there was a concept of separation of powers, and thus the duke and his clerks and chancellors who performed the governmental acts had never heard of the distinction.

To take another example, Robert A. LeVine found that variations in child-rearing practices in two African tribes had a relation to their governmental patterns. In one, judicial officials were hesitant to make a judgment or pass sentence, few conflicts were carried to the courts, and family feuds were rife. In the other, many cases were passed on by the courts; judges were firm and sentences harsh. In the first, it was found that children had been encouraged to settle their arguments by fighting it out; in the second they brought their grievances to adults, who examined the circumstances and determined who was at fault. In sum, "dispersion of authority" as a *cultural* norm coincided with *governmental* dispersion of authority.[1]

In both examples, an *analytical construct* or *concept* has been used to summarize a common type of behavior by a large number of people acting either as individuals or in concert. The concept *need not* be the property of the people doing the acting; it is improbable that the African cultures were aware that there are alternative ways to manage conflict, and certainly the British parliaments and kings that Locke and Montesquieu observed had not deliberately adopted separation of powers. (Our Founding Fathers, impressed by their accounts, did deliberately adopt it, which demonstrates that *descriptions* of government may influence, as well as be influenced by, the practices of government.) The important point for us is that the *concept* was supplied by the observer, not the actors, and that the concept is a device for summarizing in a word or phrase a multiplicity of actions which have some aspect in common. The concept, moreover, abstracts from the constant flow of human or governmental activity some particular characteristic or event upon which to focus attention.

Choosing what we shall study and which words and concepts we shall use to describe what we observe are unavoidable initial steps in making any coherent observation about political behavior. When we choose certain phenomena to consider and certain terms to describe them, though we may do this intuitively or unconsciously, we nevertheless predetermine what we will discover. Once this initial step is taken, millions of facts can no longer "speak for themselves" because we are not listening to them. Others, which we choose to hear, may say only a few things to us—only what our choice of concepts permits us to hear.

Exercises and Examples

The next section is the first of a series of Examples that either involve the application of some point that has been explained or set the stage for some point that will be discussed. They are an integral part of the presentation, and each of them should be done before you go on. Write your answer in the blank spaces provided. You will notice that the pages are perforated. If the

[1] Robert A. LeVine, "The Internalization of Political Values in Stateless Societies," *Human Organization,* 19 (1960), 51–58.

instructor wishes to check your progress or to see whether you understand what has been covered, you may be asked to hand in an Example. Periodically there are Exercises which test your understanding of some process, and they should be worked as well. Be sure that both Examples and Exercises are returned to you and filed in place, for you may find references to these pages in a later chapter.

Example : Applying Concepts

1. In the government of a student body, church, union, county, or municipality with which you are familiar, what officers perform the function of:

    legislation ___*student senators*   C___

    execution ___*student body president*   U___

    adjudication ___*administration (university)*   C___

2. Is the operation of this organization characterized by separation of powers?

    Yes ___✓___   No ___   C

3. Are there segments of American society in which children are encouraged to "fight it out" when they have differences, and other segments in which they are encouraged to bring their differences to parents and teachers for settlement? If you think this distinction can be made, name the segments:

    ___*poor ghetto*   C___ ; ___*suburban*   U___

    Do you think these child-rearing practices carry over into adult attitudes toward police, courts, and judges?

    ___*yes - distrust of legal system; authority*   C___

4. In the margin beside each of your answers, indicate with a C, U, or G whether you are *Confident* you are correct, *Uncertain* but probably right, or just *Guessing.*

5. Try to originate and define a new, original, abstract concept of your own, preferably one that is relevant to government.

Theory as Nomenclature

The formulation and application of concepts like "separation of powers" or "dispersion of authority" are undertakings quite independent of what is "out there" in the world of politics. Even though we thoroughly understand a *concept,* we can seek *examples* of it in a particular nation and find none. It is even possible to conceptualize some governmental characteristic that does not exist and has never existed, although this would not ordinarily be considered a very practical use for one's reasoning powers.

The abstraction of characteristics of political behavior, along with the invention or adaptation of terms to fit them, is one important task of theory. At some time in the past, some students or observers developed the concepts of open *vs.* closed primaries, of civil *vs.* criminal courts, of unitary and federal governments, as they appear in our texts. Plato developed the concepts of monarchy, aristocracy, and democracy to refer to government by the one, the few, and the many; and these concepts remain relevant parts of our analytic heritage.

The use of theory as nomenclature or taxonomy is perhaps most familiar in biology, geology, and psychology, where much of the introductory material consists of an intricate scheme for classification: by genus and species in biology, by age and composition in geology, by behavior syndromes (e.g., "paranoia" or "projection") in psychology. Finding appropriate names for things is the first step in theory.

Induction or Deduction?

There are two familiar ways of learning about the world. *Induction* consists of putting together your observations of what goes on around you into a pattern or generalization. If you happened to be acquainted with three persons on different campuses who majored in English literature, and all of them were vegetarians, you would conclude by induction that there is a relationship between the study of literature and vegetarianism. *Deduction* consists of applying a principle to arrive at a conclusion. For example, you might reason that studying the organization of society demonstrates the inadequacy of military techniques; hence you would infer that sociology majors tend to be pacifists.

Both methods are ancient: some say Plato's logic was deductive, while Aristotle, who collected descriptions of every government he could discover, developed the inductive approach. Francis Bacon in 1620 wrote of the "two ways of searching into and discovering the truth." The one, he said, relies on "the most general axioms, and from these principles, the truth of which it takes for settled and immovable, proceeds to judgment and to the discovery of middle axioms." This is _deduction_ . On the other hand, the method he recommended "derives from the senses and particulars, rising by gradual and unbroken ascent, so that it arrives at the most general axioms last of all." This is _induction_ .

Each has its disadvantages. Induction starts from the sound base of experience, but as soon as it seeks to enlarge the field of observation, one is faced with the problem of relevance. What phenomena are we to observe? What essential characteristics do they have that we should record? Which actions and interactions among people are the meaningful ones? Soon the observer is bogged down in an infinitely expanding collection of data in which no one fact is intrinsically more significant than another. Deduction solves this by working from some earlier theory which indicates what to look for—what is important and what is not. The difficulty is that there are already many alternative theories of social life available. Since we would not select a weak or dubious theory for a guide, we choose one in which we have some confidence. But in so doing we reduce the likelihood of turning up in the process of research any evidence that will challenge that theory. For the theory has predetermined what we shall look for and we are already half convinced that we shall find it. A social psychologist who has written a useful introduction to empirical theory calls induction "research-then-theory" and deduction "theory-then-research."[2] In the preceding paragraph, the first method Bacon refers to is *deduction;* the second, and the one he favored, is *induction.*

Some people confuse induction and deduction. The blame for this should be laid squarely upon Sherlock Holmes. His method of detection is an almost perfect example of induction: observation of "trifles," attention to details, "following docilely wherever the fact may lead me," approaching each case with "an absolutely blank mind." The trouble is that Holmes insisted upon calling it *deduction.* Indeed, when he said, "It is a capital mistake to theorize before you have all the evidence," he was explicitly condemning the deductive method. "Theorizing before one has data" might well serve as a definition of the hypothetico-deductive research technique.[3]

Learning actually moves from one process to the other to escape the induction/deduction dilemma. A hunch, based upon observation, leads to the induction of a pattern, an elementary theoretical statement. Further systematic observation then tests this pattern in a variety of circumstances and finds it supported. This produces a generalization or principle. Thereupon one reasons deductively: "If principle A is true, then corollary principle B must logically follow." Further tests are conducted to verify the corollary principles, and the generalization is broadened and more firmly believed. But if the tests do not support the theory, then it may have to be qualified in certain respects or eventually abandoned. Such a corollary principle in process of testing is called a *hypothesis.*

[2] Paul Davidson Reynolds, *A Primer in Theory Construction* (Indianapolis: Bobbs-Merrill, 1971).

[3] Jack Tracy, ed., *The Encyclopædia Sherlockiana* (New York: Doubleday, 1977), 173–174.

With common sense observation, scholarly research, descriptions, and commentaries in the media all providing a store of political ideas, one hardly ever starts the inductive process with a completely blank mind. The very language one uses is a tapestry of earlier theories, concepts, and metaphors, some appropriate, others misleading. As Keynes wrote, "Practical men, who believe themselves to be quite exempt from any intellectual influences, are usually the slaves of some defunct economist."

The testing of hypotheses—a deductive method—underlies the accumulation of information about political behavior. By comparing propositions and theories with actual observations, we confirm or reject generalizations or principles. This is the way most political scientists, sociologists, and social psychologists work. The inductive method of gathering descriptions of what is going on in government and politics and then interpreting them is the way most journalists and historians work. Government decision-makers tend to be inductive in their approach, but as the data upon which they base their decisions become more complex and harder to assimilate with the naked eye, they become more dependent upon researchers whose operations are based upon deductive logic. The problem of the decision-maker is to understand what the computer reveals and whether the conclusions of his or her research assistant are useful guidelines to policy. Thus the decision-maker too needs to understand the deductive logic behind them.

Statements of Relationship

The model sentence, "X kind of person (or institution) tends to perform Y kind of act," is the commonest way of expressing a political relationship:

> Republicans are for economy in government.
> The Bavarian kings were likely to be mad.
> Traditional societies accept autocracy.
> Young people will vote like their parents.
> Power tends to corrupt.
> The Democrats get us into wars, the Republicans into depressions.
> Physicians are pretty conservative in their political views.
> Oriental officials expect bribes.
> Young people are alienated from the system.

Such statements are called *propositions* when we do not want to imply that they are either correct or incorrect. They are called *hypotheses* when we suspect that they are true and intend to gather some evidence to find out. When several such statements combine logically to form a pattern, we call the result a *theory*.

Scientific theories appear in several forms. They may be a set of laws or tendencies which describe the behavior of certain phenomena. The term may refer to a logically integrated set of axioms and propositions. Or, more commonly in the social sciences, a theory may be a collection of cause-and-effect statements relating characteristics of phenomena to their behavior under certain conditions.[4] In politics, they suggest *why* people behave as they do. Thus a good theory not only gives rise to hypotheses but also indicates why they should be true.

Normative Theory

Montesquieu did not merely formulate the concept of separation of powers. He also advanced the proposition that, given the propensity of men in power to compete among themselves, separation of powers will reduce the government's ability to intervene in the lives of its citizens. Since this involves interlocking propositions about human nature and the structure of government, we call it a *theory* of separation of powers. But Montesquieu also concluded that separation of powers was a good thing, that governments *should* be limited in their capacity to regulate their subjects. Our Founding Fathers agreed with him and acted upon this belief. James Madison, in *The Federalist Papers,* No. 47, pronounced the "truth" that accumulation of legislative, executive, and judicial powers in the same hands "may justly be pronounced the definition of tyranny."

If you examine this theory you will discover that two distinct propositions are involved. One is that separation of power inhibits officials from intervening in the lives of citizens. The other is that such intervention is "tyranny"—in other words, it is *bad*. About a generation ago political scientists realized that this distinction was important, that the analytical processes by which we define and describe the characteristics, processes, and patterns of government are not the same analytical processes by which we decide whether we approve or disapprove of these phenomena. Since then we try to distinguish statements about *facts* (such as causes and relationships) from statements about *values* (such as morality, worth, beauty, sinfulness, or desirability). Whether governments with separated legislative, executive, and judicial branches intervene less in their citizens' affairs than do other governments is subject to empirical enquiry. Whether the consequences of this intervention are good or evil cannot be demonstrated; it is a matter of preference among the citizens.

Thus we have two kinds of theories. Those that deal with facts, quantities, and relationships

---

[4]Reynolds, Ch. 5.

are called *empirical* or sometimes *systematic* theories. Those that incorporate value judgments, goods and bads, shoulds and should nots, are called *normative* theories. The former are subject to hypothesis testing; the latter are treated by referring them to norms of what is right, good, and beautiful, which differ from person to person and culture to culture. The processes are quite different, and we shall confine ourselves to the empirical variety of theorizing in this volume.

Political Variables

To help in considering the millions of acts, roles, and institutions making up the political process, scholars have found it useful to treat certain concepts as "variables," or "dimensions." The variables may be segments of a person's whole behavior, or aspects of his or her personality, or they may be actions of a government, structures of law, or characteristic actions of officials. Almost any concept may be treated as a variable so long as it has *two or more possible values that are mutually exclusive.* Individuals vary from old to young, conservative to liberal, rich to poor, ignorant to informed. They may be classified into men or women, Democrats or Republicans, country dwellers or urbanites, citizens or aliens. Each of these concepts or pairs of contrasting attributes provides a scheme for locating a person on some variable. Similarly, characteristics of political *aggregates,* such as nations or cities, may be arrayed along continua, from large population to small, democratic government to autocratic, collectivist economics to laissez-faire, traditional values to modern, monolithic social structure to pluralistic. Acts of people are also described with reference to a variable: voting for Ford or Carter; giving nothing, less than $50, $50 to $1,000, or more than $1,000 to a candidate in the primary, etc.

Some of these continua are quite extended, such as the one from the population of a village to the population of New York City. Others are abbreviated, having only two positions—for example, civil *vs.* criminal court, unitary *vs.* federal government, citizen *vs.* alien. Even such simple dichotomies may be treated as measurable dimensions. There are some variables that cannot be encompassed in a single linear dimension, including many familiar concepts: legislative, executive, and judicial power; traditional, charismatic, and bureaucratic leadership; commission, mayor-council, and city-manager government. Though we must follow special rules, we may still treat these multidimensional concepts as variables that are measurable.

A variable, then, is a characteristic observed in any member of a class of phenomena that varies in quality or quantity from one member to the next. Before we can employ it in analysis we must (a) decide what the variable is, how it is defined, and (b) specify what class of phenomena (e.g., persons, nations, votes, budgets, etc.) the variable describes.

For example, "trust in government" is a variable that has attracted the attention of researchers since the late 1950s. It is a characteristic of individuals, some of whom have more of it than
others. It is measured by asking people's opinions about such things as whether tax money is
wasted, whether the government does right and is run for everyone's benefit, and whether officials
are honest and care what citizens think. When most people respond with positive attitudes, as
they did in the late 1950s, we can say that trust in government is high; when many respond negatively, as in the early 1970s, trust is low.[5] Both for the individual citizens and for the collectivity,
trust *varies* over time.

Relations Between Variables

By treating concepts as variables and observing the value of each of two variables for every
case in a sample or population, we can answer in a precise way certain questions which otherwise
are susceptible only to vague, impressionistic, speculative conclusions. Do riots occur more frequently in cities where council members are elected by districts? Are the well-to-do more likely
than the poor to participate in elections? Are preindustrial nations more likely than industrialized
ones to engage in conflict? Are revolutions less frequent in democracies than in other forms of
government? Do city-manager governments spend more than mayor-council governments? Are older
voters more conservative? These are simple questions involving the straightforward relationship of
two variables.

They often lead to more complex and more significant patterns. If older voters are found to
be more authoritarian than younger voters, can it be because they have less education? If mayor-
council governments spend more, is this because they are likely to be big city governments? If
Southern states spend less than Northern ones on education, is this because they have less to
spend or because they spend more on other services? If voting turnout is higher in large cities, is
this because their citizens are better educated? Do Democratic legislators vote for welfare programs because of party pressures or because of constituent pressures?

Thus trios and quartets of variables may be found to fall into patterns that "account for"
or "predict" the actions of individuals or governmental bodies.

[5]Norman H. Nie, Sidney Verba, and John R. Petrocik, *The Changing American Voter* (Cambridge, Mass.: Harvard University
Press, 1976), pp. 35–36.

Approaches to the Study of Politics

Some persons approach politics with the desire to amass and present information that will persuade others to adopt a course of action they themselves have already determined is right or proper. The accumulation and presentation of such information may be called "research," and in fact both major political parties and most pressure groups have a "research division" devoted to these activities. This is "applied" rather than basic research, more comparable to engineering than to science. It is also, in the political realm, comparable to "advocacy" as practiced by lawyers. They make their case in a one-sided fashion. Indeed, they would be derelict in their duty to their clients if they sought to present the arguments of the opposing attorney as extensively as they presented their own. A Democratic campaign speaker who extolled the merits of the Republican platform would deserve the reception he or she received. Presenting a case for a litigant, a candidate, a party, or a policy requires examination of facts and the application of appropriate concepts. Yet the way they are employed leads us to call them "advocacy" rather than "research."

Another approach, equally time-honored in the examination of political phenomena, is the search for what is good and right in government. What is the "best" structure? What course "ought" the Supreme Court to follow in its decisions? What are the "chief ends" of government: order? liberty? security? justice? Are these ends incompatible in certain respects? How may we resolve such dilemmas? How may we make the "proper" choices, individually and socially? These problems have been studied by scholars called "political theorists" or "political philosophers." Whereas the first approach to the study of politics is similar to that of the lawyer or advocate, the second one is closer to the province of the preacher or theologian. "Normative" is the term applied to this second type of inquiry.

The third approach attempts to uncover the workings of the governmental system, without concern as to who will benefit or gain by the description, or what policy should be adopted, and without an evaluation of the system in terms of "good" and "bad." It has been called "value-free" inquiry because it studiously avoids passing judgments on what ought to be. This is the approach of the researcher or scientist, in contrast to that of the lawyer or preacher.

The last approach is the one we shall adopt in these exercises, not because it is superior to the others (for each has its own purpose), but because it is often incompatible with the others. It is possible to achieve wide consensus on factual matters and statements of relationship, but difficult or impossible to achieve consensus among the same persons where values are involved, for a wide range of individual values is applicable to politics. One person may judge a policy or an entire governmental system as good because it operates inexpensively. Another may judge the same policy or system as bad because it does not provide sufficient services to its citizens. Yet both could agree that the government being described was "inexpensive" and "limited." If one of them began to inject value-laden words—for example "parsimonious and ineffective" on the one hand or "fiscally sound and prudent" on the other—the two persons who had originally agreed on the facts about this government would promptly fall out of agreement.

In the natural as well as the social sciences, "truth" is dependent upon agreement by informed persons, but the area of agreement is wider in the natural sciences, where the "facts" are more stable. Anatol Rapoport puts it this way:

> A "cat" is no less an abstraction than "progress" when you come to think of it. The problem is not one of existence but one of consensus. Not what *is* a cat, but what easily recognizable objects shall be *called* cats, is the first question. Because agreement is comparatively easy to reach on this question, we can pass immediately to the study of cats themselves, their "nature," if you wish. But where agreement is not easy, that is, where one cannot immediately agree on an easily recognizable class of events which shall be subsumed under the term "democracy" or "status" or "power," it is futile to pass to the study of these supposed entities.[6]

The agreement on facts in the social sciences is so fragile that it is likely to be ruptured by the injection of any value connotations. Political science is, of the social sciences, the most fragile. Since the facts of politics do not speak for themselves but are so complex that they must be organized according to concepts, and since the concepts are no more able than the facts to select themselves, but must be selected by fallible humans, there is bound to be a certain amount of value judgment involved in our research. What we seek to do is avoid deliberate bias or advocacy, or to make it clear when we engage in it, and to reduce unconscious bias to a minimum. To put it simply, academic students of political behavior must avoid fooling anyone else deliberately, and avoid fooling themselves unintentionally, so far as that is possible, by avoiding imprecise or value-laden terminology.

Value-Free Inquiry?

The appropriate relationship of the political researcher to the subject matter has occasioned considerable dispute. Can we really set aside our values when studying government? If we can, should we?

To deal with the first question, it is obvious that our attitude toward an entity that has the power to deprive us of money, of liberty, and even of life, but also has the responsibility to pro-

[6]Anatol Rapoport, "Various Meanings of 'Theory'," *American Political Science Review*, 52 (1958), 980. Reprinted with the permission of the publisher and author.

tect us from others who would deprive us of them, cannot always be neutral. There will be circumstances in which certain aspects of politics and government will overwhelm us with fear, pride, greed, awe, annoyance, or gratitude. There are other situations, as when listening to a U.S. Weather Service forecast, filling out an income tax return, signing a deed, or making a left turn, in which most of us manage to subordinate our emotions and values in the interests of a realistic assessment of governmental behavior. Persons who are depressed consult psychiatrists, candidates hire pollsters, defendants hire attorneys, businesses employ accountants, and surgeons avoid operating on members of their own families. All are instances where one's feelings and values are self-defeating; they interfere with clear perceptions of reality. So too with political researchers: there are some situations in which they cannot escape their values, some in which they have no difficulty in setting them aside, and some in which they go to considerable trouble to do so and even then may not succeed.

As you go through the pages that follow, you should find yourself in the position of assessing your own and others' postures toward the facts of politics and of evaluating the techniques that have been developed to counteract inappropriate biases. In the end you will make your own appraisal of the conditions under which value-free research is feasible.

Assuming value-free inquiry is possible in certain circumstances, is it wrong to attempt it? There are those who contend that in setting aside personal values researchers compromise their integrity, abdicate their responsibility to criticize existing institutions, encourage demagogy, or divert political inquiry from its higher purposes. Having just read the distinction between empirical and normative theory, you will recognize this as a normative question, and therefore one that is not amenable to resolution by the methods covered in this volume.

Terms for Reference

A *concept* (or *construct*) is a term that abstracts some generalized behavior and gives it a name, so that it may be studied and analyzed.

Induction is the process of generalizing from a number of observed facts. *Deduction* is the process of turning generalizations into statements that apply to certain other observed facts.

A *variable* is a concept broken down into a number of quantitative values or qualitative categories, so that each member of a class of phenomena may appropriately be assigned to a value or category.

14

A *fact* or *datum* (of which the plural is *data*) is something that may be observed with the senses and upon which we achieve a consensus.[7]

A *value,* in contrast, is something intrinsically desirable—something good, worthy, or estimable by the *internal, subjective* moral, ethical, or esthetic standards of the person doing the valuing. Consensus on values is harder to achieve, at least in diversified cultures.

Theory refers to a set of systematic, related concepts. If the concepts incorporate values, it is *normative* theory. If they deal with facts and the relationships between them, it is *empirical* theory. Theories are abstract, generalized statements, summarizing or linking together a number of propositions into a unified, logical structure.

A *hypothesis* is a proposition so stated that its truth may be tested by making certain observations.

More About Methodology

This chapter has treated very briefly a number of matters that have been, and continue to be, sources of discussion and dissension among theorists, logicians, methodologists, and the general run of social scientists. Paul Davidson Reynolds, *A Primer in Theory Construction* (cited earlier), is straightforward and understandable in its treatment of empirical theory and the thought processes of theorists and researchers. Thomas S. Kuhn, *The Structure of Scientific Revolutions* (Chicago: University of Chicago Press, 1962), is a classic work in the philosophy of science and has had a radical impact on social scientists. David Easton, *The Political System: An Inquiry into the State of Political Science,* 2nd ed. (New York: Knopf, 1971), treats the "value-free inquiry" issue from both sides. Duncan MacRae, Jr., *The Social Function of Social Science* (New Haven: Yale University Press, 1976), examines ethical problems. Problems of research method are treated in Robert Brown, *Explanation in Social Science* (Chicago: Aldine, 1963); Eugene J. Meehan, *The Theory and Method of Political Analysis* (Homewood, Ill.: The Dorsey Press, 1965); Abraham Kaplan, *The Conduct of Inquiry* (San Francisco: Chandler, 1964); Fred M. Frohock, *The Nature of Political Inquiry* (Homewood, Ill.: The Dorsey Press, 1967); W. Phillips Shively, *The Craft of Political Research: A Primer* (Englewood Cliffs, N.J.: Prentice-Hall, 1974); and Fred N. Kerlinger, *Behavioral Research: A Conceptual Approach* (New York: Holt, Rinehart and Winston, 1979).

---

[7] The term "data" was invented by Jeremy Bentham, the political philosopher, who derived it from the Latin for "gift." Data are the "givens" of political research.

2 / The Logic of Research

In the space of 176 years the Lower Mississippi has shortened itself 242 miles. That is an average of a trifle over one mile and a third per year. Therefore, any calm person, who is not blind or idiotic, can see that in the old oölitic Silurian period, just a million years ago next November, the Lower Mississippi River was upward of one million three hundred thousand miles long, and stuck out over the Gulf of Mexico like a fishing-rod. And by the same token any person can see that 742 years from now the Lower Mississippi will be only a mile and three-quarters long, and Cairo and New Orleans will have joined their streets together, and be plodding comfortably along under a single mayor and a mutual board of aldermen. There is something fascinating about science. One gets such wholesale returns of conjecture out of such a trifling investment in fact.
MARK TWAIN

"Theory," as we shall hereafter use the term, refers to statements about relationships between concepts or variables. In adjusting to this definition, most people have to suppress not only the alternative use of the term to mean "normative theory" but also another popular usage of the word, more familiar than either, meaning speculative rather than pragmatic, unrealistic rather than practical. Grover Cleveland used theory in this sense when he told the nation in a time of crisis: "it is a condition which confronts us—not a theory."

Persons using the word in this pejorative sense have been known to say that they have *no* theory of politics or society. In the sense in which we employ the word here, to mean organized and interlocked generalizations about politics and government, this is impossible. Without a theory of political and social behavior we would not venture from home unarmed or cross a busy street when the policeman beckoned. And, of course, if we refused to do either of these things, we would also be acting upon a theory of human behavior. We cannot live in society without resorting to some generalizations about how certain kinds of people may be expected to act.

19

Theory and Prediction

The difference between research into government and merely living under it is that to do the former we have to bring our theories to the conscious level and state explicitly what we expect to happen in certain circumstances. In other words, we deduce and *predict*. Since there are many bodies of empirical political theory, and not all of them are consistent with one another, we shall do better to explain the predictive capacity of theory with an example from the natural sciences. After centuries of observing the paths of the planets and calculating their relationships in view of the theory of gravity, astronomers developed the modern theory of the solar system. The logic of this theory was so compelling that, by noting minor inconsistencies in the orbits of known planets, astronomers predicted the presence of distant planets not hitherto observed. The hypothesis was confirmed by the observation of a planet at that spot. This is theory with a much higher degree of precision than is likely for the social sciences. The planets have been consistent in their movements since the ancient Egyptians started recording them. On the other hand, the government of the Pharaohs was supplanted by the government of the ancient emperors, then the feudal lords, and now the governments of dictators, parliaments, and presidents. With less stable phenomena, the accuracy of the social scientist's observations cannot be as great.

Nevertheless, subject to their stricter limits in time and space, social theories are capable of prediction as well. A century of study of presidential elections in the American two-party system substantiated the generalization that the major parties do not differ a great deal in their position with respect to issues or the policy recommendations of their candidates. This inductive observation, made by James Bryce as early as 1888, then stimulated inquiry into why this state of affairs might exist. An understanding of the electoral college system led to the proposition that to win presidential elections, the parties must compete for the uncommitted electors near the center of the political spectrum. Each party must be distinguishable from its opponent, but not so extreme as to repel its more indifferent, less ideological adherents.[1] From this theory we may deduce that if a party takes an extreme position, it will do worse at the polls than it otherwise would do. To test this proposition requires that a major party risk losing an election, something neither party was obliging enough to do for the sake of political researchers. However, in 1964 the Republican party (for reasons which are not relevant here) nominated the very conservative Barry Goldwater and adopted a platform in keeping with the philosophy of the candidate. They presented a vivid

---

[1] This is, incidentally, a very simplified approximation of a theory of competition that holds in certain circumstances in economics as well as politics. See Anthony Downs, *An Economic Theory of Democracy* (New York: Harper & Row, 1957).

contrast to the Democratic candidate and platform. What happened was highly predictable. Gold-water's massacre at the polls demonstrated what competent political scientists had told their classes several months before would happen. In 1972 it was the Democrats' turn. George McGovern's economic and social proposals, his appeal to youth and minorities with a more radical outlook than was comfortable for the middle-of-the-road Democratic and Republican voter, all cost him support and lost him the election.

Let us look at this presidential election strategy theory—perhaps it should be less pretentiously called a "theory fragment" or a "mini-theory"—for it is a good example of the capacities and limitations of empirical political theory.

1. It is limited in the phenomena it purports to explain; for example, it is silent on judicial behavior or international relations.

2. It treats a *pattern* of relationships. It specifies how parties and candidates act and traces this logically back to how voters behave; thus it is a "causal process" theory. In this respect it is rather subtle, for it postulates that parties tend to anticipate voter reactions and adjust to them, so that the sanctions against violating the principle do not always have to be applied.

3. It is empirically testable. One needs only to define "moderate" and "extreme" and to note how well these two types of candidates do in their campaigns.[2]

4. The pattern is stable, and hence permits prediction. In this case it has held for a century, which is an exceptionally long period for a political theory to operate. But it falls short of a "law" of the natural science sort. It might not survive a basic constitutional change in the procedure of elections or a massive reorientation of voter behavior. And one can imagine circumstances, such as the death of a candidate or a mid-October international crisis, that would make it inoperable in a particular election.

5. It is logically related to a broader set of generalizations. In this case, it is confined to a "winner-take-all" electoral system as opposed to a proportional representation system, and to a two-party as contrasted to a multiparty system. Thus it fits into the framework of comparative political party theory, which covers European and Commonwealth governments.

6. The components of the theory are logically related: election laws, parties, candidates, and voters interact in a coherent pattern which produces the expected outcome. Contrast this to the empirical observation that every president since William Henry Harrison who was elected in a year ending in zero has died in office. Evidence for the proposition's validity is overwhelming. But no logical chain of causality connects the terminal digit of an election year with the cause of death of presidents, some of whom were elderly men

[2]Actually in this case there is a slight complication. If parties *always* avoid extreme positions, the proposition could not be tested. It is when they lapse, as in 1964 and 1972, that we can test the theory. The old maxim, "the exception proves the rule," is a sound one in the archaic meaning of "proves" which is equivalent to "tests." The two exceptions test the proposition by demonstrating that failures to abide by the rule have their expected consequences.

who died in bed, whereas others fell from an assassin's bullet. Therefore we must classify it as superstition or coincidence, not theory.

We may also use this instance to provide insight into the tension between the study and practice of politics. Put yourself in the shoes of a political scientist who was a Republican loyalist in 1964 or one who was a McGovern activist in 1972. What should the role of such persons be? Should they fight in a hopeless cause, encourage their coworkers by a false show of optimism, and convince their students that they really are ignorant of the workings of the American party system? Should they protect their detachment and their reputation and thereby contribute to the even more resounding defeat of a cause they believe in?

There is not always a conflict between knowledge and goal-seeking in the study and practice of politics, but there are circumstances in which "ignorance is functional." The most effective candidate for the minority party in a one-party district is the one who is slightly out of touch with reality. There are other circumstances in which a publicized prediction will affect the course of public policy. These are known as "self-fulfilling" or "self-denying" prophecies. They occur in the social, but not the natural, sciences.

Hypothesis Testing

A *hypothesis* is a statement of what our theory leads us to expect in the "real world." We put it in the form of a declarative statement, because theory suggests that certain relationships will be found to hold when we analyze our data. If these relationships are not demonstrated, it will be advisable to revise, qualify, or discard the theory that led to the hypothesis.

It is surprising how difficult it is to adapt this process, which underlies the advance in physical sciences, to political science. In the first place, many political theories, if put into application, will benefit someone or other. The sorts of theories we have been accustomed to in political science and economics hold, for example, that if the government borrows another dollar the country is done for, or that all that is needed to restore slum dwellers to a useful life is a low-rent housing project, or that the Communists will go away if we will be firmer (or more flexible) in our foreign policy. Such theories may be correct or incorrect, but far more important to most of us is the fact that they are useful to us in other ways; they make or save us money, bolster our egos, or make us feel more secure. Most of us are very *uneager* to test them; we would prefer to argue them from *a priori* logic, to "prove" them to others and to persuade the government to act upon them. If someone should disprove the theories we really want to cling to, most of us are ingenious enough to find some reason to discredit or disbelieve him.[3] With this as their implicit premise for the examination of politics, many students are healthily suspicious when someone talks of proving or disproving theories.

Second, we suffer from a human tendency, this one a characteristic of natural, as well as social, scientists, to develop a vested interest in whatever propositions *we* have advanced. We feel it is an admission of error to say that our hypothesis failed to prove out. Students may feel as though they have given the wrong answer to an exam question when they advance a hypothesis that is disproved.

Hypothesis testing with political data quite properly takes on an unnatural, self-conscious cast, in which we challenge the accuracy of what we already "know" about politics or deliberately test the validity of factual propositions we would prefer not to see contradicted.

We always phrase a hypothesis in a positive manner—a flat, declarative sentence. We don't say, "Are old people more conservative than young ones?" but "Old people are more conservative than young ones." More precisely stated in terms of relationships between variables, the hypothesis becomes: "As age increases, conservatism increases." The categoric, positive statement is made not to persuade or convince others, much less ourselves, but because the hypothesized tendency is derived from some larger body of theory that suggests it must be so. If the data fail to support the hypothesis, then the theory from which it is derived is thrown into question.

When the hypothesis is in proper form, we then collect our data, and we give the data every chance—in fact, as we shall see, we give it a much better than even chance—to contradict our hypothesis. Our knowledge grows when hypotheses are substantiated, and our theories are shown to be an accurate picture of reality "out there." *But knowledge also grows when our hypotheses cannot be demonstrated, and we go back to reexamine and recast our theories.*

Finally, since political behavior varies with changing conditions, situations, and norms of conduct, there is no such thing as a "law" of the sort that applies to gases, heredity, or chemical compounds. There are some rather reliable generalizations about political behavior, but even the most reliable of them is likely to undergo a change as our politics and government alter with the times. We need to keep testing and probing the underlying nature of political reality.

[3]The terms "myth" and "ideology" are often applied to formulations that have values, facts, and systematic relationships so inextricably entangled that it becomes impossible to test the accuracy of their factual or systematic components. See Robert M. MacIver, *The Web of Government*, rev. ed. (New York: The Free Press, 1965), Ch. 1.

Examples : Graphing Relationships

Casual observations that people make about social behavior may be readily accepted, or they may lead to a brisk argument. They may also be treated as hypotheses and tested against available evidence. Here are three statements that occasionally pop up in conversations, along with data from the Census Bureau's *Historical Statistics of the United States: Colonial Times to 1970* (pp. 170, 381, 414). Beside each is the outline of a graph. Plot the points and then draw your conclusions. (These charts reveal "correlations" between two variables. Beginning in Chapter 17 we shall describe a more satisfactory method of appraising the strength of correlations.)

It is customary to draw straight lines linking successive points when *time* is the variable along the bottom of a graph, but not to connect the points in most other instances.

1. Hypothesis: "People aren't working as hard as they used to."

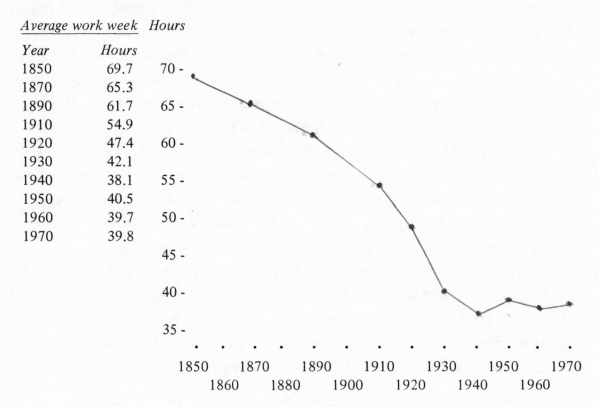

Average work week Hours

Year	Hours
1850	69.7
1870	65.3
1890	61.7
1910	54.9
1920	47.4
1930	42.1
1940	38.1
1950	40.5
1960	39.7
1970	39.8

Conclusion: Hypothesis is confirmed _____ disconfirmed _____

Other (explain) *neither - people are working shorter hours but not necessarily less harder*

24

2. Hypothesis: "More and more people are being murdered." (You label the left-hand scale.)

Homicides per 100,000
population

Year	Rate
1900	1.2
1910	4.6
1920	6.8
1930	8.8
1940	6.3
1950	5.3
1960	4.7
1970	8.3

Conclusion: Hypothesis is confirmed _____ disconfirmed _____

Other (explain) _neither - fluctuating_
murder rate - not a constant increase
or decrease

3. Hypothesis: "Education pays." (You label both scales.)

Males 25 years of age and older, 1970

Years of school completed	Average annual income
Fewer than 8	$ 4,434
8 years	6,035
1–3 yrs. high school	7,627
4 yrs. high school	9,185
1–3 yrs. college	10,891
4 yrs. college	13,372
Over 4 yrs. college	15,732

Income

16,000 -

14,000 -

12,000 -

10,000 -

8,000 -

6,000 -

4,000 -

-8 8 1-3 4 1-3 4 4+

Education

Conclusion: Hypothesis is confirmed ___✓___ disconfirmed _____

Other (explain) _____

_____

Operational or "Working" Definitions

We "operationally" define a theoretical concept or relationship when we put it in terms that may be treated as a variable, i.e., may be "measured." Thus we translate concept into data available to the researcher. An operational or "working" definition is thus essential to testing a hypothesis; it is a bridge between the more abstract "conceptual" definition in the theory and the actions of people that we observe and record as our data.

As you did the Example, did you feel some discomfort about the discrepancy between the wording of the hypothesis and the nature of the data you were given? The first hypothesis dealt with "working hard" but the data dealt with working *long hours.* These are not quite the same thing.

The operational definition is a bridge, and it may rest upon shaky ground at either end—or at both ends. On the theory end, we often generalize in imprecise fashion, especially in everyday discourse. "Working hard" might mean working long hours, or working at unpleasant or exhausting tasks, or it might mean concentrating intently upon one's work. In scholarly writing, imprecise meaning may escape the reader's, and even the writer's, notice. In the social sciences we sometimes deal with concepts so difficult that we cannot agree upon them. "Power" is a very central concept that has defied operationalization to the satisfaction of most political scientists. "The public interest" is another such concept, this time one with value connotations, that is widely used despite the difficulty of defining it crisply.[4]

At the other end of the bridge, the data end, our trouble is finding the information we need in exactly the form we want it. The Census Bureau (for good reasons) combines grade levels, and this makes it difficult to locate the exact point on the horizontal axis where "fewer than 8 years" should fall.

An "assumption" in research is something that is taken for granted rather than tested. One does not seek to prove or disprove an assumption in the course of that particular operation or experiment. An operational definition is an assumption in this respect. One may examine it for logic, reliability, internal consistency, face validity, or availability of data to see how it will work. Sophisticated research often uses several operational definitions to get at some theoretical concept. There are other assumptions, implicit or explicit, in every research project: that observations are accurate, that a sample is representative, that conditions have not changed over time, etc. For example, you were forced to make some assumption about the period during which the statement that more people are being murdered was to be tested, and this affected your conclusion.

Clever researchers have derived "unobtrusive" measures to operationalize variables that are troublesome to measure directly. At a Chicago museum, floor tiles in front of some exhibits had to be replaced more frequently than others, giving an index of the popularity of those displays. Another researcher measured the level of whisky consumption in a "dry" town by counting bottles in the garbage cans.[5] One way of comparing several towns' community spirit would be to find the per capita amount contributed to charity drives, but this would be distorted by the rela-

---

[4]For a book-length pursuit of this concept, see Glendon Schubert, *The Public Interest* (Glencoe, Ill.: The Free Press, 1960).

[5]Eugene J. Webb, Donald T. Campbell, Richard D. Schwartz, and Lee Sechrest, *Unobtrusive Measures: Nonreactive Research in the Social Sciences* (Chicago: Rand McNally, 1966), p. 2.

tive wealth of the town. A better way might be to ascertain the proportion of the population volunteering to donate blood.

An operational definition usually represents a compromise. Some uncompromising theorists prefer to elaborate their conceptual structures in so complicated and airy a fashion that they can never be subjected to any test but that of impressionistic plausibility. One may argue with them, but one cannot collect evidence that will disprove them, which gives the theorist a sense of security, no doubt. At the other extreme are the rugged empiricists. They will not accept the evidence of any test in which the conceptual definition and the operational definition are not exactly the same. This equivalence is not easy to achieve with sophisticated concepts, so their research is likely to confirm only obvious or trivial propositions. Most useful studies represent a compromise between the demands of the pure theorist and those of the mechanical empiricist. They operationally define some, but not all, important theoretical concepts in terms that are approximately equivalent to data that can be collected without too formidable an effort.

The operational (or working) definition, then, bridges the gap between concept and data. It is a researcher's assumption, which means that the definition is taken for granted for the time being and not tested in the course of that research (though it may be validated in earlier or later stages of research on the subject). If a reader finds a serious flaw in an operational definition, he or she will not accept the conclusions of the study. Since there must always be some compromise, the most useful standard is whether the researcher, given the resources, might have operationalized the concepts more precisely.

Review

The terms which have been introduced up to this point will be used throughout this book. To check that you are familiar with these terms as employed in the context of political research, fill in the blanks below. If you fail to remember them, use the page numbers for guidance.

1. A term that is used to abstract, summarize, or refer to a particular type of behavior is an analytical _construct_ or _concept_ . (4, 14)

2. Observing similarities of actions or events and formulating a generalization to cover them is the process of _induction_ . (6, 14)

3. Deriving conclusions from previous generalizations and applying them in some specific instance is the process of _deduction_ . (6, 14)

4. A concept in which each member of a class may be assigned a value or category is referred to as a _variable_ . (10, 14)

5. Abstract, generalized statements linking relationships in a unified structure constitute a ___theory___ . (15)

6. Theories which explicitly or implicitly incorporate evaluations of "good" or "bad" are ___normative___ theories. (9, 12, 15)

7. Theory dealing with the relationship between observable facts or variables is ___empirical___ theory. (10,15)

8. A statement expressed in positive form but meant for testing against data to be collected is called ___a hypothesis___ . (15, 23)

9. The bridge between theory and data which puts an abstract concept into a form that may be tested against reality is an ___operational___ or ___working___ definition. (26)

10. Phenomena which may be observed by the senses and upon which people can reach agreement are called ___facts___ or ___data___ . (15)

11. Any element of a research operation which is taken for granted and is not tested in that particular project is an ___assumption___ . (27)

Operational Definitions in Practice

A classic example of the use of historical data in the behavioral sciences is a study by Herbert Goldhamer and Andrew W. Marshall, who set out to study the increase of mental illness over the past century. The definitional and data-gathering problems they faced in testing their hypothesis have been described by W. Allen Wallis and Henry V. Roberts.[6] First, it might be observed that many of us have talked in an offhand fashion about the reasons for the increase in insanity—for example, the pressures of urban living, rapid change in norms and customs—without bothering to check our impression that mental disease has in fact increased. These authors ascertained, not without effort, that almost complete records from mental hospitals and town almshouses in Massachusetts between 1840 and 1885 have survived. Then they faced the decision of how to operationally define "mental disease." First, they had to eliminate some milder forms of disturbance, such as neuroses and maladjustments, which have only recently been studied and are not always diagnosed the same by modern practitioners. Then, for lack of information, they had to omit privately treated cases and confine their study to hospital admissions. "Narrowing the study

[6]The study was Herbert Goldhamer and Andrew W. Marshall, *Psychosis and Civilization* (Glencoe, Ill.: The Free Press, 1953), and the description of it appears in W. Allen Wallis and Henry V. Roberts, *The Nature of Statistics* (New York: The Free Press, 1956).

to hospital first admissions is dictated not by the desire for definiteness and precision, but by the availability of data. A shift has been made from what should be studied ideally, namely, rates of first onset for the whole population, to what can be studied practically, namely, rates of first admission to hospitals. Such shifts are commonly necessary in research. They require especially good judgment, for neither a precise study of irrelevant trivialities nor a meaningless study of the central issue is of any value. Good researchers must balance tenacious adherence to strategic objectives against attacks on targets of opportunity."[7] They made appropriate adjustments for size of population, availability of hospital space, and other complicating factors and concluded that there is no evidence of an overall increase in the incidence of mental disease, although there has apparently been an increase in hospitalization for conditions associated with senility.

To turn to an example of operationalization in political research, Herbert McClosky and his associates sought to test the proposition that the leaders of the Republican and Democratic parties were more extreme in their positions on a liberal-conservative scale than were their respective followers. Several definitional problems arose. Who are the "party leaders"? "Followers"? What is "conservatism"? "Liberalism"?

They defined "leaders" as those members of the parties who had been designated to attend the previous national nominating convention. "Followers" were citizens who responded to questionnaires given them by representatives of the Gallup poll. "Liberalism" and "conservatism" were defined by responses to a set of questions, asked of both groups, concerning public ownership of resources, government regulation of the economy, welfare policies, taxation, and foreign policy.[8] Would you expect leaders _____ or followers _√_ to be more extreme?

[7]Wallis and Roberts, p. 48.

[8]Herbert McClosky, Paul J. Hoffman, and Rosemary O'Hara, "Issue Conflict and Consensus among Party Leaders and Followers," *American Political Science Review*, 54 (1960), 406–427.

One or More Variables?

To know the value of a single variable may be helpful in understanding the political environment. The amount, or the proportion, of the United States budget spent on defense, the percentage of voters who currently think the president is doing a good job, the average income of a family in Brazil, the proportion of Catholics in Northern Ireland—each of these *univariate* (one-variable) statistics gives some insight into a governmental situation. But a single figure is often inadequate.

When fellow Athenians would greet him with the inquiry, "How's your wife?" Socrates is said to have responded: "Compared to what?" Early in 1971 the Harris poll reported that 27% of 18- to 21-year-olds felt that Vice-President Spiro Agnew was doing a good or excellent job. What does this mean?

Obviously the statistic is a great deal more meaningful when it is compared to something else: what young people thought about other vice-presidents, or what they thought about President Richard Nixon, or what older persons thought about Agnew. For example, the figure takes on more meaning when Harris reported in the same article that 47% of those over 30 thought Agnew was doing a good or an excellent job as vice-president.

Any insightful analysis of social or political phenomena is likely to involve the cross-tabulation of two variables, in this case *attitude* and *age*. In the examples given on pp. 29-30 the variable *insanity rate* was analyzed in terms of the variable *time;* the variable *liberalism-conservatism* was analyzed in terms of the variable *Republican-Democratic* and the variable *leader-follower*. Attitudes of the educated and the uneducated might be compared in studying support for civil rights. Unemployment rates among blacks and whites are often compared.

Psychological and biological research ordinarily utilizes an *experimental* and a *control* group, the control group being one which has not been subjected to experimental treatment. In sociological and political surveys the comparison of two or more groups with different values on an analytical variable serves somewhat the same function.

Dependent and Independent Variables

Independent variables are those which for the purposes of the analysis at hand cannot be considered to be the result or consequence of other variables—or, at least, not of other variables we are concerned with. *Dependent* variables are those presumably affected or determined by the other, independent, variables. If this strikes you as a roundabout way of saying "independent" means "cause" and "dependent" means "effect," you are entirely correct. Why do we have to adopt this circuitous language? If you have read David Hume and John Stuart Mill, you are aware of the intricate epistemological and philosophical arguments that can be provoked by the concept of causality. If you have not, the following greatly simplified discussion may summarize them.

When we observe phenomena, we may ascertain that they vary together: when A is low, B is also low, and when A increases, B increases. Mill's "Canon of Concomitant Variations" states that "Whatever phenomenon varies in any manner whenever another phenomenon varies in some particular manner, is either a cause or an effect of that phenomenon, or is connected with it through some fact of causation.[9] We must *infer* which is cause and which is effect. In the physical sciences, where experiments may be conducted in which every quality is measured, every independent variable controlled, extraneous factors eliminated by careful laboratory work, and the experiment repeated over and over again, we may make fairly certain inferences about cause and effect. This is hardly ever possible in the social sciences, where we observe concomitant variation but cannot control the many factors involved and sometimes cannot even describe or measure them. We can never be certain that variable C, which we cannot detect, is not responsible for both A and B, or that B is not in fact the cause of A. (More about this in Chapter 14.)

We are caught in a dilemma. Unless we make some inferences about cause and effect, it is hardly worthwhile to do research on social phenomena, for it could never be put to use. Yet we know that the inferences we make are quite tentative. To prevent misinterpretation, we use the words "cause" and "effect" carefully, for they may imply that we know more than we actually do.[10]

We do have some logical rules that help us with inference as to which variable is independent. The best is *temporal order.* Which *came first,* the hen or the egg? If we knew which really came first, we would know which was cause and which effect. By the same logic we speak of age, sex, ethnicity, religion, region, urban or rural residence and other such variables in political analysis as *independent.* They "came first." They occur, or have their roots, *before* other variables we are interested in. Voting behavior, campaign participation, opinions on current political questions, political activities—these are usually considered *dependent* variables.

[9]From John S. Mill, *A System of Logic,* 8th ed. (New York: Harper and Brothers, 1900). A useful discussion of Mill's canons will be found in John Madge, *The Tools of Social Science* (New York: Doubleday-Anchor, 1965).

[10]Within the last few years some mathematical techniques have been developed that parcel out the relations between several postulated independent variables in a way that permits much stronger inferences about causality than have hitherto been considered safe. It is possible that social scientists of the future will use the term "cause" more frequently and less guardedly than is presently the fashion. See Hubert M. Blalock, *Causal Inferences in Non-Experimental Research* (Chapel Hill: University of North Carolina Press, 1964), and *Methodology in Social Research* (New York: McGraw-Hill, 1968), Ch. 5. Arthur S. Goldberg, "Discerning a Causal Pattern Among Data on Voting Behavior," *American Political Science Review,* 60 (1966), 913–922, demonstrates the technique, which is called "causal modeling."

Independent variables are more stable, unchangeable. For example, one might theorize that men tend to choose the Democratic presidential candidate; women, the Republican. It would not be logical to suppose that a man going into a polling booth would come out of it a woman as a result of having voted Republican. Voting behavior may depend upon sex; sex is independent of voting behavior.

3 / The Research Report: An Example

*When you cannot express it in numbers, your knowledge
is of a meagre and unsatisfactory kind.*
LORD KELVIN

Many articles in political science and sociology journals report the results of research. Books and research monographs describe more elaborate research projects. We are now in a position to take the ideas and terms discussed so far and organize them into an outline for a research report.

1. *Theory*. This is the source of the concepts; it suggests the expected relationship between variables; it is deduced from what is already known about the subject. The research report usually opens with a survey of the literature of the discipline, indicating in footnotes the principal books or articles that bear on the subject. It explains and defines the concepts and constructs as others have developed them. It states the pattern of relationships among the concepts.

In exploratory research, or in testing very revolutionary theories, the theory may consist largely of the hunches and tentative observations of the researcher. In some student research the object is to test "common sense" beliefs about the political world, and this may be well worthwhile, because common sense is often wrong. In any event, the theory must be explicitly stated or the whole undertaking is a waste of time.

2. *Hypothesis*. The relationships posited in the theory are expressed as hypotheses to be tested. They specify that variables are related in one way rather than another. They must be stated in such a way that the data gathered will definitely confirm or reject them. Most research reports contain a number of reinforcing or interlocking hypotheses.

3. *Data*. The observations used to test the hypotheses are described; the reader is told how, when, where, and by whom they were collected. Any inadequacies or qualifications

about the data that would bear upon the conclusions must be called to the reader's attention.

4. *Operational definitions.* These are the bridges from theory to data. Working definitions represent the theoretical concepts in terms of observations that can be made with some reliability.

Variables are concepts operationally defined so that they may be observed to vary along a continuum or between mutually exclusive categories. *Independent* variables are posited as "causal" in nature (using the word warily). *Dependent* variables are those that are believed to vary with changes in the independent variables. The way the hypothesis is framed often controls which variable is to be considered dependent in a particular test, although some variables, such as time, must always be considered independent.

The researcher must make his operational definitions explicit. For example, if a variable is measured by a survey question, the exact wording must be given. If census data are used, the categories must be fully explained.

5. *Testing the hypotheses.* The relationship revealed in the data is compared with the expectation established by the theory. This is normally done by reducing the variables to quantities that may be presented in tables or graphs. The accompanying text points out the relationship, and the author may also add inferences or speculations about what lies behind the data. He *must* make clear whether the data support the hypothesis (thus confirming the theory) or contradict the hypothesis (leading to reexamination and probably revision of the theory).

6. *Conclusions.* Finally the theory is evaluated in terms of the results of the combined hypothesis tests. What revisions or amplifications are needed? Do the findings suggest other questions left unresolved, or new hypotheses that need to be tested? Do they have any implications for governmental or social policy?

Not every research article presents these components in exactly this order, and some of the steps may be abridged, especially in brief research notes. Sometimes the hypotheses or conclusions may be implicit and may not be labelled as such.

A model article, which is almost classic in the precision with which it follows this outline, is James C. Davies' "Charisma in the 1952 Campaign." See page 45.

CHARISMA IN THE 1952 CAMPAIGN*

James C. Davies

The term charisma—miraculously-given power—was transferred by Max
Weber from its original religious meaning to politics. He described it as "the
absolutely personal devotion and personal confidence in revelation, heroism,
or other qualities of individual leadership."[1] He contrasts charisma with
leadership based on custom and tradition or on competence related to "ra-
tionally created rules" of law. The charismatic leader is thus the one whose
claim to rule is neither as a perpetuator of traditional values nor as one who
resolves conflicting interests by reasonable and just means but as one en-
dowed with superhuman powers to solve political problems. In the abstract,
pure case he is seen by his followers as being *all*-powerful, *all*-wise, and mor-
ally *perfect*.

One of the outstanding characteristics of charismatic rule is its mass base.
Unlike the palace revolutionary or the condottiere, the charismatic ruler is
not content with gaining and maintaining control merely over the machinery
of government—the police, administrative offices, legislature, and courts. He
consciously seeks to gain control over the individual citizen, not just by the
threat of force but perhaps more significantly by appealing for affirmative
and enthusiastic devotion. The leader seeks not passive acceptance of his rule
but an active identification of the citizens' needs and expectations with his
own and those of the nation. The political demands of individuals become
uniform, at least on the manifest level, and are absorbed in and merged with
the economic, social, and ethnic demands of the nation, as these are expressed by the leader. A greater portion of the individual's life finds its expression in politics. The charismatic follower becomes an undifferentiated,
cancerous cell in the body politic.

Charisma is therefore not a characteristic of leaders as such but a relationship between leader and followers. It depends both on the construction by a
leader and his associates of an image of him as infallible, omniscient, and in-
corruptible and on a positive, active response to this kind of image-building by
those who are predisposed toward such leadership. The "compleat" charismatic follower is oriented in politics toward candidates in a particular way,
rather than toward parties or issues. He tends to divide political figures on
the basis of strength or weakness, omnicompetence or utter incompetence,

Source: James C. Davies, "Charisma in the 1952 Campaign," *American Political Science Review*,
XLVIII (December 1954), 1083–1102. Reprinted with the permission of the publisher and author.

*This analysis is derived from data gathered in the study of the 1952 presidential campaign and
election that was made by the Survey Research Center of the University of Michigan. The general
study was under the sponsorship of the Committee on Political Behavior of the Social Science Research Council under a grant from the Carnegie Corporation. The study is published as *The Voter
Decides*, by Angus Campbell, Gerald Gurin, and Warren H. Miller (Evanston, Ill., 1954). I wish
simultaneously to thank very warmly these three people and others who advised on and facilitated
this analysis and to free them, the SSRC Committee on Political Behavior, and the Carnegie Corporation of any responsibility for the data and conclusions herein presented.

[1]*From Max Weber: Essays in Sociology*, ed. H. H. Gerth and C. W. Mills (New York, 1946),
p. 79

righteousness or iniquity. He is unable to see any but good qualities in the leader he accepts or to see any good qualities in the one he rejects. Although strong liking for a candidate is not in itself evidential, for charismatics the emotional attraction of a candidate is predominant and is coupled with the feeling that the leader is the incarnation of all virtues.

In contrast, the non-charismatic person who is nevertheless oriented toward leader rather than party or issues tends to evaluate candidates quantitatively, saying that one is generally better than the other—rather than that one is good, the other bad—and assessing them in terms of specific characteristics indicative of relative competence, skill, experience, or integrity.

Pure charismatic leaders and followers are ideal types unlikely to be found in actual situations. There are doubtless some charismatic tendencies in all candidates for popularly elected office above the level of sanitation supervisor. The well-known panegyrics of those who introduce candidates at public gatherings as often as not are full of hackneyed phrases suggesting the power of their men to move mountains, stop the tides, and gain or regain Utopia within two weeks of taking office. There are doubtless some tendencies in all voters to believe that the candidate of their choice is superhuman and that his opponent is infrahuman. For, campaign hyperbole aside, the phenomenon of strong leadership is perhaps only rarely divorced completely from the will to be or to follow a leader who will make no mistakes and suffer no defeat at the hands of malignant, real enemies and hostile, shadowy forces. In politics, neither St. George nor the dragon is ever quite dead. . . .

The political phenomenon of charisma is new only in name. Its demagogic and irrational basis was described by Plato in the discussion of rhetoric in the *Gorgias*. The tyrants in the Greek city-states, Alexander the Great and the succession of Roman Emperors starting with Augustus, were to some extent dependent on charisma for their rule. Augustus appears to have tolerated and unofficially encouraged the building of his popular image as a superhuman. Three centuries later the Emperor Aurelian had medals of himself struck with the inscriptions "Lord" and "God." More recent charismatic rulers, like Napoleon I, Hitler, Stalin, and Huey Long have avoided the label "god," being content with possessing, in the minds of their followers, more than mortal but perhaps only demigodly powers.

Charisma seems most likely to occur during periods when the force of neither tradition nor reason appears to be adequate to cope with mounting political crisis. In the course of the French Revolution, when ancient monarchical tradition had failed and its successor, Reason, brought only evident anarchy, a superman was able to unite France in the pursuit of its supposed destiny to rule all of Europe. Similarly, in Germany, after the breakdown of Imperial rule and even pre-Bismarckian tradition, came the seemingly impotent Republic with its rule of law through the Weimar constitution and parliament. Again a superman gained control in the pursuit of a similar, even more ambitious destiny.

II

The domestic and international situation during the 1952 national election campaign was a crisis of the sort resulting from persistent, unresolved conflict.

There was relatively little insecurity about basic needs of food, shelter, and health—and only the memory of the depression. There was no great outcry to put down malefactors or even accumulators of great wealth. But war, the threat of war, and the memory of two wars which was reinforced by the on-going Korean conflict, were all factors gnawing at individuals' peace of mind like an eagle plucking daily the liver of Prometheus, the Titan who stole fire from the gods to benefit mankind. A comparison of this crisis period with others in the United States and elsewhere is impossible in terms of its psychic impact on the general public. One can hazard the guess that as a crisis the years after World War II and the Korean conflict do not seem so capable of producing a sense of individual insecurity as the shock of the depression years. Nevertheless the vagueness and pervasiveness of the current conflict, involving as it does the fear of all-out war, the fear of Communist encircle-ment, the real and—even worse—the imaginable danger of domestic subver-sion, and the socio-economic threat implicit in the term communism itself, are strong enough to elicit more than the minimum number of charismatic responses that normalcy would entail.

The 1952 candidates for the presidency offered considerable opportunity for charismatic response. Unlike Truman and Dewey in 1948, Stevenson and Eisenhower were dramatic candidates, both expressing a sense of destiny and both successful—as the size of the vote indicates—in evoking widespread and enthusiastic support. Eisenhower in particular had characteristics which made it possible for those in search of an infallible leader to find comfort in attaching themselves to him. His record as supreme commander of allied forces during World War II, after a swift rise from relative military obscurity; his prestigeful presidency of Columbia University; and his successful inaugu-ration of the North Atlantic Treaty Organization—all indicated a capacity for leadership in such diverse fields as military command, educational administra-tion, and diplomacy. For those who so chose to regard his record, these and other achievements could be the evidence for gifts of leadership far beyond those of any mere mortal.

The study of the 1952 election undertaken by the Survey Research Center of the University of Michigan provided an opportunity for analysis of charis-ma as a factor influencing the way people voted for president. On the basis of a sample drawn by area probability techniques, 1799 adults[2] living in private dwellings were interviewed between mid-September and the election on No-vember 4. Of these 1799 individuals, 1644 were successfully reinterviewed after the election. Among the many questions asked in the pre-election inter-view was a battery of four on the candidates. These four questions asked what there was about Stevenson and Eisenhower that might make the re-spondent want to vote for or against each of the candidates. When combined with responses to several other questions, it was possible by a process out-lined below to select those cases[3] in which the factor of charismatic

American context 2.

---

[2]An additional 222 in the Far West were interviewed before the election but were deliberately dropped from the post-election sample. These 222 are not here considered because of the need for information available only in the post-election questionnaire.

[3]The selection procedure is described in the Note on Method at the end of this article.

perception of one candidate or the other was evidently predominant over other grounds for evaluating the candidates.[4]

Out of this sample of 1799 respondents, who within the limits of sampling error constitute a representative national cross-section of the adult population living in private dwellings, there were only 32 cases in which three judges agreed unanimously that charisma was predominant in the candidate perceptions.

The fact that less than two per cent of even a carefully chosen national sample gave clear evidence of a charismatic orientation is of only tentative significance. Latent charisma may be considerably more widespread among the general public. The responses available in the interviews may have for various reasons failed adequately to report the phenomenon. For one thing, analysis of charisma was not a primary objective of the election study undertaken by the Survey Research Center. For another, there is considerable variation in the fullness of the recorded responses, reflecting presumably some variation in the proportion of the spoken answers that were put down on paper and some variation in the degree of rapport between interviewer and respondent. It is also possible that some respondents felt strongly a charismatic attachment to one or the other of the candidates but were unable or unwilling to express such feeling.

Nevertheless, the predicted relationships that are described below in most instances proved to be considerably closer, considerably more significant statistically, on the basis of the 32 cases finally selected for analysis than on the basis of a preliminary analysis using 252 cases chosen solely because respondents used such expressions as "he is a real leader," or "he is strong and decisive," or "I have confidence in him." The 32 cases, in other words, gave evidence of being a much more homogeneous category on the charisma

---

[4]The interview questions used to derive evidence of charismatic responses toward the candidates were:

a. "I'd like to ask you what you think are the good and bad points about the two parties. Is there anything in particular that you like (don't like) about the Democratic (Republican) party?" If necessary: "What is that?" (This is a condensed version of the four actual questions.)

b. "Do you think it will make a good deal of difference to the country whether the Democrats or the Republicans win the elections this November or that it won't make much difference which side wins?" If the answer was "Yes": "Why is that?" If "No": "Why do you feel it won't make much difference?"

c. "Now I'd like to ask you about the good and bad points of the two candidates for president. Is there anything in particular about Stevenson (Eisenhower) that might make you want to vote for (against) him?" If necessary: "What is it?" (This version is similarly condensed from the actual.)

d. "Now, adding up the good points and the bad points about the two candidates, and forgetting for a minute the parties they belong to, which one do you think would make the best president?"

e. "Some people say that Eisenhower is not a real Republican. What do you think about this? Is he the kind of man that *you* think of as being a real Republican?"

f. "What about Eisenhower's ideas and the things he stands for? Do you think that he is pretty much the same as most other Republicans or is he different from them?" If necessary: "Why do you say that?"

g. (After asking for whom the respondent planned to vote:) "What would you say is the *most important reason* why you are going to vote for Stevenson (Eisenhower)?"

h. (If the respondent has said he was not going to vote:) "What would you say is the most important reason why you would vote for Stevenson (Eisenhower)?"

dimension than a category eight times as large chosen because of the use of words and phrases that could have—but in fact did not have—clearly charismatic connotation. The evidence is strong that charisma, at least in a manifest form, was not a major factor determining the candidate choice of the very large majority of the respondents interviewed.

All 32 of the cases involved charismatic perceptions of Eisenhower. No clear-cut cases of Stevenson-oriented charisma were found. Of these 32 cases, 26 voted for Eisenhower, four said they would have voted for him but failed to vote. One of the 32 voted for Stevenson.[5] (And one was not reinterviewed after the election.) For those who were charisma-prone, it is therefore evident on two scores that Eisenhower and not Stevenson was overwhelmingly the candidate to whom they turned. By no means all of these 32 individuals were traditional Republicans. Nine reported voting Democratic in 1948, 14 said they voted Republican, and nine either didn't vote in 1948 or their vote was not ascertained.

It is possible that additional charisma-oriented people would have been found on the basis of responses to the interview question about vice-presidential candidates. This was not attempted because probably few people see the vice-presidential nominee as a potential president and there was only one question in the interview on the basis of which perceptions of Nixon could be assessed.[6] It would thus be difficult to determine whether Nixon's popularity among a fourth of the sample was charismatic or was of the relatively apolitical sort that might be accorded any national hero.

III

To explain why some individuals have a relatively stronger need than others for infallible political leaders, we must hypothesize differences in individual personality structure and environment that will produce differential reactions to aspects of politics other than leadership as such. Being exposed by and large to substantially the same political phenomena—the same threat of war, the same threat of Communist encirclement and subversion, the same issues of inflation, taxes, corruption, etc.—those who react charismatically to leaders must do so because they differ from others in relatively basic needs and in ways of structuring the external world.

The determinants of these differences are doubtless numerous. Among the causal factors may be a deep-seated sense of insecurity because of a particular kind of upbringing or other formative experiences with parents and others during childhood and adolescence, unusual upward social mobility aggravated by a failure to achieve actual status corresponding to aspirations, or even traumatic experiences such as prolonged unemployment or the loss of son or spouse in consequence of war or automobile accident. Determinants

[5]Eleven additional borderline cases (nine pro-Eisenhower and two pro-Stevenson) were rejected because the evidence satisfied only two of the three judges that charisma was the chief factor in the respondent's perception of the candidates. Thirty more cases (all pro-Eisenhower) were rejected because only one judge regarded the evidence of charisma to be adequate. See the Note on Method for further explanation. The Stevenson voter is discussed in note 10 below.

[6]The question was: "How about the candidates for vice-president: aside from their parties, do you have any strong opinions about either of them?" If necessary: "How is that?"

such as these, or actual socio-economic status (including income, education, and occupation), could not be examined because of the complete absence of such data in the interviews or the quite meaningless distribution of these variables among the 32 cases analyzed.

But it is unnecessary to find the causes for a particular aspect of personality structure which results in charisma in order to recognize that the pattern exists and has manifestations in politics other than in the reaction to leaders. The following hypotheses as to the charismatic aspect of personality structure are suggested.

1. The individual with charismatic tendencies is less able to tolerate indecision and crisis.
2. He is less able to maintain ambiguous perceptions—the phenomena he observes must be classified. He is, in other words, more likely to make categoric judgments.[7]
3. He is more likely to believe that other people share his opinions and act as he acts.
4. He is less likely, because of his preoccupation with leaders, to have strong ties to political parties.

These are hypotheses on which data are available from the election study. The relative intolerance of the charismatic follower for indecision and crisis is posited on the assumption that he is an exceptionally insecure, anxious, or frustrated individual and in consequence incapable of tolerating political conditions which aggravate his sense of insecurity or frustration. There is a sort of restlessness about uncertain situations, a relatively strong demand that something be done to alleviate the uncertainty. The demand is in part for action as such rather than for a particular kind of action. This is not to say that the charismatic person is unconcerned with the kind of action taken, but that his tensions will be *more* relieved if any action is taken and

TABLE I. RESPONDENT'S PREFERENCE FOR U.S. POLICY IN KOREA*

	Republican Charismatics (N = 30)	Republican Non-charismatics (N = 544)
Pull out	7%	10%
Keep trying for peaceful settlement	17	38
Take stronger stand	63	44
Either pull out or take stronger stand, respondent refusing to make choice	7	1
Don't know	0	4
Not ascertained	7	3

*The question asked was: ' Which of the following things do you think it would be best for us to do *now* in Korea? Should we: (1) Pull out of Korea entirely? (2) Keep on trying to get a peaceful settlement? (3) Take a stronger stand and bomb Manchuria and China?"
Note: Because of rounding, percentages do not always add to 100.

[7] See Else Frenkel-Brunswik, "Intolerance of Ambiguity as an Emotional and Perceptual Personality Variable," *Journal of Personality*, Vol. 18, pp. 108-43 (Sept., 1949).

that he will be *less* concerned with appraising the possible consequences of alternative kinds of action than will non-charismatic individuals. ⌐

The most striking evidence of this phenomenon appears in comparing the attitude of charismatic and non-charismatic people on the question of what should be our current policy in Korea. In contrast to the 44 per cent of the Republican non-charismatics who said we should take a stronger stand and bomb Manchuria and China and the 38 per cent of these who said we should keep on trying to get a peaceful settlement, 63 per cent of the Republican charismatics said we should take a stronger stand and 17 per cent favored continued efforts toward a peaceful settlement.[8] Table I presents the total picture.[9]

Further evidence of intolerance for indecision among the charismatic respondents comes from an examination of the relative promptness with which they made up their minds on the candidates. The promptness is apparent and highly significant whether one considers only Republican charismatics or the entire category. Four out of five of the charismatics after the election reported having decided to vote for Eisenhower before or during the Chicago conventions; only about half of the non-charismatics had decided by then.

Similarly, far fewer of the charismatics reported that they had considered voting for the candidate they rejected at the election. Although one out of five non-charismatic Republican voters said he had considered Stevenson,

TABLE II. TIME OF VOTING DECISION*

	Republican Charismatics (N = 30)	Republican Non-charismatics (N=544)	All Charismatics (N = 31)	All Non-charismatics (N = 830)
Before or during the Chicago conventions	80%	53%	77%	51%
After the convention	7	22	10	24
Didn't vote	13	21	13	23
Don't know	0	†	0	†
Not ascertained	0	3	0	2

*The question was: "How long before the election did you decide that you were going to vote the way you did?"
†Less than one-half of 1 per cent.
Note: Because of rounding, percentages do not always add to 100.

[8]Despite the small number of cases, these differences are highly significant statistically; significant, that is, at the one per cent level of confidence using a Chi-square test. This means that there is only one chance in a hundred that the differences between the two categories of individuals are due to chance. The Chi-square formula used here and elsewhere in this article, except where another formula is given is the basic one of $x^2 = (0-e)^2/e$. Since both difference between the two categories and the direction of difference were predicted here, the level of significance is doubled here and elsewhere in the article where direction was predicted.

[9]Respondents who voted or would have voted Republican tended more often than Democrats either to say we should pull out of Korea or to say we should take a stronger stand. Since being Republican in terms of the 1952 vote is thus related to this policy issue, this factor was controlled in Table I by eliminating Democrats and comparing only Republican charismatics and non-charismatics. This practice is followed in all comparisons where there is evidence that voting or intending to vote Republican is related to the response given to a particular question. In such cases, the charismatics and non-charismatics are labeled Republican in the tables.

only one charismatic Republican respondent out of 25 who voted for Eisenhower said he had considered Stevenson. The difference is again highly significant and the proportions are about the same for all charismatic and non-charismatic voters.[10]

The second hypothesis concerns the intolerance of the charismatic follower for ambiguity of perception, just as the first concerns his intolerance

TABLE III. CONSIDERATION OF OTHER CANDIDATES*

	Republican Charismatics (N = 30)	Republican Non-charismatics (N = 544)	All Charismatics (N = 31)	All Non-charismatics (N = 830)
Voted for Eisenhower, considered Stevenson	3%	15%	3%	10%
Voted for Eisenhower, did not consider Stevenson	83	63	81	42
Voted for Stevenson, considered Eisenhower	0	0	0	9
Voted for Stevenson, did not consider Eisenhower	0	0	3	15
Other voting possibilities	0	1	0	1
Didn't vote	13	21	13	23
Don't know or not ascertained	0	†	0	†

*The question was: "Did you ever think during the campaign that you might vote for (opposite candidate)?"
†Less than one-half of 1 per cent.
Note: Because of rounding, percentages do not always add to 100.

for ambiguity of action or for what he regards as inaction or indecision. The two hypotheses are as related to and as separate from each other as are action and perception in the individual. Table III, discussed above, represents the borderline between perception and action and is relevant to both hypotheses. The second hypothesis relates more strictly to the way the charismatic follower goes about forming his judgments. It says that he tends to see the world in blacks-and-whites, to fit persons and ideas into compartments, and generally to regard the withholding of judgment as being as unpleasant as the withholding of action.

The general tendency to view the political world in blacks-and-whites was measurable in the election study by a comparison of the pattern of responses on the general party and candidate questions in which the respondent was asked to state what he regarded as the good and bad points about each party and candidate.[11] As might be expected, some respondents had favorable and unfavorable things to say about both parties and both candidates. Others had

[10]Curiously, but consistently with this hypothesis, the one charismatic respondent who voted for Stevenson said after the election that he had never considered voting for Eisenhower and that he had decided to vote as he did "three months at least" before the election. When he was first interviewed on September 25, just six weeks before the election, he said he was going to vote Republican, had only favorable things to say about Eisenhower, and unfavorable things about Stevenson.

[11]The wording of these questions is given in footnote 4, items a and c.

only favorable things to say about one candidate or one party. Others had only unfavorable things to say about one candidate or party. The different patterns are presumably related to several things, including level of political interest and information, political involvements, party preference and voting preference for example. The patterns are related also to charisma.

For present purposes, those charismatic and non-charismatic respondents (labelled least black-and-white in the tables to follow) who had both good and bad things to say about both Stevenson and Eisenhower were compared with those (labelled most black-and-white) who had only good things to say about one candidate and bad about the other. A similar comparison is presented on the parties. In both comparisons, only those who voted or would have voted Republican are considered, to eliminate the distorting influence of the relationship between vote and pattern of response.

TABLE IV. PATTERN OF RESPONSE ON CANDIDATES

	Republican Charismatic (N = 30)	Republican Non-charismatics (N = 544)
Least black-and-white	3%	13%
Most black-and-white	50	27
Other response patterns	47	60

TABLE V. PATTERN OF RESPONSE ON PARTIES

	Republican Charismatics (N = 30)	Republican Non-charismatics (N = 544)
Least black-and-white	10% 3	18%
Most black-and-white	47 14	29
Other response patterns	43 13	53

The charismatics are clearly much more inclined to judge both candidates and parties on a cops-and-robbers basis.[12] On candidates, the charismatic Republicans are 16 to 1 most black-and-white, as contrasted with a 2 to 1 ratio among non-charismatics. On parties, the corresponding ratios are 4½ to 1 and 1½ to 1.

Another indication of the charismatic person's relative inability to sustain perceptual uncertainty appears in the forecast respondents made before the election of how close the national race for the presidency would be. As the following table indicates, charismatics were about evenly divided as to whether the race would be close or would approach a landslide. The non-charismatics were about 3 to 1 inclined to think the election would be close. The difference is highly significant.

[12]The difference is significant in both cases at the five per cent level of confidence. In Table IV, because the expected frequency among the least black-and-white charismatics was less than five, the following formula was used:

$$\chi^2 = \frac{N\left(|AD - BC| - \frac{N}{2}\right)^2}{(A + B)(C + D)(A + C)(B + D)}$$

See Quinn McNemar, *Psychological Statistics* (New York, 1949), p. 207.

TABLE VI. PREDICTION OF CLOSENESS OF PRESIDENTIAL RACE*

	Republican Charismatics (N = 30)	Republican Non-charismatics (N = 544)	All Charismatics (N = 32)	All Non-charismatics (N = 922)
(Very) close race	50%	68%	53%	68%
One candidate will win by (quite) a lot	46	21	44	19
Respondent answered but gave no clear-cut prediction	0	7	0	7
Don't know or not ascertained	4	4	3	6

*The question was: "Who do you think will be elected president in November? Do you think it will be a close race or will (respondent's choice) win by quite a bit?"

The intolerance for perceptual ambiguity is evidenced also in the discrepancy between the candidate respondents voted for and the one they said would make the best President aside from the party. Few people can be expected to believe or to state that in their opinion there is a difference between the candidate of their choice and the best potential President. Nevertheless, here again the charismatic Republicans differ from the non-charismatics; there is slightly more than one chance in twenty that the difference is due to chance. The difference therefore falls short of statistical significance.

The third hypothesis—that the charismatic individual is more likely to believe that other people share his opinions and act as he acts—is related to the second in that the inability to maintain ambiguous perceptions is presumably part of the same psychic inability to tolerate diversity. The third hypothesis, however, introduces the additional factor of the charismatic's need for group

TABLE VII. CANDIDATE BEST SUITED FOR THE PRESIDENCY*

	Republican Charismatics (N = 30)	Republican Non-charismatics (N = 544)
Eisenhower	97%	83%
Stevenson	3	10
Either; neither; it depends	0	2
Don't know or not ascertained	0	5

*The question was: "Now, adding up the good points and the bad points about the two candidates, and forgetting for a minute the parties they belong to, which one do you think would make the best president?"

support for his own judgments, his relative inability to stand alone. In the pre-election interview respondents were asked how they thought various groups would vote. The groups in question were farmers, the working class, Negroes, the middle class, big businessmen, union members, Protestants, Catholics, and Jews. The Republican charismatic respondents were much more likely to believe that farmers, working class, and middle class would vote Republican. There were slight differences also between charismatic and

non-charismatic respondents on the other groups, but the differences were [handwritten: confirmed]
generally so small that they must be attributed to other factors or to chance.

The fourth hypothesis states that the charismatic follower will have [handwritten: 6.4]
weaker ties to party than others because his main concern is to attach [handwritten: indep. 4]

TABLE VIII. PREDICTION OF VOTE OF VARIOUS GROUPS OF REPUBLICANS

	Farmers		Working Class		Middle Class	
	Charismatics (N = 30)	Non-charismatics (N = 544)	Charismatics (N = 30)	Non-charismatics (N = 544)	Charismatics (N = 30)	Non-charismatics (N = 544)
Will vote Democratic	17%	24%	23%	38%	3%	11%
Will vote Republican	40	20	27	14	47	35
Will split	30	33	30	32	30	31
Don't know and not ascertained	13 [handwritten: dep.]	23	20	16	20	23

himself to an infallible leader. The evidence in support of this notion is not
so strong as for the other hypotheses. In terms of classifying themselves as
either strong or weak Republicans or Democrats rather than as Independents
with or without leanings toward one or the other of the parties, there is
some evidence—which falls slightly short of statistical significance at the five
per cent level—that charismatics are more likely than the non-charismatics
to attach themselves to party.

But when asked what they would do if confronted with voting for a candidate of their own party whom they liked less than the candidate of the
other party, the charismatics differ markedly from the non-charismatics.
Three-fourths of the former would vote for the candidate rather than the
party of their preference, while less than half of the latter would do so. Only
one out of eight of the charismatics in such a conflict situation would stick
by his party or else not vote at all, whereas one out of four of the non-
charismatics would choose one or the other of these alternatives that

TABLE IX. VOTING FOR CANDIDATE OR PARTY*

	Republican Charismatics (N = 30)	Republican Non-charismatics (N = 544)	All Charismatics (N = 32)	All Non-charismatics (N = 922)
Would vote for candidate of other party	74%	49%	72%	42%
Would vote for candidate of own party	10	10	9	14
Would not vote for either candidate	3	14	3	17
Don't know or not ascertained	13	27	16	27

*The question was: "Suppose there was an election where your party was running a candidate that
you didn't agree with. Which of the following things comes closest to what you think you would do?
(1) I probably would vote for him anyway because a person should be loyal to his party. (2) I probably
would not vote for either candidate in that election. (3) I probably would vote for the other party's
candidate."

maintain his party ties. The relationship is evident whether one contrasts all charismatics or only those who voted or would have voted Republican in 1952.

The interesting aspect of this information is that, if charismatics are indeed more likely to attach a party label to themselves, the label means less for them than for non-charismatics. The former may declare rather more strongly or more often their loyalty to party, but this loyalty means less to them than the attraction of a strong candidate. One can speculate on an explanation for this, saying that conventional loyalties are prominent among charismatics but that the convention is honored mostly on the verbal level and will be flouted in action—without the flouters being particularly aware that their party loyalty is largely sham. The available evidence from the election study, however, offers no clue other than the data presented to explain a phenomenon—apparent real weakness of verbally strong party ties—that is by no means self-explanatory. . . .

V

The foregoing analysis of charisma in the 1952 campaign was undertaken for three reasons: to assess the researchability of an important political phenomenon which heretofore has remained largely in the intuitive realm of thought, to find out how prevalent the phenomenon is in contemporary American politics, and to test the validity of certain intuitive hypotheses as to the way charismatic followers will act.

The analysis presented is neither exhaustive nor deeply etiological. Because of the broad scope of the election study undertaken by the Survey Research Center, it was not possible to insert in the interview questions which could be designed to explore in depth the causes and in breadth the manifestations of charisma. The absence of prior research that is of directly probative value would have made imprudent the large expenditure necessary to gather a large national sample for the sole or primary purpose of research in patterns of leadership perception. But it was in fact possible by relatively exact, though crude, techniques to isolate a category of respondents whose primary orientation to politics indicated a strong predilection for a particular kind of leadership. And meaningful as well as statistically significant relationships between this predilection and kinds of political attitude and action did in fact emerge. I believe the analysis does indicate that a concept which up to now has been confined largely to intuitive observation can be subjected to empirical observation and test.

As we have noted, less than two per cent of the very precisely representative and random sample of the national adult population gave clear evidence of a primarily charismatic orientation. This fact is indeed significant, in more than a statistical sense, but its significance should not be overestimated. There is evidence in the interviews suggesting that more than such a tiny fraction of the general public has some charismatic reactions to politics. There is indeed no evidence that only about one person in fifty would actively support a man with a halo on a white horse. However, the fact that 32 cases produced striking relationships whereas more cases less precisely selected did not—despite the pronounced statistical advantage of large numbers—indicates rather clearly that charisma judged by fairly clear-cut criteria and exhibiting specific behavioral manifestations is not now epidemic in our society.

The four intuitive hypotheses stated at the beginning of Section III find considerable support in the data presented. It does seem clear that charisma-oriented individuals are relatively intolerant of political crisis, incapable of maintaining ambiguous perceptions, and more likely to see others as sharing their opinions and actions. The fourth hypothesis on relative weakness of party ties among the charismatics is supported by less convincing evidence. The hypotheses are by no means proven, but they state differences which are theoretically consistent, and the relevant data are consistent with the hypotheses. Further research should not only test anew such hypotheses as these but also seek to examine in greater depth and breadth the causes and political counsequences of charisma.

As is true with all research, a danger of investigations in charisma is that they lead the analyst and the reader to believe that the concept is the sole one having portent for our political future. Social analysts having an established set of work interests are prone to see charisma or anomie or authoritarianism or class struggle as *the* crucial concept, in terms of which the past can be explained and the future predicted with a confident sadness. No claim is here made for the primacy of charisma. Liberal and democratic political institutions are surely fostered or destroyed in consequence of a wide range of phenomena operating together and during the same time period. The isolation and abstraction of a particular phase of political life is necessary but should not lead to the crowning of kings when it seems clear that causal regency is plural.

We have noted that certain hypothesized relationships exist between underlying behavior patterns and charisma. Those who are looking for an omnipotent leader are doing so because they cannot tolerate either ambiguous thought or uncertain action. They tend to seek group support for their judgments and perhaps to be less firmly attached to political parties than others. More elaborate analysis would surely produce a wider range of knowledge about the dynamics of charisma.

The major caveat I would make is that there is danger of inferring from general behavior patterns to political behavior and vice versa. No claim can legitimately be made that, because charismatics cannot tolerate ambiguous thought and action, all those who cannot tolerate such ambiguity are charismatics. The term charisma refers to a particular pattern of political behavior and not to a general characterological type. The charismatic individual is not a personality type any more than the person with cancer is an organic type. Charisma is in this paper conceived of as a characteristic of a particular aspect of the individual's total pattern of behavior—the political aspect. No more is asserted than one would say in describing a person as having cancer when he had a cancerous lung or liver. As a political behavior pattern, charisma is probably more fundamental than Republican or Democratic, but much less basic psychologically than, let us say, sado-masochistic or paranoid.

There is a growing tendency in current social research to jump with verbal ease from political to psychological concepts and back again. This saltatory process is presumably designed to establish profound relationships between the two areas of investigation. Profound relationships do exist, and are researchable, but the facile leap is likely to impede rather than facilitate the growth of our knowledge of political behavior. Until such time as we can demonstrate that all those who are insecure or intolerant of ambiguity or paranoid are of a single political type (whether charismatic or authoritarian or anomic) and can demonstrate that all charismatics or authoritarians can be subsumed under a particular broad psychological type, it seems likely that progress in knowledge can be more rapid the more cautiously we generalize. All individuals who are characterologically intolerant of ambiguous thought and action may share a political predisposition not to tolerate indecision and crisis in politics. But for some of them, family tradition or community pressure may preclude identification with candidates in a charismatic manner. Some political non-charismatics may have a strong tendency to attach themselves charismatically to leaders in business or trade union or to religious fanatics or even to their spouses. Preliminary efforts to establish relationships between general and specifically political behavior patterns must be recognized as such and regarded as initial efforts to appraise the significance of only some of the wide range of determinants of people's political attitudes and actions.

The broader context in which charisma is here conceptualized is the irrational tendency not to solve but to suppress major political problems of the age. Isaiah Berlin has said that the new belief of the 20th century "consists, not in developing the logical implications and elucidating the meaning, the context, or the relevance and origin of a specific problem . . . but in altering the outlook which gave rise to it in the first place. . . ."[16] Charisma is regarded as only one of the major forms which this tendency takes. The evidence here presented indicates that the factor is not now prevalent on the manifest level. The extent to which it is a latent disease in the body politic cannot here be judged. If our political institutions remain strong and prove generally though falteringly able to handle the crises of our times or if the crises abate, charismatic leaders and followers alike may be frustrated in their combined search for power and glory.

NOTE ON METHOD

The central methodological problem was selection of the charismatic cases. This process went through three stages. The first stage was facilitated by the elaborate code established for appraising respondents' perception of Stevenson and Eisenhower. A range of over a hundred different kinds of responses favorable to each of the candidates and about the same number of unfavorable responses was established in the code. From this range of possible responses were selected those that indicated some possibility of charismatic

[16]Isaiah Berlin, "Political Ideas in the 20th Century," *Foreign Affairs*, Vol. 28, pp. 351–85, at p. 371 (April, 1950).

content, such as the one that he is a natural leader, he is above politics, people have confidence in him, etc. A machine sorting produced a total of 252 interviews in which one or more such possibly charismatic remarks had been made about Eisenhower or Stevenson. I then read through each of these interviews to determine which contained defensible evidence of charisma and which did not. This reduced the number to 50. The final sifting process involved having two other judges independently read through the 252 interviews and apply the criteria described in the next paragraph. There was some difference of opinion among the two independent judges and myself. Cases on which agreement was not unanimous among the three of us were discussed. Those on which there was not final unanimous agreement were discarded. On 32 cases there was final unanimous agreement, and this group provided the basis for analysis.

The criteria used in judging were established in a four-page, single-spaced "code." It described the concept of charisma, specified the questions in the interview (those listed in footnote 4) that were to be first examined for evidence of the characteristic and the questions that specifically were not to be examined (such as the one on vice-presidential candidates and how the respondent expected to vote), and gave examples of responses which did and did not meet minimal standards for charisma. Since the examples were so important in establishing a cutting point, the most relevant responses in three different interviews are given below:

1. An interview classified as not sufficiently charismatic to be included: (What do you like about the Republican party?) "Nothing except their choice of candidate, General Eisenhower. I'm a particular admirer of him." (What do you like about Eisenhower?) "His qualities of leadership. His ability to accept responsibility and make up his mind."

The respondent says he is "a particular admirer" of Eisenhower and praises his qualities of leadership, but speaks of his ability to accept responsibility and make up his own mind, which are not uniquely charismatic qualities.

2. An interview classified as minimally charismatic: (Why will it make a difference if the Republicans win?) ". . . I am trusting to the Republicans and Ike to end this awful war." (What do you dislike about Stevenson?) "Truman got the nomination for him, and, instead of being himself, Stevenson is being a little second Truman. We don't need a weak sister now . . ." (What do you like about Eisenhower?) "His past record has shown him a man of decision and honor. He will do the wise thing about Korea and get our boys out of there . . ." (Is Eisenhower a real Republican?) ". . . In some ways he may differ, but only in ways he feels it best for the country, and then the Republicans will listen, as they know they have a wise man to listen to."

The charismatic clues are: (1) Stevenson is "a little second Truman" and "a weak sister"; (2) Eisenhower is trusted to end the Korean war; (3) Eisenhower is "a man of decision"; (4) the Republicans will listen to "a wise man"; (5) there is belief in the *certainty* that Eisenhower will end the war and that he will lead the Republicans.

3. An interview classified as clearly charismatic:
(What do you like about Eisenhower?)
"I think Eisenhower is God-sent in our moment of strife. He will, I believe, get us out of this turmoil and back on our feet again. He is a leader of men, and he can do the job if anyone can."
(Are Eisenhower's ideas pretty much the same as other Republicans?)
"I'd say a little different, maybe. His ideals of right and wrong are much higher than most politicians. He has been at the head of an army, a college, and men all over have looked up to him and respected him. Why, he is just the man to lead this country and put it on a firm footing."
The belief in Eisenhower's omnipotence and moral excellence are rather clear-cut here.

There were inevitably some borderline cases. It was because our primary interest was in assessing the characteristics found to be clearly associated with charisma rather than in reaching a firm conclusion on the number of individuals whose approach to politics is charismatic, that we excluded all cases on which the three judges could not agree. This proved to be sound because the predicted relationships were more clear-cut among the 32 cases than among the 50 that I had chosen without the aid of judges—despite the fact that the criteria used by the other two judges were my own.

A statistical measure of the amount of agreement between the three judges indicated reliability of judgments considerably above the level of chance. Using a measure of agreement between judges labeled π by its author, William A. Scott,[17] we found that the completely independent classification of interviews as charismatic by the three judges (including myself) had a π of .40, where 0 indicates only chance agreement and 1 indicates complete agreement. The π score for agreement between the two independent judges, who had no part in preparing the criteria for charisma, was higher (.53) than the agreement scores (.32 and .36) between each of them separately and me. If I had gone through the 50 interviews I originally classified as charismatic and judged them in accordance with the more rigorous formal criteria used by the two judges, agreement would have been statistically higher but would have needlessly involved my being both judge and jury.

[17]Wherein $\pi = P_0 - P_e/1 - P_e P_0$ signifies observed per cent of agreement between two or more judges selecting a particular characteristic out of a group. P_e signifies expected or chance per cent of agreement between two or more judges selecting such cases.

4 / Techniques of Analysis

Mathematics has become the dominant language of the natural sciences not because it is quantitative—a common delusion—but primarily because it permits clear and rigorous reasoning about phenomena too complex to handle in words. This advantage of mathematics over cruder languages should prove of even greater significance in the social sciences, which deal with phenomena of the greatest complexity, than it has in the natural sciences.

HERBERT SIMON

The most useful tool for analyzing political and social phenomena is the oldest and, fortunately, the easiest to understand and to perform. It is simple proportionate analysis in the form of percentages. The percentage table is a form of communication comparable in its directness, economy, and precise formal structure to a sonnet or a Japanese painting. As a logical device it admits more subtlety than you might think. An entire book has been devoted to the analysis of data that may be compressed into a pair of percentages.[1]

Percentage Tables

We shall go through the process of analyzing some hypothetical data in a step-by-step fashion, examining the decisions the researcher must make at each point. This will serve as a model for the reports you will be asked to do later.

Let us suppose that you live in a town with 897 adult residents that passed a referendum prohibiting the staging of rock festivals. You hypothesized that age was a factor in the vote, with

---

[1]Roy G. Francis, *The Rhetoric of Science* (Minneapolis: University of Minnesota Press, 1961).

older persons favoring prohibition. You and some colleagues went from door to door asking citizens how they voted and what their age was. By some miracle (which never occurs in real surveys) you found everyone at home. On a separate three-by-five card for each person, you wrote that person's age and vote: *for, against,* or *non-voter.*

To analyze the results you first sort the cards into three stacks: Age 21–35, Age 36–50, and Age 51 and over. Then you sort each of these stacks into *For, Against,* and *Non-voter.* But even before you make this cross-tabulation you should outline the table that will inform your readers whether your hypothesis is demonstrated. Each cell in the table will show the number of cards in one of your nine stacks. Your title for this table should name the two variables you are analyzing. You also must compose brief but meaningful headings for your columns and rows. And you must decide which will be the column variable and which the row variable. (See below for more about this.)

Most important, you must decide which way to run your percentages. You have three options. The first option is to make 897 equal to 100% and express each pile of cards as a percentage of it. This would not reveal much, for the percentages would remain in the same proportions to one another as the stacks of cards.

The second option is to add up all persons *For* and take each of the age stacks as a percentage of that number, then do the same for those *Against.* That would permit the reader to learn which group had more young people and which had more old people in it.

The third option is the most revealing. Here you use as your percentage base the age group totals. You take the percentage *For* in each age group. Is it largest in the young, the middle-aged, or the old? Is there much difference between the groups? How about the *Against* and the *Non-voter* percentages: how do the groups compare? When you do it this way, you are following an important rule of thumb in research: *percentage on the independent variable.* Age, of course is the independent variable; people did not grow older because they voted against rock festivals. Rather, they reflected the effects of their age or generation in their choice of voting alternatives. Later, when we deal with two independent variables and one dependent variable, we shall find even more compelling reasons why it is absolutely necessary to "percentage on the independent variable."

Deciding which variable is independent determines which will be the column and which the row variable. While there is some variability, the custom in political research is to make the column headings the categories on the independent variable and the rows the categories on the dependent variable. This means that the percentages in each column will add up to 100%. Note that all these

62

decisions can be made before you cross-tabulate your data. In principle they should be, though most of us are too eager to see our results to make up dummy tables in advance. Our decisions have led us to Table 4.1.

TABLE 4.1   VOTE ON REFERENDUM PROHIBITING ROCK FESTIVALS, BY AGE

	Age			(Total)
	21–35	*36–50*	*51 and over*	
For Prohibition	____%	____%	____%	(____)
Against Prohibition	____	____	____	(____)
Non-voter	____	____	____	(____)
	100%	100%	100%	
Total	____	____	____	897

The totals in the right-hand column are in parentheses because we shall omit them when we present the table to our readers. We put them in our working table to check that the row sums add up to 897. The column sums (which also add up to 897) will appear in our report, for they indicate how many people are in each age bracket, in case the reader wants to get back to the raw data by multiplying each column total by the voting percentage. Column totals also show whether our age distribution approximates that in the population of our city.

In cross-tabulating our two variables we sorted our cards into three stacks, by age, and each of these into three stacks, by vote. We count each stack and check the totals, with the following results:

	Age 21–35	Age 36–50	Age 51 and over	Total
Voted				
For prohibition	93	127	168	388
Against prohibition	91	84	42	217
Non-voter	102	90	100	292
Total	286	301	310	897

Communicating the Results

The next decision comes when you start percentaging. To how many places do you carry out your results? Here are two alternatives:

	21–35	36–50	51 and over		21–35	36–50	51 and over
For	32.5%	42.2%	54.2%		33%	42%	54%
Against	31.8	27.9	13.5		32	28	14
Non-voter	35.7	29.9	32.3		36	30	32
	100%	100%	100%		101%	100%	100%
	$N = 286$	$N = 301$	$N = 310$		$N = 286$	$N = 301$	$N = 310$

Each has its merits. The method on the left gives an appearance of accuracy, with all the loose ends of the percentages neatly tied up in tenths of a percentage point. However, a little reflection will suggest that, with samples of about 300 indivisible human beings in each age group, this ostensible tidiness is achieved by chopping persons into thirds. We are implying more accuracy than the data warrant, and in this sense our communication is inaccurate. The fractional percentages, however, make it possible for a reader who wishes to know the number of cases in each cell to reconstitute the original data by multiplying the Ns at the bottom by the proportions in each cell.

The method on the right expresses the relationship about as well, but it gives an uncomfortable appearance of sloppiness in the first column, where percentages add to 101%. In other instances, we might get 99%. We must go to the trouble of putting an asterisk by the offending total, and a footnote: "percentages add to 101% (or 99%) due to rounding," simply to inform the punctilious reader that we, too, know how to add. And the reader cannot reconstitute the table precisely. For example, in the 51-and-over category 32% of 310 is 99 rather than 100, the correct figure. But either method is acceptable if followed consistently.

The text of your report, accompanying the tables, would compare the relevant percentages *beside* one another in each row. For example, you would note that 9.7% more people in the middle-aged group voted for prohibition than in the young group (42.2% compared to 32.5%). And 12% more voted for it in the elderly than in the middle-aged group. Thus the tendency to support prohibiting rock festivals increases with age. There is a substantial relation between the variables of age (independent) and prohibitionist vote (dependent).[2]

[2]Hans Zeisel, *Say It With Figures*, 4th ed. (New York: Harper and Brothers, 1957), which was written to be understood by one with no statistical background, shows what versatile instruments of exposition the percentage table and the bar chart can become. Though the examples come from market research, the logic is entirely applicable to political research.

One other alternative might have been, but was not, taken. Since the proportion that did not vote was not much different in the three age groups, we might have omitted them from the table entirely and percentaged on all voters, leaving only two percentages in each column. Sometimes the "Don't know" or "No answer" responses are omitted in this way to further simplify the table. Whether you should do this depends upon their number (newspaper polls usually omit DK/NAs if they are less than 10% of the sample), upon their meaning (the number who are ignorant may be the most important fact), and whether they clutter up the table with unnecessary information. If they are left out, you must inform the reader and specify how many are omitted.

Here is a checklist to follow whenever you prepare a table for a research report:

1. Does the title describe the variables?

2. Which is the independent variable? Have you made it the column variable? If not, have you a good reason?

3. Are the categories for column headings clear? For row headings?

4. Have you percentaged on the independent variables? Do your percentages total 100%?

5. Does the reader know the column Ns? The source of your data?

6. Have you explained any omissions, such as "no answer," "don't know," or "non-voter"?

Tables you hand in for subsequent assignments, as well as any reports you make to governmental, party, or administrative agencies, should be checked against this list. Finally, ask yourself: "Do my tables tell a reader who knew nothing about the subject before seeing my report everything needed to understand it?"

Data and Instructions for Exercise 5

Arthur Banks and Robert Textor, in a volume entitled *A Cross-Polity Survey*,[3] collected a large amount of information about the 115 nations in existence as of 1963. They summarized this in the form of 57 variables, and each nation was assigned a position on each of these variables after an examination of its history, government, and social system. Some of the decisions as to which category a nation fell into were difficult, and for some nations the necessary information was not available.

[3](Cambridge, Mass.: The M.I.T. Press, 1963.)

Sixteen of these variables have been selected and reproduced for your use. The "code" beginning on p. 67 enables you to interpret the values assigned to each nation located on pp. 72-74. (You will note that the values range from 1 to 9, which enables these data to be analyzed by punch card, with one variable per card column.) The *variable number* in the code is a convenient reference number to substitute for the title of the variable. *Number of cases (N)* indicates the number of nations in each category of each variable. The *code number* (the "punch" number on a computer card) is a reference number standing for the category into which each nation falls on that variable. The *operational definition* is the one given by Banks and Textor. Not all scholars agree with their assignment of every nation, and you may have some information which leads you to reclassify some nation or nations. This is all right if you add a footnote to your analysis indicating what you did and why you did it.

To check that you understand how the data are presented, turn to p. 72. The first nation, Afghanistan, has a 1 underneath Variable Number 1. On p. 67 you find that a 1 on this variable means that Afghanistan is among the 56 nations coded 1 because they have a high proportion (over 66%) of the population engaged in agriculture. Albania and Algeria fall into the same category, but Argentina, with a 3 in Col. 1, has a "low" percentage of the population (between 16% and 33%) engaged in agriculture. Moving to Col. 2 on p. 72, we find that Afghanistan, with a code of 5, has a "very low" gross national product per capita. And soon, in performing the clerical task of tabulating, you will notice that you may handle the numbers without regard for their meaning. Thus, for a short while, you are playing the role of a computer, which counts but does not think.

Now prepare to test Proposition 2 from Exercise 3 (p. 37). For this test we shall use Variable 2, "Per capita gross national product," as an index of "economic advance," but you will have to make the operational definition as to where the dividing line between "advanced" and "underdeveloped" economies should fall. You will communicate this decision to your readers when you phrase your column headings. For the other variable, "democracy," you must construct a definition by selecting categories in Variable 10. You will also have to decide what to do about the nations in the three categories where the data are missing. Construct a table with proper labels, percentage on the *independent* variable, give the reader enough information to check your figures by reconstituting the cell entries, and present this table with your analysis and conclusions as the answer to Question 1 of Exercise 5.

Variable Number	N	Code Number	Operational Definition
1			*Agricultural Population as Percent of Total Population* ✗
	56	1.	High (over 66 percent)
	33	2.	Medium (34–66 percent)
	17	3.	Low (16–33 percent)
	7	4.	Very Low (under 16 percent)
	2	9.	Unascertained
2			*Per Capita GNP*
	11	1.	Very High ($1200 and above)
	13	2.	High ($600–1199)
✗	18	3.	Medium ($300–599)
	22	4.	Low ($150–299)
	51	5.	Very Low (under $150)
3			*Literacy Rate*
	25	1.	High (90 percent or above)
	30	2.	Medium (50–89 percent)
	24	3.	Low (10–49 percent)
	26	4.	Very Low (under 10 percent)
	10	9.	Unascertained
4			*Degree of Freedom of the Press*
	43	1.	Complete (no censorship or government control of either domestic press or foreign correspondents)
	17	2.	Intermittent (occasional or selective censorship of either domestic press or foreign correspondents)
	21	3.	Internally absent (strict domestic censorship; no restraint on foreign newsgathering, or selective cable-head censorship)
	16	4.	Internally and externally absent (strict direct or indirect censorship or control, domestic and foreign)
	4	7.	Unascertainable
	1	8.	Ambiguous
	13	9.	Unascertained

Variable Number	N	Code Number	Operational Definition
5			*Newspaper Circulation per 1,000 Population*
	14	1.	High (300 and over)
	23	2.	Medium (100–299)
	41	3.	Low (10–99)
	35	4.	Very low (below 10)
	2	9.	Unascertained
6			*Racial Homogeneity*
	82	1.	Homogeneous (90 percent or more of one race)
	27	2.	Heterogeneous (less than 90 percent of one race)
	4	8.	Ambiguous
	2	9.	Unascertained
7			*Linguistic Homogeneity*
	52	1.	Homogeneous (majority of 85 percent or more; no significant single minority)
	12	2.	Weakly heterogeneous (majority of 85 percent or more; significant minority of 15 percent or less)
	50	3.	Strongly heterogeneous (no single group of 85 percent or more)
	1	8.	Ambiguous
8			*Constitutional Status of Current Regime*
	51	1.	Constitutional (government conducted with reference to recognized constitutional norms)
	23	2.	Authoritarian (no effective constitutional limitation, or fairly regular recourse to extra-constitutional powers; arbitrary exercise of power confined largely to the political sector)
	16	3.	Totalitarian (no effective constitutional limitation; broad exercise of power by the regime in both political and social spheres)
	9	7.	Unascertainable
	5	8.	Ambiguous
	11	9.	Unascertained

Variable Number	N	Code Number	Operational Definition
9			*Representative Character of Current Regime*
	41	1.	Polyarchic (broadly representative system)
	8	2.	Limited polyarchic (mass-sector representative or broadly oligarchic system)
	43	3.	Pseudo-polyarchic (ineffective representative, or disguised oligarchic or autocratic system)
	6	4.	Non-polyarchic (non-representative in form as well as content)
	8	7.	Unascertainable
	7	8.	Ambiguous
	2	9.	Unascertained
10			*Current Electoral System*
	43	1.	Competitive (no party ban, or ban on extremist or extra-constitutional parties only)
	9	2.	Partially competitive (one party with 85 percent or more of legislative seats)
	30	3.	Non-competitive (single-list voting or no elected opposition)
	21	7.	Unascertainable
	11	8.	Ambiguous
	1	0.	Irrelevant
11			*Degree of Freedom of Group Opposition*
	46	1.	Autonomous groups free to enter politics and able to oppose government (save for extremist groups, where banned)
	18	2.	Autonomous groups free to organize in politics, but limited in capacity to oppose government (includes absorption of actual or potential opposition leadership into government)
	24	3.	Autonomous groups tolerated informally and outside politics
	11	4.	No genuinely autonomous groups tolerated
	13	7.	Unascertainable
	3	8.	Ambiguous
12			*Political Enculturation*
	15	1.	High (integrated and homogeneous polity with little or no extreme opposition, communalism, fractionalism, disenfranchisement, or political non-assimilation)
	38	2.	Medium (less fully integrated polity with significant minority in extreme opposition, communalized, fractionalized, disenfranchised, or politically non-assimilated)

Variable Number	N	Code Number	Operational Definition
	42	3.	Low (relatively non-integrated or restrictive polity with majority or near majority in extreme opposition, communalized, fractionalized, disenfranchised, or politically non-assimilated)
	2	8.	Ambiguous
	18	9.	Unascertained

13   *Sectionalism*

	N	Code	
	27	1.	Extreme (one or more groups with extreme sectional feeling)
	34	2.	Moderate (one group with strong sectional feeling or several with moderate sectional feeling)
	47	3.	Negligible (no significant sectional feeling)
	3	8.	Ambiguous
	4	9.	Unascertained

14   *Party System—Quantitative*

	N	Code	
	34	1.	One-party (all others nonexistent, banned, non-participant, or adjuncts of dominant party in electoral activity; includes "National Fronts" and one-party fusional systems)
	13	2.	One-party dominant (opposition, but numerically ineffective at national level; includes minority participation in government while retaining party identity for electoral purposes)
	3	3.	One-and-a-half-party (opposition significant, but unable to win majority)
	11	4.	Two-party or effectively two-party (reasonable expectation of party rotation)
	30	5.	Multiparty (coalition or minority party government normally mandatory if parliamentary system)
	5	6.	No parties, or all parties illegal or ineffective
	12	7.	Unascertainable
	7	8.	Ambiguous

15   *Political Participation by the Military*

	N	Code	
	21	1.	Interventive (presently exercises or has recently exercised direct power)
	31	2.	Supportive (performs para-political role in support of traditionalist, authoritarian, totalitarian, or modernizing regime)
	56	3.	Neutral (apolitical or of minor political importance)
	7	8.	Ambiguous

Variable Number	N	Code Number	Operational Definition
16	.		*Role of Police*
	66	1.	Politically significant (important continuing or intermittent political function in addition to law enforcement)
	35	2.	Not politically significant (role confined to law enforcement only)
	2	7.	Unascertainable
	12	9.	Unascertained

Listing	1	2	3	4	5	6	7	8	9	10	11	12	13	14	15	16
001 Afghanistan	1	(5)	4	4	4	2	3	2	3	(8)	3	2	2	6	2	1
002 Albania	1	(4)	2	4	3	1	1	3	3	3	4	9	2	1	2	1
003 Algeria	1	(4)	(3)	3	3	1	3	2	3	3	7	2	2	1	2	1
004 Argentina	3	(3)	2	2	2	1	1	8	8	1	1	3	8	5	1	1
005 Australia	4	1	1	1	1	1	1	1	1	1	1	1	2	4	3	2
006 Austria	3	2	1	1	2	1	1	1	1	1	1	1	3	4	3	2
007 Belgium	4	1	1	1	2	1	3	1	1	1	1	3	1	5	3	2
008 Bolivia	1	(5)	(3)	2	3	2	3	1	1	1	1	3	3	2	3	1
009 Brazil	2	(4)	2	2	3	2	1	1	2	1	1	3	1	5	1	9
010 Bulgaria	2	(3)	2	4	2	1	2	3	3	3	4	9	2	1	2	1
011 Burma	1	(5)	2	2	3	1	3	2	4	(7)	7	2	1	7	1	1
012 Burundi	1	(5)	4	9	4	1	1	9	9	2	2	9	3	2	3	9
013 Cambodia	1	(5)	(3)	3	4	1	2	2	3	3	3	2	2	1	2	1
014 Cameroon	1	(5)	4	1	4	1	3	7	8	(7)	2	2	2	2	3	1
015 Canada	4	1	1	1	2	1	3	1	1	1	1	2	1	4	3	2
016 Central Afr. Rep.	1	(5)	4	9	4	1	3	2	3	3	3	3	3	1	3	1
017 Ceylon	2	(5)	2	7	3	1	3	1	1	1	1	2	2	5	3	2
018 Chad	1	(5)	4	1	4	2	3	9	3	2	2	3	2	1	3	9
019 Chile	3	(3)	2	1	2	8	1	1	2	1	1	3	3	5	3	9
020 China	1	(5)	9	4	3	1	8	3	3	3	4	9	2	1	2	1
021 Colombia	2	(4)	2	1	3	2	1	1	2	(8)	1	2	1	4	3	1
022 Congo (Brazzaville)	1	(5)	4	9	4	1	3	9	3	2	2	3	2	2	3	1
023 Congo (Léopoldville)	1	(5)	4	2	4	1	3	7	7	(7)	7	3	1	5	8	1
024 Costa Rica	2	(4)	2	1	2	1	1	1	1	1	1	1	3	5	3	9
025 Cuba	2	(3)	2	4	2	2	1	3	3	7	4	9	3	1	8	1
026 Cyprus	2	(3)	2	1	2	1	3	1	1	8	1	3	3	5	3	9
027 Czechoslovakia	2	2	1	4	2	1	3	3	3	3	4	9	1	1	2	1
028 Dahomey	1	(5)	4	9	4	1	3	9	3	3	3	3	2	1	3	1
029 Denmark	3	2	1	1	1	1	1	1	1	1	1	1	3	5	3	2
030 Dominican Repub.	2	(4)	2	1	3	2	1	1	1	1	1	2	3	5	3	7
031 Ecuador	2	(4)	(3)	1	3	2	3	1	2	1	1	3	1	5	2	1
032 El Salvador	2	(4)	(3)	9	3	2	1	2	3	3	2	3	3	5	1	1
033 Ethiopia	1	(5)	4	3	4	2	3	2	3	(8)	3	3	2	6	2	1
034 Finland	2	2	1	1	1	1	2	1	1	1	1	2	3	5	3	2
035 France	3	1	1	2	2	1	1	1	1	1	1	2	2	2	8	2
036 Gabon	1	(5)	4	9	4	1	3	9	3	3	2	3	2	1	3	1
037 Germany, East	3	2	1	4	1	1	1	3	3	3	4	9	3	1	2	1
038 Germany, Fed. Rep.	4	2	1	1	1	1	1	1	1	1	1	2	2	3	3	2
039 Ghana	1	(5)	(3)	3	3	1	3	2	3	3	3	2	2	1	2	1

72

Listing	1	2	3	4	5	6	7	8	9	10	11	12	13	14	15	16
040 Greece	2	3	2	8	2	1	1	1	1	1	1	2	3	2	3	2
✳ 041 Guatemala	1	4	3	9	3	2	3	7	7	7	7	3	3	5	1	1
042 Guinea	1	5	9	3	4	1	3	2	3	3	3	2	2	1	2	1
043 Haiti	1	5	3	3	3	2	1	8	3	3	3	3	3	6	1	1
044 Honduras	1	4	3	9	3	2	1	1	2	1	1	2	3	4	1	1
045 Hungary	2	3	1	4	2	1	1	3	3	3	3	9	3	1	2	1
046 Iceland	3	2	1	1	1	1	1	1	1	1	1	1	3	5	3	2
047 India	1	5	3	1	3	1	3	1	1	1	1	2	1	2	3	2
048 Indonesia	1	5	2	3	3	1	3	2	3	7	2	3	1	8	2	1
049 Iran	1	5	3	3	4	1	3	2	4	7	2	3	1	7	2	1
050 Iraq	1	4	3	7	3	1	3	7	7	7	7	3	1	7	1	1
051 Ireland	2	2	1	1	2	1	1	1	1	1	1	1	3	5	3	2
052 Israel	4	2	2	2	2	1	3	1	1	1	1	2	3	5	3	2
053 Italy	3	2	2	1	2	1	1	1	1	1	1	2	2	5	3	2
054 Ivory Coast	1	5	4	9	4	1	3	8	3	3	3	2	3	1	3	1
055 Jamaica	2	3	2	1	3	2	1	1	1	1	1	2	3	4	3	2
056 Japan	2	3	1	1	1	1	1	1	1	1	1	1	3	3	3	2
057 Jordan	2	5	3	4	3	1	1	2	3	8	8	3	1	7	2	1
058 Korea, North	1	5	9	4	9	1	1	3	3	3	4	9	3	1	2	1
059 Korea, Repub. of	1	5	2	3	3	1	1	2	7	7	7	3	3	7	1	1
060 Laos	1	5	4	2	4	1	3	2	3	8	8	3	1	5	8	1
✳ 061 Lebanon	2	3	9	2	3	1	1	1	8	8	1	3	2	5	2	1
062 Liberia	1	5	9	2	4	1	3	2	2	3	3	3	2	1	2	1
063 Libya	1	5	3	2	4	1	1	1	8	8	2	2	1	6	3	9
064 Luxembourg	3	1	1	1	1	1	1	1	1	1	1	1	3	5	3	2
065 Malagasy Repub.	1	5	3	1	4	8	1	1	1	1	1	2	1	2	3	2
066 Malaya	2	3	3	1	3	2	3	1	1	1	1	3	2	8	3	2
067 Mali	1	5	4	1	4	2	3	9	3	3	3	9	9	1	3	9
068 Mauritania	1	5	9	1	4	2	3	1	3	3	2	2	2	1	3	2
069 Mexico	2	4	2	1	3	2	1	1	1	8	2	2	8	2	3	2
070 Mongolia	1	5	9	4	2	1	1	3	3	3	4	9	3	1	2	1
071 Morocco	1	5	9	2	3	1	3	1	1	7	2	2	1	8	3	1
072 Nepal	1	5	4	3	4	8	3	2	4	7	3	3	9	7	8	1
073 Netherlands	3	2	1	1	2	1	1	1	1	1	1	2	2	5	3	2
074 New Zealand	3	1	1	1	1	1	1	1	1	1	1	1	3	4	3	2
075 Nicaragua	1	4	3	9	3	2	1	2	3	2	2	3	9	8	1	1
076 Niger	1	5	4	1	4	2	3	9	3	7	3	3	9	1	3	9
077 Nigeria	2	5	3	2	4	1	3	1	8	7	7	3	1	5	3	1

Listing	1	2	3	4	5	6	7	8	9	10	11	12	13	14	15	16
078 Norway	3	1	1	1	1	1	1	1	1	1	1	1	3	5	3	2
079 Pakistan	2	(5)	3	3	4	1	3	2	3	8	7	3	1	7	1	1
080 Panama	2	(4)	2	1	2	2	2	1	1	1	1	3	3	5	1	9
081 Paraguay	2	(5)	2	4	3	8	1	2	3	2	2	9	3	2	1	1
082 Peru	2	(4)	3	2	3	2	3	7	7	7	7	3	2	5	1	7
083 Philippines	2	(4)	2	1	3	1	3	1	1	1	1	2	2	4	3	2
084 Poland	2	(3)	1	3	2	1	1	3	3	3	3	1	3	1	2	1
085 Portugal	2	(4)	2	3	3	1	1	3	3	3	3	9	3	1	2	1
086 Rumania	1	(3)	1	4	2	1	2	3	3	3	4	9	3	1	2	1
087 Rwanda	1	(5)	4	9	4	1	1	9	9	7	2	9	3	2	3	9
088 Saudi Arabia	9	(4)	4	4	4	9	1	2	4	0	3	3	3	6	2	1
089 Senegal	1	(5)	4	9	4	1	3	7	3	2	7	2	2	1	2	1
090 Sierra Leone	1	(5)	4	1	4	1	3	1	1	1	1	2	2	4	3	2
091 Somalia	1	(5)	4	1	4	1	1	9	8	2	2	2	1	2	8	1
＊092 South Africa	3	(3)	3	2	3	2	3	8	2	(8)	8	3	2	8	2	1
093 Spain	2	(3)	2	3	3	1	2	3	3	3	3	3	2	1	2	1
094 Sudan	1	(5)	4	3	4	2	3	2	4	7	3	2	1	7	1	1
095 Sweden	3	1	1	1	1	1	1	1	1	1	1	1	3	5	3	2
096 Switzerland	3	1	1	1	1	1	3	1	1	1	1	8	1	5	3	2
097 Syria	1	(4)	9	2	3	1	2	7	7	7	7	3	2	7	1	1
098 Tanganyika	1	(5)	4	1	4	1	3	9	2	2	2	2	3	1	3	2
099 Thailand	1	(5)	2	3	3	1	2	2	4	7	3	1	2	7	1	1
100 Togo	1	(5)	4	7	4	1	3	7	7	7	7	2	2	7	1	1
101 Trinidad	3	(3)	2	1	3	2	2	1	1	1	1	2	3	3	3	2
102 Tunisia	1	(4)	3	3	3	1	1	1	1	3	2	2	3	1	3	1
103 Turkey	1	(4)	3	2	3	1	2	1	1	1	1	1	3	8	1	1
104 Uganda	1	(5)	4	1	4	1	3	1	8	1	1	3	1	5	3	2
105 U.S.S.R.	2	2	1	3	2	1	3	3	3	3	4	9	1	1	2	1
106 United Arab Rep.	2	(4)	3	4	3	1	1	2	3	7	3	9	3	1	1	1
107 United Kingdom	4	1	1	1	1	1	1	1	1	1	1	1	1	4	3	2
108 United States	4	1	1	1	1	2	1	1	1	1	1	2	2	4	3	2
109 Upper Volta	1	(5)	4	9	4	1	3	9	3	2	3	3	3	1	3	9
110 Uruguay	3	3	2	1	2	1	1	1	1	1	1	8	8	8	3	2
111 Venezuela	2	2	2	3	3	2	1	1	1	1	1	2	3	5	8	1
112 Vietnam, North	9	(5)	9	4	9	1	2	3	3	3	4	9	3	1	2	1
113 Vietnam, Repub. of	1	(5)	2	3	3	1	2	8	3	3	3	3	3	2	2	1
114 Yemen	1	(5)	4	7	4	9	1	7	7	7	7	3	1	7	1	1
115 Yugoslavia	1	3	2	3	3	1	3	3	3	3	3	3	1	1	2	1

5 / Simplifying Things

In small proportions we just beauties see,
And in short measures life may perfect be.
BEN JONSON

Our life is frittered away by detail. . .
Simplify, simplify.
HENRY DAVID THOREAU

In Exercise 5 you confronted the world in something remotely approaching its natural complexity, even though Banks and Textor had done a staggering amount of data-gathering. Every nation on which they had information was listed by name, along with sixteen facts about it. They had reduced the full range of diversity by coding each of these characteristics into nine or fewer categories, and you reduced this even further, so that you wound up with a table of four, six, or nine cells. The remaining busywork was a chore, but nothing compared to what it would have been had you attempted to cope with the variables in their initial diversity.

This chapter consists of (a) suggestions as to ways you can reduce the clerical and arithmetical drudgery involved in reaching conclusions about political tendencies, and (b) explication of some measures that will further simplify and summarize the complexity of the socio-political world.

Counting and Thinking

An adage that was popular several decades ago held that "counters don't think and thinkers don't count." Since "count" has more than one meaning in this context, the purport of the aphorism is obscure. In any event, with mechanical and electronic aids now available, the tedium of counting and calculating may be reduced considerably, so that machines can do the counting and people the thinking.

You may make your adjustment to this technological revolution at one of four levels, depending on your previous learning, your goals, and the resources available to you.

Level 1: Hand Calculation

Hardly anyone with serious computation to do relies on paper and pencil anymore. It is slow and inaccurate.

Level 2: Pocket Calculator

If you do not have one already, you can get one that will do the exercises in this book for less than $20. It should have at least eight digits display, a square root key ($\sqrt{}$) and a memory (indicated by M+, M−, CM, and RM or equivalent keys). If you also plan to use it for science, statistics, or mathematics classes, you may wish to get one of the more versatile machines, which start at about $30. Scientific (E) notation is helpful in handling the larger numbers you will encounter.

Level 3: Programable Calculator

There is much variety, including pocket calculators with programs that do *chi square,* regression, and some of the other statistics we shall cover in this book, desk-top models that print results on a tape, and teletype terminals connected to minicomputers. For some, you write the programs yourself; for others, you get them already written from the manufacturer. You punch in the data and the machine then does all the computation for you. These machines are most useful when you have relatively small amounts of data which can be accurately entered by hand, and when you need to calculate the same statistics again and again. The programing feature will not be particularly useful to you in this course, since you will rarely be asked to calculate the same measure more than twice. You should do this step by step in order to learn what the statistic means.

Level 4: The Computer

Campus computer centers are geared for more complex operations than this text requires, but when you have completed it you will be able to make some use of the computer. This has two major advantages. First, masses of data that have been gathered by others—census results, election returns, national voter surveys, opinion polls, legislative roll calls, United Nations votes, and a host of other studies, including the Banks-Textor material used in the last exercise—are available in the form of magnetic tapes or punch cards. Many colleges and universities have access to this material through the Interuniversity Consortium for Political and Social Research. Second, elaborate "canned" programs have been written to perform most of the statistical operations in this book plus many others, some of them quite sophisticated. The researchers, then, select variables from the codebooks of the available studies and specify how the computer is to process them. In a short time the tables and statistics come tumbling out, all neatly arranged and ready for analysis. The computer does the counting, but the researchers must do more thinking than ever. They must learn how the data were gathered, any weaknesses in the sampling methods, and how they were processed and recorded. They must understand the statistics they choose, what assumptions underlie them, and how they are to be interpreted. Otherwise researcher and machine may have supported each other in an intricate but meaningless, or even misleading, endeavor.

Examples : Testing Hypotheses

Most hypotheses state a relationship between two or more variables. This relationship may be strong or weak. The strength of the relationship may be measured by one of a number of statistics which summarize the table as a whole. Electronic technology has freed us from the tedium of arithmetic, but we still have to decide which statistic will best reveal to the reader the configuration of our data. Here are two examples to put the hypothesis test to work. They will then be used to illustrate some simple statistics that summarize the relationship between two variables. These are known as "measures of association."

1. Hypothesis: "Whites are less concerned with achieving progress in civil rights than are racial minorities in the United States."
Data: A survey in 1964 asked people whether they thought the civil rights movement was going too fast or too slow. Here are the responses:

	Too fast	About right	Too slow	Don't know
Whites	211	63	13	7
Orientals	1	1	0	0
Negroes	1	15	13	1

Decide which is the independent variable, put it at the top of your table, percentage upon it, and make up a table, complete with title and all the other necessary elements. If you choose to combine or omit categories, be able to justify your decision. Put your table here:

In a sentence, sum up the findings of the table as they bear upon your hypothesis.

_____

_____

2. There has been a great deal of controversy about the effects of election-night predictions. On the basis of the first returns from East Coast precincts, the television networks start making projections which predict the winner before the polls close on the West Coast. In the 1964 presidential election these predictions were made between 4:30 P.M. and 5 P.M. Pacific Coast Time. They indicated that Lyndon B. Johnson would defeat Barry Goldwater. Phrase a hypothesis as to the effect of these predictions upon those West Coast voters who had not yet gone to the polls.

Hypothesis: Those late voters *who had heard the telecasts* would tend to vote more for

_____ than *those who had not heard them* because _____

_____

_____

Data: A California survey asked late voters whether they listened to the predictions before they voted, with these results:[1]

	Listened be- fore voting	Did not listen before voting
Voted for Johnson	129 ____ %	850 ____ %
Voted for Goldwater	101 ____	639 ____
Refused to tell vote	14 ____	141 ____
Total	244 ____ %	1630 ____ %

Calculate the percentages and indicate whether your hypothesis is confirmed: _____

_____

Demonstrating the Obvious

In the Examples just completed, your testing of the first hypothesis told you something that "everybody knows already"—that blacks in 1964 were less satisfied than whites with the progress of civil rights. The second hypothesis also dealt with something that "everybody knows"—the tendency of people to side with a sure winner, often called the "bandwagon effect," but the evidence collected in this instance showed that what "everybody knows" about the bandwagon effect was *not* correct.

One difference between the natural and the social sciences is that we accept findings of the former as non-obvious and difficult to discover. With the latter we may have already made unsystematic observations and come to impressionistic conclusions, to which we cling fervently. When elaborate research undertakings merely confirm what we already believe to be so, we dismiss them as trivial. But if they fail to confirm what we believe, we may question the methods of the researcher, the size of the sample, etc. Much of the utility of the social sciences consists in testing whether what we take for granted about human nature can be demonstrated to be true under specified conditions.

[1]For more results from this study, see Harold Mendelsohn, "Election-day Broadcasts and Terminal Voting Decisions," and Douglas A. Fuchs, "Election-Day Radio Television and Western Voting," *Public Opinion Quarterly*, 30 (1966), 212–236.

Measures of Association: D and d_{yx}

It has already become apparent that an important part of analyzing political data involves reducing the infinite complexity of the real world to more simple summary measures. Now we shall consider several measures that reduce the relationship between two variables to a single figure. Let us begin with the percentage table from the previous Example, Hypothesis 1, combining or "collapsing" the data into four cells.

	Whites	Others			Whites	Others
Too fast	211	2	which, in per-		74%	6%
About right *and*			centage table			
too slow	76	29	form becomes		26	94
					100%	100%
					$N = 287$	$N = 31$

One can see that the percentage table, though effective as a communicating device, is redundant as a summary measure. The entire meaning of the table hangs upon a single figure. That is the difference between 74% and 6% on the top line, which is 68%. (The difference on the second line is, of course, the same: $94\% - 26\% = 68\%$.) We can define this difference as D, and note that D varies from 0, when there is no difference between the two percentages, up to 100%, which would occur if two of the cells diagonal to one another had no cases in them. This would be the situation if all whites had said "too fast" and none of the others had given this response—a perfect association between the two variables.

D has the advantage of being completely understandable, but it has a drawback as a single indicator that sums up these four percentages. Let us begin with the same raw figures but violate our rule and percentage across on the *dependent* rather than the independent variable. The result is:

	Whites	Others		
Too fast	211 (99%)	2 (1%)	=	213 (100%)
About right *and*				
too slow	76 (72%)	29 (28%)	=	105 (100%)

In this case, although the raw data are the same, $D = 99\% - 72\% = 27\%$, and that's a long way from 68%. A measure that is so unreliable cannot be used to sum up a fourfold table. This difficulty is overcome by calling it d_{yx} where x is the independent variable (usually the column variable) and d_{xy} where y is the independent variable.[2] Sometimes D is known as ϵ (epsilon). Statisticians have the exasperating habit of calling the same thing by different names. We just learn to live with it.

Yule's Q

Another measure for summarizing a fourfold table is Yule's Q.[3] It is quite simple to compute from raw data by the formula:

$$Q = \frac{ad - bc}{ad + bc}$$

The letters refer to the values in the cells of a fourfold table located as follows:

a	b
c	d

In our Example:

$a = 211$ $b = 2$

$c = 76$ $d = 29$

$$Q = \frac{(211 \times 29) - (2 \times 76)}{(211 \times 29) + (2 \times 76)} = \frac{6119 - 152}{6119 + 152} = \frac{5967}{6271} = .95$$

(handwritten marginalia:)

	0-20	over 20
voted	60	45
novote	40	55

$\dfrac{1500}{5100}$

$\begin{matrix} 70 & 40 \\ 30 & 60 \end{matrix}$ $.29 = Q$

$\dfrac{3000}{5400} = .55 = Q$

Q varies from +1.0 for perfect positive association to −1.0 for perfect negative association. Therefore Q is zero when there is no association at all. In this case, $Q = .95$ means there is a very strong positive relationship between the two variables. A perfect positive association of $Q = +1$ would occur if there were no cases at all in the b cell or none in the c cell, or none in either b or c. This would be the case if no non-whites said "Too fast," or if no whites said "About right" or "Too slow," or if all whites said "Too fast" and all non-whites said "About right" or "Too slow." Perfect negative association would occur in the circumstances (improbable in this Example) of all

[2] R. H. Somers, "A New Asymmetric Measure of Association for Ordinal Variables," *American Sociological Review*, 27 (1962) 799–811.

[3] It bears the name of its inventor, G. Udny Yule, to distinguish it from another statistic called Q, the interquartile range, which has no relationship to it.

minority members saying that civil rights had proceeded too fast and/or all whites saying that it had not gone too fast.

"Positive" and "negative" in this instance have no intrinsic meaning. Researchers routinely put the values of the variables they expect to be associated in the first column (independent) and the top row (dependent). If there were the same proportion of whites and of others in the "Too fast" cells, there would be no relationship between the variables. Q would be 0.

Now compute Q for the following collapsed data from the second hypothesis test in the last Example:

	Listened before	Did not listen before
Johnson	129	850
Goldwater	101	639

$$Q = \frac{-3419}{168281} = -.02$$

Q is ——————, which means that ————————————————————————————

——————————————————————— .

Let us compare Q with D as a measure of association. Q has the major disadvantage of having no obvious, intrinsic meaning, unlike the difference between two percentages. We must learn to interpret Q to appreciate whether a value of $-.02$ is a high or a low one. Knowing that 0 represents complete lack of association, +1 the maximum possible positive association, and -1 the maximum negative association makes it apparent that $-.02$ shows virtually no relationship between the variables. Q, in its range of variation from +1 through 0 to -1, resembles other members of the family of *coefficients of correlation,* some of which will be discussed later. The sign (+ or −) indicates the direction of the relationship:

> Plus means that the cases tend to fall in the *ad* (upper left and lower right) cells, i.e., the *descending* (\ ) diagonal.
> Minus means that the cases tend to fall in the *bc* (lower left and upper right) cells, i.e., the *ascending* (/) diagonal.
> This direction, of course, is determined by how we construct our table.

In our Example, if non-whites had been put in the left-hand and whites in the right-hand column, Q would have come out as $-.95$ instead of $+.95$. Similarly, if the top and bottom rows on the dependent variable are transposed, the sign is reversed. Although the choice is arbitrary, it is customary for researchers to arrange their tables so that a positive Q corresponds with support for their hypotheses.

The Phi Coefficient

There are other measures of association with different properties from Q. One of them is ϕ, or *phi,* pronounced either "fie" or "fee" and calculated as follows:

$$\phi = \frac{ad - bc}{\sqrt{(a + b)\,(c + d)\,(a + c)\,(b + d)}}$$

Let's calculate ϕ for the last example, where

$$
\begin{aligned}
a &= 129 & b &= 850 \\
c &= 101 & d &= 639
\end{aligned}
$$

$$\phi = \frac{(129 \times 639) - (850 \times 101)}{\sqrt{979 \times 740 \times 230 \times 1489}} = \frac{-3419}{\sqrt{248,105,820,000}} = \frac{-3419}{498,102} = -.01$$

Phi reaches $+1$ or -1 only if *both* cells in the diagonal are empty, that is, when the response to one variable is *completely* determined by the response to the other. Let us think of a legislative committee voting to pass or kill a bill. If the outcome of the voting were as follows:

	Dem.	Rep.			Dem.	Rep.
Pass	10	0		Pass	5	0
Kill	0	5	or	Kill	0	10

then both ϕ and Q would be $+1$.

But if the outcome were:

	Dem.	Rep.			Dem.	Rep.
Pass	5	0		Pass	5	5
Kill	5	5	or	Kill	0	5

then the ϕ value for the relationship between party and vote would be only $+.50$, but the Q value would still be $+1$. Thus ϕ reaches its maximum value when all the cases are on the diagonal and the two other cells are empty. Q, on the other hand, can reach a maximum when only one cell is empty. For the same table, ϕ gives a lower value than Q except where ϕ reaches unity. To decide which you should use, consider how a logician would look at the following tables:

	Dem.	Rep.			Dem.	Rep.
Pass	10	10		Pass	15	0	ϕ
Kill	0	10	or	Kill	0	15

Q

He would say that in the case at the left, being a Republican is a *necessary* but not a *sufficient* condition for voting to kill the bill, whereas at the right being a Republican is both a necessary and a sufficient condition for a "kill" vote.

The choice between Q and ϕ is one you have to make solely in terms of the meaning of your research. For example, if you were studying legislative votes and wished a measure that reached high values only when the majorities of the members of the two parties were opposed to one another, you would choose ϕ over Q.

Example: Strength of Association

1. A study of party leaders in Ohio produced the following income, age, and education distributions. Calculate Q and ϕ for each.

	Democrats	Republicans		
Under $7,500	55	64	$Q =$ _____	$\phi =$ _____
Over $7,500	65	61		
Under age 45	41	38	$Q =$ _____	$\phi =$ _____
Over age 45	85	91		
No college	57	54	$Q =$ _____	$\phi =$ _____
Some college	66	73		

Source: These data are reconstituted from Tables V and VI in Thomas A. Flinn and Frederick M. Wirt, "Local Party Leaders: Groups of Like Minded Men," *Midwest Journal of Political Science,* 9 (1965), 77–98.

Which variable shows the strongest relationship to party affiliation? _____

2. What in general would you conclude about the relationship of these three variables to party affiliation among party leaders? _____

_____

The Imprecision of Prose

Observations about the relationship between political or social variables may be expressed in five ways:

1. In prose: "Manual workers tend to vote for the Democratic party."

2. In algebra:

$$\frac{W_d}{W_d + W_r} > \frac{O_d}{O_d + O_r}$$

where W_d means manual workers voting Democratic

W_r means manual workers voting Republican

O_d means persons other than manual workers voting Democratic

O_r means persons other than manual workers voting Republican.

3. In percentage tables, if we have data supporting the observation:

	Workers	Others
Democratic	55%	51%
Republican	45	49
	100%	100%

4. In summary statistics, for the table above:

$$D = 4\%$$

5. In graphs of various sorts, for example:

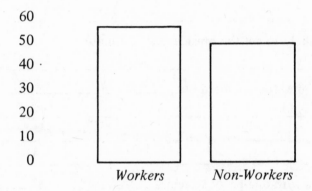

PERCENTAGE DEMOCRATIC OF WORKERS AND NON-WORKERS

Each of these methods of communication has its advantages and disadvantages, but where precision is valued, prose is probably the worst. Consider the following dialogue, which may resemble one you have heard on occasion:

"Don't light that cigarette; you know that smokers die of lung cancer!"

"Really? All of them?"

"No, of course not. I mean they *tend* to die of lung cancer."

"You mean that's what the majority of smokers die of?"

"No, but they're more likely to die of it."

"Oh, you mean that lung cancer kills more smokers than do heart failure and automobile accidents."

"Not that, either. What I mean is that more smokers die of lung cancer than do non-smokers. In fact, the death rate from lung cancer among heavy smokers is about 1.66 per thousand deaths."

"That's very small. It's obvious that smokers *don't* tend to die of lung cancer."

"Yes, they do. The comparative death rate among non-smokers is only .07 per thousand."

The difficulty here is that any statement of relationship involves a comparison with a control group, although what the control group is may not be expressed. Here are some statements about politics. Examine each of them, not for truth but for completeness. If there are any parts of the statement that have not been made explicit, complete the statement to put it in testable form. Otherwise, write "Complete" in the space provided. If the statement is not testable, write "Value judgment" beside it.

1. Protestants tend to vote Republican; Catholics, Democratic. _____

_____

2. Fewer cities had the commission form of government in 1960 than in 1930. _____

_____

3. Candidates from populous states are likely to get the presidential nomination. _____

_____

4. The United States defense budget is higher than it should be. _____

_____

5. Politicians are dishonest. _____

_____

6. Strong pressure groups appear in states with one-party systems. _____

_____

7. In roll-call voting, legislators from competitive districts follow their party line. _____

_____

8. Monarchy is characteristic of underdeveloped nations. _____

_____

There is a moral to this chapter. We start off with the real world in its infinite diversity. We simplify it by choosing two variables, reducing the possible categories on each to two, and compute D, Q, or ϕ. Thus we reduce 318 individuals in our sample, all of them with their own racial identities and idiosyncratic opinions on civil rights progress, first to a 12-cell table, then to a 4-cell table, and finally to a single index of relationship between the variables. "$Q = +.95$" is a truly economical statement. We pay a price for this reduction. We have to do some arithmetic, we have an index which the man in the street does not understand, and we have had to learn to interpret D, Q, and ϕ in order to choose between them and to interpret the result. But we have achieved the ability to say *how strong* a relationship exists between these two variables in terms that are comparable with any other pair of variables in the gamut of political and social attitudes. We have overcome the inadequacies of English prose for stating the relationship between two variables.

For a lively discussion of the various fourfold measures, going back to the political observations made by Aristotle, read Hayward Alker, Jr., *Mathematics and Politics* (New York: Macmillan, 1965), Ch. 4. The most lucid statistics text on this subject is Morris Zelditch, Jr., *A Basic Course in Sociological Statistics* (New York: Holt, Rinehart and Winston, 1959).

6 / Statistical Significance

*The induction of which the logicians speak, which
proceeds by simple enumeration, is a puerile thing;
concludes at hazard; is always liable to be upset by
a contradictory instance. . .and leads to no result.*
FRANCIS BACON, 1620

The Davies article on charisma (p. 51, fn. 8) says that percentage differences are "highly significant statistically; significant, that is, at the one percent level of confidence using a Chi-square test." Elsewhere Davies observes that a finding "falls slightly short of statistical significance at the five per cent level." This chapter deals with what "statistical significance" means, using a very simple test. Chapter 8 describes *chi square,* the most frequently used test of statistical significance.

Let us assume that you have a hypothesis you have deduced from theory. You need some empirical evidence, upon which you will decide either to bring your discovery before your colleagues, crying "Eureka!" or return sadly to your desk and scratch pad. So you collect observations by conducting a survey of American citizens. The data you collect will either support or reject—confirm or disconfirm—your hypothesis. But before you start to analyze your data, you pause to ponder: how much contradictory evidence must I have before I will give up this hypothesis? How much assurance will I need before I stake my reputation on it? Obviously *you* must already have considerable confidence in it, or you would not have gone to the cost of testing it. Perhaps you are so committed that you would not recognize contradictory evidence if it should appear in the data you have gathered.[1]

---

[1]This desire to believe in one's own theories is not confined to social researchers. C. P. Snow's early novel, *The Search* (New York: Scribners, 1934, 1958), deals with a physical scientist's desire to find support for his theories and the subtle effect this has upon his research. Snow revised and reissued the novel in the 1950s upon the urging of scientists who felt that it was an effective portrayal of the nature of their work.

The strongest case for quantitative techniques in political (or any other) research is that, properly used, they protect you against this very human frailty by permitting you to apply a standard of truth outside of—independent of—your own judgment. They will force you, reluctantly, to reject something you *want* to believe if it is not sufficiently substantiated by the evidence.

Back to your problem. Let's assume your hypothesis deals with a certain characteristic that is operationalized as a "yes" answer to one of the questions in your survey. Your hypothesis will be supported by the finding that *men* tend to give a "yes" response to a greater extent than *women.* You have a random sample of 200 cases, a true cross-section. Before starting to analyze your data, you ask yourself: how strong must the evidence be before I am convinced? You try to foresee various ways in which the results might turn out. If you can decide *in advance* what your standards will be, you can avoid fooling yourself into accepting quite trivial differences as convincing evidence, just because they happen to run in the right direction.

Before making your survey, you consider the following possible outcomes (remember: these are *numbers,* not percentages):

(a)	M	W	
Yes	50	50	
No	50	50	Obviously, this would not support your hypothesis at all. No
	100	100	difference appears.

(b)	M	W	
Yes	55	65	This outcome would not only fail to confirm your hypothesis,
No	45	35	it would appear to contradict it, for in this case women say
	100	100	"yes" more than men. In this instance the whole theory that led to your hypothesis should be re-examined.

(c)	M	W	
Yes	61	41	Now, that's more like it. The difference is in the right direc-
No	39	59	tion; that is, men are more likely to give the "yes" response,
	100	100	and by a substantial margin: a difference of 20 ($61 - 41 = 20$).

(d)	M	W	
Yes	91	71	Here the difference is just as great: 20. Would it disturb you
No	9	29	that both men and women give predominantly "yes" respon-
	100	100	ses? It shouldn't. You are looking for tendencies, not majorities.

(e)	M	W	
Yes	51	49	If you were to get these results, what would you conclude? Is
No	49	51	your hypothesis supported or not? How much confidence would
	100	100	you have in your answer?

Standards of Confidence

At this point you might well decide that you should set a standard in advance and say: I'll not convince myself, and I'll certainly not expect to convince anyone else, unless I get a difference of 5 or more. By setting your criterion in advance, you would ward off the tendency to say, whatever you found, "Well, there is a difference of 4. It's not much, but I'll settle for it." Which you could just as easily talk yourself into doing with a difference of 3. Or a difference of 2, as in example (e).

But where to set the standard? One solution would be to let each researcher do it. But some would be lax and suggest revision of theories whenever they found trivial departures from expectation. Others would set their standards high, and we would never get the advantage of their research unless they achieved overwhelming verification. The best research by the most meticulous scholars would remain unpublished, and the worst research would clutter up the journals. Some conventional standard is necessary. The standard that came to be accepted is expressed in terms of *probability*. It can best be illustrated by returning to your original hypothesis.

When we say the difference of 2 in example (e) is so small that it could easily be caused by chance, we are saying, in effect, that in the whole population men and women may be equally likely to respond "yes" to our query, but by sheer luck you ran across two more men giving that response than you did women. How likely are you to be this "lucky"?

Or to put it another way: Suppose men and women responded to your question after flipping a coin, both sexes replying "yes" if it fell heads and "no" if it fell tails. What is the likelihood of getting this 2-person difference between the groups—which you would then interpret as support for your hypothesis—when in fact there is only a random difference, the result of the odds involved in coin-tossing?

At this stage, we find we have a standard. Mathematicians long ago calculated the probabilities involved in coin-tossing, among them the odds that if you tossed two batches of 100 coins each, you would find two more heads than tails (in our example, two more "yesses" than "noes") in the first batch (in our example, men) than in the second batch of coins (women). They have figured these odds by algebraic logic (theoretically) and have tested the odds by tossing coins (empirically); the results have been reduced to tables in the back of statistics books. In this particular instance, the answer is that *three times out of every eight* you would get a difference as great as 2—i.e., you would get evidence in support of your hypothesis—even though nothing but chance was at work, as in flipping coins.

So you would reluctantly conclude, if your study should come out as in example (e), that no one would be very convinced. Nor should they be. On the other hand, if you were to get a difference as great as 20, as in examples (c) and (d), the statistical tables would show that the chances are fewer than 1 out of 1,000 that this is due simply to chance. In other words, with odds of 999 to 1 that your finding represented a *real* difference in the population, and not just the luck of the draw, you would be quite justified in advancing your hypothesis before a critical audience.

Levels of Significance

The conventional standard that social scientists have agreed upon is expressed in such probability terms. The actual level has been set by convention. Political scientists customarily decide in advance that their findings must reach the level of probability where the odds are 19 to 1 against their being due to chance. Hence the phrase you have noted (or will someday see) in an article in a journal of political science, sociology, or social psychology: "$p < .05$" or "$p < 5\%$." It means that the probability (p) of the results found occurring by chance is less than 1 in 20, or 5 in 100, or .05, or 5%—all of which mean the same thing. Psychologists, who have larger samples and more refined measures, may demand more of their data ($p < .01$), and biologists or agronomists who accumulate large samples of plants or animals may enjoy the luxury of requiring that their findings have only 1 chance in 1,000 of being due to chance ($p < .001$). It is worth noting that no one who works with samples ever claims to be *absolutely* sure about his conclusions. He merely states *how probable* it is that he is right, taking into account the size of the sample.

At the other end of the scale, particularly when samples are unavoidably small, a political scientist or sociologist may report a finding that is significant only at $p < .1$.[2]

"Statistical significance" is a technical term with a specialized meaning. Therefore you must be careful to avoid using "significant" in its ordinary connotation of "important" or "noteworthy" in a report in which you also use "significant" in the technical sense.

Precisely applied, tests of significance tell us *how likely* it is that a *tendency* we find in a *sample* is sufficiently strong for us to conclude that it also occurs in the *population* from which the sample is drawn. Some assumptions are involved. One is that we know what population we

---

[2] And, to confuse the beginner, we are forced to point out that some scholars persist in reporting the probability of their being *right*, not wrong. So if you read that some finding is "significant at the 95% level," you may infer that it means the same thing as "significant at the 5% level." Similarly, $p > .01$ usually means the same as $p < .01$.

are generalizing about. Another is that our sample is truly *representative* of this population in the sense that only *chance* fluctuations can throw it off. To take an example: in 1936 the *Literary Digest* poll predicted that Alfred M. Landon would win the presidency with nearly 60% of the popular vote. Its sample size was 3 million persons. Landon got only 38% of the vote. Significance tests would show that the chance of an error of this size with a 3 million sample was infinitesimally small. What was wrong was that the huge sample was not at all typical of the American electorate. It consisted of persons whose names were taken from telephone directories and automobile license lists. Phones and cars were luxuries found only in middle- and upper-class homes in the 1930s. Thus the *Digest's* estimate for the entire electorate was based upon an upper-income sample, not a random one. Such errors are called "biases," in contrast to "random errors." Statistical tests are applicable only to random errors, not biases. Such tests are based on the assumption that the sample is random, which means that every person has exactly the same chance of being drawn into it.

A sample drawn by taking names from a *listed population,* picking them by drawing slips from a hat, spinning a wheel, or some other completely unpredictable random-number device would meet this specification. Since there is no list of the American population or the electorate, this is impossible. Interviewing systems only approximate the ideal. Those people who live in remote places, and those who move frequently, are often out of town, work at odd hours, or spend most of their time at the poolroom or the country club thereby reduce their chances of being located by the interviewer. Good survey organizations make massive, and expensive, efforts to reduce biases. The egregious errors of the *Literary Digest* are not repeated. However, surveyors realize that they only approach, but never quite reach, the randomness assumed in statistical tests. They apply the tests nevertheless, to estimate how much error is attributable to sample size. This is the only part of the error they can even estimate.

No further effort will be made here to explain either the logic or the algebra behind the derivation of formulae and tables. If you have an inquisitive and thoughtful turn of mind, you should seek the answers in an introductory statistics book or course. You will find much more satisfaction in understanding the principles involved than in taking them on faith, which is what you are asked to do here. To summarize:

1. Statistical significance gives us one answer to the question: how strong a relation between variables must I find in a survey before I should conclude that the apparent relationship is "real" and not just due to chance?
2. The answer is not in unequivocal terms, but in probabilistic terms: how big a chance do you want to take that you may be wrong?
3. The conventional answer to the above question is: only 1 chance in 20.

4. Two factors contribute to a high level of significance:
   A. a strong relationship, and
   B. a large number of cases.
5. These tests assume that your sample is representative of the population. They are irrelevant if it is seriously biased.

Testing for Significance

Let's assume you have a hypothesis that the "rich" differ from the "poor" in some respect that may be operationalized by a simple yes–no attitude question. Your sample contains 211 cases, distributed as follows:

	Rich	Poor
Yes	58%	71%
No	42	29
	100%	100%
	(N = 58)	(N = 153)

There is a percentage difference (D) of 13 points (42% − 29% = 13%; or 71% − 58% = 13%). Is this difference significant at the .05 (or 1-in-20) level? The answer may be found in Table 6.1.

TABLE 6.1

Minimum Size (N) of Group	Minimum Size (N) of Group					
	50	90	150	300	600	1000
50	20	18	16	15	15	15
90	18	15	14	12	12	11
150	16	14	12	10	9	9
300	15	12	10	8	7	7
600	15	12	9	7	6	6
1000	15	11	9	7	6	5

The Ns, or number of cases, on which the two percentages are based are 58 for the Rich group and 153 for the Poor group. The smaller group, 58, is above the minimum group size of 50, and the larger N of 158 is above the minimum of 150. The 50 column and the 150 row intersect at the figure 16. *This is the smallest percentage difference that is significant at the .05 level.*

98

Since the observed difference of 13% between Rich and Poor is smaller than this, we must conclude that the results of the survey are not statistically significant. A difference of this size could result from chance oftener than 1 time in 20.

Note the effect of sample size. Had we increased our sample to bring the number of rich respondents to 150, then our hypothesis would have been confirmed by the data, with the same percentage difference of 13 points, since it is larger than the 12% in the table.

Study of this table will reveal something important about sampling. The richer rewards in reliability occur with the first small increases in sample size. Put yourself in the position of the survey researcher with a limited budget, deciding how large a sample he or she can afford. Interviewing costs for an accurate nationwide sample will run at least $10 per case. If it is assumed that any two categories to be compared have about the same number of members in the sample— a most optimistic assumption—the researcher first considers a sample of about 100 cases, which will cost $1,000. If the researcher should find differences smaller than 20% (for example, if 41% of 50 men gave some response, compared to 60% of 50 women, he or she would be dubious about the applicability of the finding to the national population. An alternative is to go up to 100 men and 100 women, or a sample of 200 in all. This will cost another $1,000 but will produce differences of 15% or more, a 5% improvement in probable accuracy. Let us project this computation, in Table 6.2.

TABLE 6.2

Sample	Cost	Limit of Accuracy	Improvement in Accuracy per $1,000
100	$ 1,000	20%	
200	2,000	15	5%
300	3,000	12	3
600	6,000	8	1.3
1200	12,000	6	0.3
2000	20,000	5	0.1

Facing estimates like this, surveyors and pollsters do not often increase their samples beyond 3,000 cases. They prefer to spend their money on painstaking interviewing and sampling, seeking responses that accurately convey what each interviewee thinks in a collection of persons that accurately mirrors the characteristics of the population being studied. The extra money goes to locate hard-to-find cases whose absence would bias the sample.

Table 6.1 is a conservative one in the sense that it will not tell you that a hypothesis is confirmed when in fact there is not a large enough sample to warrant this conclusion. But it may tell you that a borderline difference is *not* significant when a more refined test would tell you that it is. We shall now expand the table to make it a little more accurate in this respect, taking into account another element.

If your two percentages are 45 and 50, then a 5% difference is *relatively* rather small. But if your two percentages are 10 and 15, then the 5% difference between them is comparable in size to the percentages themselves. If 10 and 15% give a "yes" answer to some question, we could just as well say that 90 and 85%, respectively, do *not* give a "yes" answer. Therefore, $X\%$ and $(100-X)\%$ have the same meaning so far as this characteristic of the table is concerned. The rule is that the closer the percentage split comes to 50–50, the smaller will be the percentage difference as a proportion of the percentages themselves. We are now going to take this principle into account in the expanded table.

Significance of Difference Between Two Percentages

For every test of a hypothesis expressed in percentage terms, we have the following information:

    1. The size of each of the two groups compared. They are called "subsamples," and the number of cases in each is designated N_1 and N_2. (It makes no difference which subsample is called N_1 and which N_2.)

    2. The percentage of each group giving the response we are analyzing. One of these percentages will be *closer* than the other one to 50%, and this one will be designated P_c. The other, the percentage *farther* from 50% (and hence nearer to 0 or 100%), is called P_f.

    3. The difference (D) between these two percentages (discussed on p. 82) is:

$$D = |P_c - P_f|$$

This means to subtract whichever percentage is smaller from the one that is larger, i.e., to subtract and ignore the sign.

For example, is the hypothesis that women tend to favor the incumbent mayor supported by the following data?

	Men	Women
Favor	$61\% = P_c$	$68\% = P_f$
Neutral	11	9
Oppose	28	23
	100%	100%
	$N_1 = 261$	$N_2 = 238$

$$D = |P_c - P_f|$$
$$= |61\% - 68\%|$$
$$= 7\%$$

Whether the 7% difference is large enough to rely upon as representing a real difference in the population is influenced by two factors:

1. How large each subsample is. The larger the Ns, the greater the probability that the percentages in the *sample* are close to the true proportion in the *population*. The closer the sample estimates are to the true proportions, of course, the greater is the probability that whatever difference between them is found in the sample is close to the true difference, if there is in fact a difference, in the population.

2. How close the percentages are to 50%. It is easier for a large difference to occur by chance if the two percentages are close to 50% than if they are close to 0 or 100%.

Table 6.3 takes account of these principles. P_c will tell you which block of the table to work in. N_1 tells you which row to use, and N_2 which column. D must be *as large as or larger than* the number found in the cell of this table if the hypothesis is to be confirmed at the .05 level of significance.

In the example, P_c (61%) is between 60 and 69%, so we enter the second block. Both Ns (261 and 238) are over 150 but less than 300, so we find the intersection of the 150 row and the 150 column, which gives us a difference of 11%. Therefore our difference of 7% falls short of significance. This means that there is more than 1 chance in 20 that this great a difference could be caused by sampling error in view of the number of cases in the two subsamples.

This procedure is conservative, in that it will err in the direction of *rejecting* your hypothesis. The two Ns were closer to 300 than to 150, and with Ns of 300 an 8% difference is significant. If you interpolate and ask whether in this instance a difference of 10% might be significant, you may want to apply a more accurate, less conservative, test. Later we will present an exact method of testing for significance, *chi square*.

TABLE 6.3 TABLE OF SIGNIFICANT DIFFERENCES BETWEEN PERCENTAGES*

Where P_c is:	N_1 is at least:	N_2 is at least:									
		30	50	90	150	300	600	1000	1500	2000	3000
Between	30	25%	23%	21%	20%	19%	19%	19%	19%	19%	18%
41% and	50	23	20	18	16	15	15	15	15	15	14
59%	90	21	18	15	14	12	12	11	11	11	11
	150	20	16	14	12	10	9	9	9	9	9
	300	19	15	12	10	8	7	7	7	7	6
	600	19	15	12	9	7	6	6	5	5	5
	1000	19	15	11	9	7	6	5	4	4	4
	1500	19	15	11	9	7	5	4	4	4	4
	2000	19	15	11	9	7	5	4	4	4	3
	3000	18	14	11	9	6	5	4	4	3	3
Between	30	23%	22%	20%	19%	19%	18%	18%	18%	18%	18%
31% and	50	22	19	17	16	15	15	14	14	14	14
40% or	90	20	17	14	13	12	11	11	11	11	11
between	150	19	16	13	11	10	9	9	9	9	9
60% and	300	19	15	12	10	8	7	7	7	6	6
69%	600	18	15	11	9	7	6	5	5	5	5
	1000	18	14	11	9	7	5	5	4	4	4
	1500	18	14	11	9	7	5	4	4	4	4
	2000	18	14	11	9	6	5	4	4	4	3
	3000	18	14	11	9	6	5	4	4	3	3
Between	30	21%	20%	19%	18%	17%	17%	17%	17%	17%	17%
21% and	50	20	17	15	15	14	14	13	13	13	13
30% or	90	19	15	13	12	11	11	10	10	10	10
between	150	18	15	12	10	9	9	8	8	8	8
70% and	300	17	14	11	9	8	7	6	6	6	6
79%	600	17	14	11	9	7	6	5	5	5	4
	1000	17	13	10	8	6	5	4	4	4	4
	1500	17	13	10	8	6	5	4	4	4	3
	2000	17	13	10	8	6	5	4	4	3	3
	3000	17	13	10	8	6	4	4	3	3	3
20% or	30	17%	16%	16%	15%	15%	15%	15%	15%	15%	15%
under;	50	16	14	13	13	12	12	12	12	12	12
80% or	90	16	13	11	10	10	9	9	9	9	9
over	150	15	13	10	9	8	7	7	7	7	7
	300	15	12	10	8	7	6	6	5	5	5
	600	15	12	9	7	6	5	4	4	4	4
	1000	15	12	9	7	6	4	4	4	3	3
	1500	15	12	9	7	5	4	4	3	3	3
	2000	15	12	9	7	5	4	3	3	3	3
	3000	15	12	9	7	5	4	3	3	3	2

*Numbers in the cells are the minimum percentage differences necessary for statistical significance at .05 for two-tailed tests and .025 for one-tailed tests, given the proportions and the subsample Ns. The table is based upon *chi square*, which will be explained in Chapter 8.

Example : The Effect of Education on Voter Decision-Making

Let us test the hypothesis that educated persons are slower in deciding for whom they will vote than uneducated persons. Respondents to the Survey Research Center study of the 1964 election were divided into three groups: those with grade-school education or less, those with some high school or college, and those with a college degree. This is the independent variable. They were asked on the survey when they made up their minds to vote for Johnson or Goldwater. This is the dependent variable, and it has three categories: those who said they knew all along how they would vote or that they always vote for the same party, those who said they decided around convention time or as soon as they knew who the candidates would be, and those who decided during the campaign or waited until they went into the polling booth.

1. In which group would your hypothesis call for the largest percentage saying they knew all along? _____ The smallest percentage saying they knew all along? _____ .

   In which group would your hypothesis call for the largest percentage saying they decided during the campaign, up to election day? _____ The smallest percentage giving this response? _____ .

2. Here are the percentages actually giving each response:

	Grade school	High school	College graduate
Knew all along	26%	17%	8%
Decided at convention time	47	48	55
Decided during campaign	27	35	37
	100%	100%	100%
N =	223	719	142

   Are the percentages in the right direction to support your hypothesis? _____

3. Hypothesizing that education is a factor leading to delay in deciding, let us first test for the significance of the difference between the grade-school and high-school groups. The difference between the proportions who did not delay, but knew all along, is 9%. Is this difference in the right direction? _____ Is it significant at .05? _____

4. Now perform the same operation, comparing the high-school and college groups. Write the difference and your conclusion: _____

   _____

   _____

   _____

103

5. Now figure the differences and their significances, if you had used the proportion saying they decided during the campaign as your operational definition of "delay in deciding." Your conclusions: _____

_____

_____

7/ The Null Hypothesis

*If the signs hit twenty times
for one missing, a man may lay a
wager of twenty to one of the
event; but may not conclude it for
a truth.*
THOMAS HOBBES

To this point we have discussed the testing and confirming or disconfirming of hypotheses which postulate anticipated relationships between variables. There is another way of looking at this. Instead of seeking support for the hypothesis that our variables are related, we may seek to *reject* the proposition that they are *not* related. This double negative is called the *null hypothesis.* On first encounter, your reaction is likely to be that this is a roundabout and perverse way of treating something that is already sufficiently complicated. Once the principle is understood, however, it becomes apparent that the distinction is not a fine-spun triviality, but is essential to grasping what we do when we undertake to disentangle the complexities of the world about us.

In Chapter 1 we contemplated the millions of political acts, the thousands of characteristics that might be selected to describe the people who performed those acts, and the multifarious institutions that try to organize these activities. Each time we formulate and test a simple bivariate hypothesis, we are selecting from this almost infinite pool of variables one independent and one dependent variable and postulating that we will discover that the two variables are correlated. We may state this hypothesis in prose, in arrow diagram, or in tabular form:

(1) X sort of person (or institution) tends to perform Y sort of action.

(2) Independent variable (X)→Dependent variable (Y)

(3) Dependent (Y)

	Independent (X)	
	+	−
+	Many cases	Few or no cases
−	Few or no cases	Many cases

Only rarely are we able to collect information about the entire population, so we usually have to depend upon samples. But there is a possibility (greater with small samples than with large ones) that we will find support for our hypothesis, even though the null hypothesis of no relationship applies in the population as a whole. We appraise the possibility of this happening by a familiar standard: the known probability distributions obtained from flipping coins, rolling dice, etc. Suppose we have a proposition to test: "women are more likely than men to support political candidates with beards." Let us also assume that we have no problem in sampling the United States electorate and have a means of operationalizing our hypothesis, e.g., by showing respondents pictures of the same candidate before and after shaving and asking their preference. Now let us compare this test with a similar proposition that dimes are more likely to turn up heads than pennies:

General (non-directional) hypothesis	Sex is related to political barbophilia		Coin denomination is related to heads/tails outcome	
Directional hypothesis	Women	Men	Dimes	Pennies
	Pro-beard x		Heads x	
	Anti-beard	x	Tails	x
Population to generalize about	Men and women in United States electorate		Dimes and pennies in circulation	
Our sample	100 men, 100 women		100 dimes, 100 pennies	
Outcome	Unknown: hence the survey		Known: half heads, half tails	

Since the coin-tossing probabilities have long since been worked out theoretically and also demonstrated empirically by generations of statistics classes, we know how frequently we would get more heads among dimes than among pennies due just to sampling, even though the null hypothesis holds true for the population as a whole. If we were to draw many samples of 100 pennies and 100 dimes from all the coins in circulation, flip them, and then record the number of heads in each lot of 100, what would we find? The most frequent occurrence would be 50 heads and

50 tails. The next most likely outcome would be 49 heads and 51 tails. Equally likely would be 51 heads and 49 tails. Slightly less likely would be 48 heads or 52 heads. We would only rarely get 40 heads or 60 heads, and hardly ever as few as 30 heads or as many as 70 heads. It is almost, but not quite, impossible that we would get 100 heads or no heads at all. The frequency with which each proportion of heads would come up may be calculated from probability theory. The graph would look something like the curve in Figure 7.1. Along the bottom is the frequency of each number of heads out of 100 coins tossed; along the side is the number of times this proportion of heads would occur if 100 coins were tossed 100 times.

FIGURE 7.1

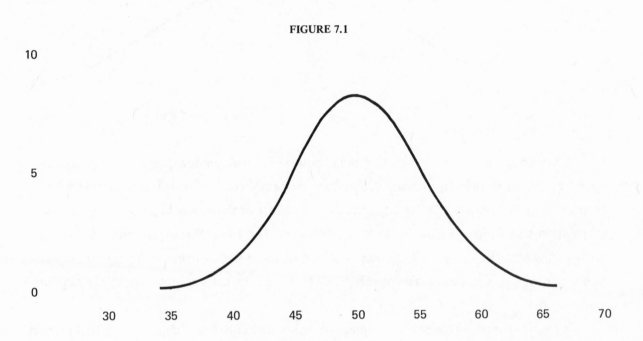

The probability of getting fewer than 30 or more than 70 heads is not zero, as the diagram suggests, but so small that it cannot be indicated graphically.

You may think of this chart as representing either the *number of times* an outcome would occur in *100 tosses* of 100 coins or the *probability* of that outcome occurring in *one toss* of 100 coins. If you haven't encountered that idea previously, it may require a little reflection to realize that for practical purposes the two statements are identical.

In our sample of pennies the most likely occurrence is 50 heads, and the same goes for our sample of dimes. Thus the most likely difference D is $50 - 50 = 0$. If this occurs in our sample, it gives no support for the proposition that dimes turn up heads more frequently. But it is almost as likely that the dimes would show 51 heads and the pennies 50, for a difference of 1. And it is slightly less likely that dimes would show 52 heads and pennies 50, or dimes 51 and pennies 49, or all the other possibilities that would give $D = +2$ in favor of dimes. (Of course, we also might get more heads among the pennies—indeed, this is equally likely—but since it would not confirm our hypothesis, we shall disregard it for the present.) The probability of each *difference* occurring is graphed in Figure 7.2.

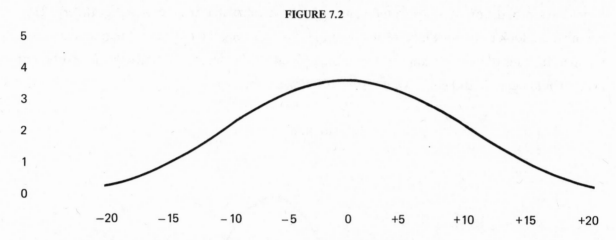

FIGURE 7.2

Considering that the + differences would show more heads among dimes and support the hypothesis, while 0 differences and − differences would not confirm it, you can see that a fair proportion of the samples, though somewhat short of half of them, would give support to the proposition that dimes are more likely to fall heads up. And some of these differences may be +5 or +10, which the unsophisticated might accept as impressive evidence in favor of a proposition which we know *not* to be true of the population, i.e., the total number of dimes and pennies in circulation.

Our beard survey has only one sample, not many, and only one D representing the difference between men and women in their responses. But we know there can be differences between heads-on-pennies and heads-on-dimes in samples, even though there would be none if the entire population of coins were flipped. We also know that nearly half these coin sample differences would lead us to reject the null hypothesis—no difference—and that some of these rejections would be based on sample results that appeared quite impressive, all this even though there is no real difference in the coin population. Finally, we know (from the calculations on which Figure 7.2 is based) how often each difference of +1, +2, +3, and so on would occur by chance. It is against this standard that we appraise the D found in the one sample in our beard survey and discover how often a difference of this size could occur by chance even when the null hypothesis of $D = 0$ is true in the population of the United States.

Though we have illustrated the process with only one pair of subsamples, each consisting of

100 cases, it is possible to calculate a comparable distribution for any combination of subsample sizes.[1]

Theory and the Null Hypothesis

A variable, remember, is anything that can be measured and has more than one value. If we picked two variables at random from the large grab bag of possible variables in the world of behavior, paired them up for investigation, and used sampling to collect our data, we would be sampling a universe in which entropy—another word for the null hypothesis—prevailed. Except, of course, to the extent that we selected variables which are related because there is some order imposed upon this random world. And that order, to be sure, is what our theory leads us to deduce in this case.

Instead of men and women, we might have selected as our hypothesized independent variable any one of an almost infinite number of variables: young *vs.* old, tall *vs.* short, rural *vs.* urban, Democratic *vs.* Republican, left- *vs.* right-handers, optimists *vs.* pessimists. Testing for effects of all such variables, using samples, is like tossing our samples of 200 coins. There is a known probability each time of getting an apparent relationship, even where there is no real relationship in the population as a whole.

In a world with an almost infinite number of variables that might be cross-tabulated, the sensible expectation is that any pair of them selected haphazardly will not be related. Any relationship found will be due to random sampling. And that is the *null hypothesis*—the hypothesis that no relationship will be found, that the difference between percentages will be zero. But if our theory is sound, if we understand reality well enough to have posited a true relationship, then a difference in the expected direction will be found and it will be rather large. Then the null hypothesis will be rejected on the grounds that either there is a real relation between our two variables in the population or else an improbable accident has occurred.

The null hypothesis approach to research is not a fanciful exercise in epistemology but rather a sane and reasonable view of the world of human behavior: the belief that relationships between variables are not credible unless, first, there is a logical *theoretical* reason to expect them to be,

---

[1]The two tests are analogous in every respect but one: we know that the ratio of heads to tails is 50:50, but we do not know the ratio of barbophiles to barbophobes in the total population. Also, a finite population of coins might depart trivially from a difference of zero. These points have some statistical relevance but need not confuse our explanation.

and second, that there is demonstrated *empirical* evidence that rises to a high probability.[2]

In statistics books the null hypothesis is often presented as H_0 and the corresponding working hypothesis as H_1. Though researchers speak loosely, for convenience, of demonstrating their hypothesis, H_1, they will quickly admit that all they have done, strictly speaking, is to gather impressive evidence to reject, disconfirm, or falsify the null hypothesis, H_0. Persons who long for certainty may feel disappointment on learning that the so-called scientific method does not purport to *prove* anything. We can never say we have proved our hypothesis, and even less the theory that gave rise to it. We have merely demonstrated that in a specific instance, empirical data have shown a relationship between variables that is highly unlikely to be due to chance. This is evidence in support of the theory, always assuming that the operational definitions adequately represent their conceptual equivalents. Our confidence in it is enhanced. But no theory is ever proved, for theories deal with abstractions and with statements that are applicable to the past, present, and future, and no one can "prove" a statement about the future.[3] Students who use the word "prove" in their research papers generally lose points on their grade.

Example : Framing The Null Hypothesis

1. Go back to Table IV in Davies' article (Chapter 3). Express the *null hypothesis* that Davies seeks to reject:

   _____

   _____

   _____

2. Do the data run in the right direction to reject the null hypothesis? _____

3a. Is the percentage difference in the "least black and white" category large enough to reject the null hypothesis at the .05 level? _____

   b. Is the percentage difference in the "most black and white" category large enough? _____

---

[2] I sometimes suspect that social science performs a greater service by confirming than by rejecting null hypotheses. A fair proportion of the trouble in this world stems from our belief in plausible, romantic propositions about human behavior, many of them more appealing than the dull reality that can be demonstrated. Notions that one race or nation is braver, nobler, more energetic or brighter than another, that a set of people is engaged in a conspiracy against us, that some proposed policy will have a dramatic effect for good or ill are appealing. The most enlightening aspect of political behavior research is to discover how few of the relationships we take for granted are statistically demonstrable. In other words, much of what we "know" about politics is sheer moonshine.

[3] Paul Davidson Reynolds, *A Primer in Theory Construction* (Indianapolis: Bobbs-Merrill, 1971), Ch. 6.

Direction of the Hypothesis

We phrased the hypothesis in our introductory example, "Women are more likely to support political candidates with beards." Since a difference larger than 15 percentage points is significant at the .05 level, results such as the following would be accepted as a rejection of the null hypothesis:

	(a) Men	Women	
Pro-beard	52%	68%	$D = 16$
Anti-beard	48	32	
	100%	100%	

Any of the following differences would be considered not significant and would be taken as support for the null hypothesis.

(b) Men	Women		(c) Men	Women		(d) Men	Women	
Pro-beard 58%	64%	$D = 6$	60%	60%	$D = 0$	64%	56%	$D = -8$
Anti-beard 42	36		40	40		36	44	
100%	100%		100%	100%		100%	100%	

But take a look at this one:

	(e) Men	Women	
Pro-beard	70%	50%	$D = -20$
Anti-beard	30	50	
	100%	100%	

What would you conclude?

You can't conclude that there is no difference in the population (H_0). There is evidence of a difference, but it runs in the direction *opposite* to that supporting H_1. For this hypothesis test, we must count it as supporting the null hypothesis. But it suggests that we should re-examine our theory, since it led us in a direction not supported—indeed contradicted—by the evidence.

The Two-Tailed Test

There is a form of hypothesis not yet discussed. Instead of specifying that women prefer bearded candidates, or that men prefer them, our theory might hold that sex is somehow related to preference for bearded candidates. With such a hypothesis, it is twice as easy to find supporting evidence by chance, since differences *in either direction* would reject the null hypothesis.

This sort of non-directional hypothesis may appear to be vague, equivocal, and something less than rigorous. Indeed it is, but sometimes our theory does not provide a better one. Freud noted the ambiguity of love-hate and love-fear relationships. We know that there is a relationship between fathers' political views and those of their sons. But in what situations would sons follow their fathers' orientations, and when would they rebel against them and go in the opposite direction? The proposition that whenever presidents bungle, their popularity in the polls goes down would seem to be too trivial to bother testing. But John F. Kennedy's popularity went *up* after the Bay of Pigs debacle.[4] Or we might want to examine the proposition that religious background influences voting behavior in some elections without being able to specify in advance how Protestants might differ from Catholics, or how either might differ from Jews or non-believers. These *non-directional* hypotheses are often characteristic of exploratory research on a new topic. For such hypotheses we need a "two-tailed test." The name stems from the principle that the hypothesis can be supported by either positive or negative differences that are unlikely to be due to chance. Figure 7.3 illustrates the principle.

FIGURE 7.3

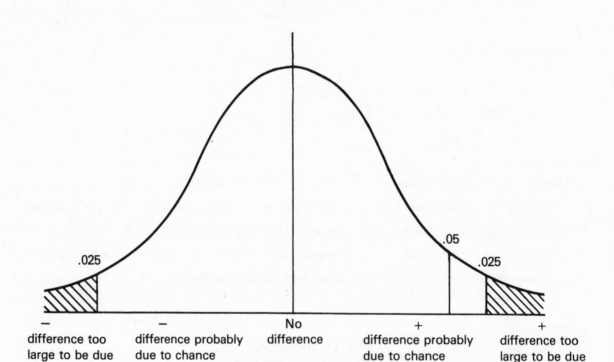

NOTE: One-tailed test is on the right; two-tailed test is on both right and left.

[4]John E. Mueller, "Presidential Popularity from Truman to Johnson," *American Political Science Review*, 64 (1970), 18–34.

The table of significant differences at .05 on p. 102 and the *chi square* test to be treated in the next chapter are designed for two-tailed tests, where large differences in *either* direction will reject the null hypothesis. That is, the 5% of results so improbable that we must conclude that our finding is genuine are distributed equally between the two tails of the distribution. Hence the tables are very "conservative" for one-tailed tests; they will accept the null hypothesis more often than is warranted. If you have specified the direction in advance and consider even large differences in the wrong direction as confirming the null hypothesis, then you may halve the .05 significance level and say that $p = .025$.

Conservatism of Tests

Whether the null hypothesis is accepted or rejected at a given level of significance depends upon two things: (a) how large the overall sample is and (b) how large a difference is found. With small samples we may have to accept the null hypothesis of no difference between the groups— that is, no relation between the variables—when with larger samples, achievable by spending more money on the research, we might reject the null hypothesis and conclude there is a relationship. Our conclusions are thus inextricable from the quality of our research undertaking.

In general, the scientific method is conservative in that it does not consider it so serious a mistake to reject a "true" finding on the grounds of small sample and probable random error as it does to accept a false finding. Thus the researcher stacks the odds against himself at 19 to 1 or 99 to 1. This insistence on overwhelming evidence, and acceptance of even this as tentative and subject to eventual revision, is symbolized by the familiar story of the scientist riding with a companion in a train. Observing a flock of sheep, the companion observed that they were all black. After a moment's thought, the scientist expressed modified agreement. "At least," he said, "they are all black on this side."

Statistical methods also provide for estimates of the probability of accepting the null hypothesis when in fact there is a difference not caused by chance and it ought to be rejected. The researcher also runs this risk. It is harder to estimate, because it turns upon *how large* a difference he or she is refusing to recognize. Of course, the scientist does not know how large the *real* difference in the population is. If this were known, he or she would know that there *was* a real difference and would reject the null hypothesis. Suffice it to observe here that there is more chance of accepting the null hypothesis if the real difference (whatever it is) is small, and less likelihood if it is large. And the probabilities can be figured out. If you wish to pursue this problem, you will find it in statistics books under the rubric of "Type I" errors (falsely rejecting the null hypothesis) and "Type II" errors (falsely accepting the null hypothesis).

Steering a course between the two types of errors is not exclusively a preoccupation of statisticians, but concerns all of us who must base decisions upon imperfect knowledge. A doctor commits a Type II error (false positive) when he or she diagnoses a healthy person as having a pathological condition. However, a physician who mistakenly dismisses a sick person as being healthy commits a Type I error (false negative). Either type is unfortunate for the patient; Type I errors are also unprofitable for surgeons. For a jury to call a guilty person innocent (Type I) is considered less damaging in our society than for it to hold an innocent person guilty (Type II). Our legal processes are structured to reflect this difference.

Occasionally students are tempted to phrase their working hypothesis to state that there is *no* significant difference in percentages, or no relationship between a pair of variables. That is, they want to prove, rather than disprove, the null hypothesis. If that is their purpose, they cannot employ the approach of seeking evidence that the behavioral world is not random but conforms to the pattern predicted by theory. Such tests can be constructed, but they require a greater knowledge of the statistics than we present here.

There are other complications. For example, if we examine a series of tables, with no theory indicating what to expect, and look for significant differences at the .05 level, we will probably find 1 out of every 20 tables we look at to be significant, even though the tables themselves have only random differences. Alternatively, if 40 researchers, unknown to each other, were to test the same hypothesis, which in fact is false, the odds are that 2 of them will encounter significant results, at $p < .05$. The 38 would accept the null hypothesis, give up and not publish their results. But the other 2 would write articles describing their findings, and readers of the journals would say: "It must be so, because two researchers independently got the same results." The protection against this happening is, of course, the reliance on a *theory* for the generation of hypotheses. This requires that individual findings be fitted into a pattern of similar evidence.[5]

Academic *vs.* Applied Research

We have noted that the decision to believe only when the odds are at least 19 to 1 against the null hypothesis is no more than an accepted convention among social scientists seeking reliable

---

[5]To explore such problems further, read William H. Kruskal, "Significance, Tests of," *International Encyclopedia of the Social Sciences* (New York: The Free Press, 1968), vol. XIV, pp. 238–250.

generalizations about relationships in their environment. According to this convention, it is much worse to accept misinformation than to reject truths that are not firmly supported by evidence.

A politician or statesman might set quite different standards in deciding whether to act upon information gathered by research. If the suggested policy involved serious consequences—an epidemic, an environmental catastrophe, or a nuclear holocaust—he might demand a much more stringent standard. On the other hand, if the research supported a policy where the costs to the taxpayers were minimal and the results highly beneficial, he might settle for odds of, say, 3 to 1 that the policy would be successful.

In recent years, public policies have increasingly been based upon research statistics involving tests of significance. Public works to contain floods, policies to cope with environmental damage such as oil spills, regulations for the sale of drugs suspected of causing cancer, and estimates of the probability of default on government-guaranteed loans are examples. Underlying such calculations is the logic of the null hypothesis.

8 / Chi Square

Ah, what a dusty answer gets the soul
When hot for certainties in this our life.
GEORGE MEREDITH

The Table of Significant Differences (Table 6.3, p. 102) has the advantages of dealing with data in their most understandable form, percentages, and of being calculable for any table in a report where the author has failed to indicate whether the data are significant.

It has several disadvantages: (a) It is conservative and may show a borderline difference not to be significant at .05 when a more precise test would show it to be significant; (b) It does not report significance of subgroups with N less than 30; (c) It tells only whether a difference is significant at .05—it does not tell what the significance actually is, whether .01 or .001, or something else; (d) In a table with more than four cells, you have to choose which pair of percentages to use. Sometimes, as in the Example on p. 103, dealing with education and delayed voting decision, the choice makes a difference. When you used the "Knew all along" category as your operational definition, you got significant differences. But when you used "Decided during campaign," you found a difference that was not significant.

The measure most frequently used in working with political and social data, since it avoids these difficulties, is a statistic called *chi square* (pronounced "kye-square") and written χ^2. The formula for it is:

$$\chi^2 = \Sigma \; \frac{(O - E)^2}{E}$$

and it appears formidable only if you have not been told that the *sigma* sign (Σ) means to add up a series of numbers as you learned in the second grade.

O refers to the *observed* values in each cell of a table.

E refers to the values you would *expect* to find in the cell if there were no relationship between the variables, that is, if the null hypothesis were absolutely true.

The Connecticut Crackdown

Let us start with a very simple example. The number of highway deaths in Connecticut in 1955 was 324. In December, Governor Abraham Ribicoff announced that persons convicted of speeding would thenceforth have their driver's licenses suspended for 30 days, with even more severe penalties for second and third offenses. The death toll for 1956 was only 284.

Was the drop in traffic fatalities due to the governor's action or to chance fluctuations? First, let's calculate the *expected* frequency. What would you expect the number of fatalities to be in any two consecutive years if no other factors were in operation? They should be the same, so we take as our expectation an average of the two years; in this instance:

$$E = \frac{324 + 284}{2} = \frac{608}{2} = 304$$

Now we calculate the difference between observed and expected frequencies and square these differences. Then we divide the result by *E*.

Year	O	E	$(O-E)^2$	$\dfrac{(O-E)^2}{E}$	
1955	324	304	$20^2 = 400$	400/304 =	1.315
1956	284	304	$20^2 = 400$	400/304 =	1.315
	608	608			2.63

Now to sum up:

$$\chi^2 = \Sigma \frac{(O-E)^2}{E} = 1.315 + 1.315 = 2.63$$

Before we can go further, we need to calculate something called "degrees of freedom." The observed frequencies add up to 608. If we know the number for either year, we can find the other by subtraction. Therefore, we are "free" to insert only one number; the other is determined. There is one degree of freedom.

Our *chi square* value of 2.63 is meaningless unless we know how likely it is to occur by chance. This has been worked out by statisticians and is presented in the back of every statistics text. Table 8.1 is an abridged table of *chi square.* Knowing that degrees of freedom (*d.f.*) is 1, we look across the first row and find that our value of 2.63 falls between 1.64 and 2.71. Reading the column headings, we see that such a value would occur by chance between .20 (1 chance in 5) and .10 (1 chance in 10).

1 chance in 10
1 chance in 20

TABLE 8.1 ABBREVIATED TABLE OF *CHI SQUARE**

Degrees of Freedom	[.10]	[.05]	*Level of Significance*			
	.20	*.10*	*.05*	*.02*	*.01*	*.001*
1	1.64	2.71	3.84	5.41	6.64	10.83
2	3.22	4.60	5.99	7.82	9.21	13.82
3	4.64	6.25	7.82	9.84	11.34	16.27
4	5.99	7.78	9.49	11.67	13.28	18.46
10	13.44	15.99	18.31	21.16	23.21	29.59
20	25.04	28.41	31.41	35.02	37.57	45.32
30	36.25	40.26	43.77	47.96	50.89	59.70

*This abbreviated table of *chi square* is taken from Table IV of Fisher and Yates: *Statistical Tables for Biological, Agricultural and Medical Research,* published by Longman Group Ltd., London (previously published by Oliver & Boyd, Edinburgh), and reprinted by permission of the authors and publishers.

An academic researcher would accept the null hypothesis that revocation of licences is unrelated to traffic deaths at the conventional level of $p. < .05$. But a governor might well decide that a policy that involved some extra work for the courts but kept some citizens alive was worth pursuing if the odds are better than 5 to 1 that there is a relationship between the independent and dependent variables. The case of the Connecticut speeding crackdown is a famous one in the annuals of evaluation research, and we shall refer to it again.

Chi Square for a Fourfold Table

Now let's consider the answers to a simple question such as: "Should the budget be balanced this year?" Suppose the responses were as follows:

	Dem.	Rep.	Total
Yes	9	8	17
No	10	6	16
Total	19	14	33

The numbers within the table are called "cell entries" or "cell frequencies," and the numbers in the Total column in the right margin and at the bottom are called "marginals." Using our familiar cell labels:

a	b
c	d

E for cell a is $\dfrac{17 \times 19}{33} = 9.8$

E for cell b is $\dfrac{17 \times 14}{33} = 7.2$

E for cell c is $\dfrac{16 \times 19}{33} = 9.2$

E for cell d is $\dfrac{16 \times 14}{33} = 6.8$

As you can see, the E (expected) frequencies are entirely determined by the marginals. You can confirm this by noting that $a + b = 9.8 + 7.2 = 17$, and $a + c = 9.8 + 9.2 = 19$, the proper marginals. Now check to see that the E value you calculated for cell d fits in with its respective marginals.[1]

What is meant by an "expected" frequency in a cell? E is found (in fourfold tables like this and in larger tables as well) by multiplying the marginal for the row in which the cell is located by the marginal for the column in which it is located and dividing the product by N for the table as a whole. This gives an expected value for each cell that is exactly proportionate to the distribution of the marginals. Thus if one were to percentage a table of expected values in either direction, across or down, and figure the percentage difference (D) for any comparable pair of percentages,

---

[1] If you prefer algebra, E for cell a is $(a+b)(a+c)/a+b+c+d$; for cell b, $(a+b)(b+d)/a+b+c+d$; for cell c, $(a+c)(c+d)/a+b+c+d$; for cell d, $(c+d)(b+d)/a+b+c+d$.

D would be zero. Such a table could be described in a number of ways. We could say that the cell values are *determined* by the marginal totals, that $O = E$, that the variables are *independent* of one another, that there is no *relationship* between them, that we cannot *predict* one from the other, and that *the null hypothesis is confirmed.* However, if observed frequencies differ from expected frequencies, i.e., $O \neq E$, one variable depends on the other (in this example, whether a respondent says "Yes" depends in some degree on whether he or she is a Republican or a Democrat), and we can predict the response more successfully if we know the party than if we don't know it. The null hypothesis could be rejected.

The *chi square* test is to determine whether this dependence or relationship is strong enough to be meaningful or so trivial that the departure from independence might well be due to chance. To do this, we must calculate the departures from expectation, $O - E$, in each cell. Then we must square $O - E$, and divide $(O - E)^2$ by E. Finally, we must sum up the resulting values for the table as a whole. This will measure how much the actual results depart from the expectation of no relationship. If it is large enough, we can reject the null hypothesis.

For cell a, $O - E = 9.0 - 9.8 = -0.8$
For cell b, $O - E = 8.0 - 7.2 = 0.8$
For cell c, $O - E = 10 - 9.2 = 0.8$
For cell d, $O - E = 6 - 6.8 = -0.8$
For the final operation, obeying the Σ or summation sign:

$$\chi^2 = \Sigma \frac{(O - E)^2}{E}$$
$$= \frac{-0.8^2}{9.8} + \frac{0.8^2}{7.2} + \frac{0.8^2}{9.2} + \frac{-0.8^2}{6.8}$$
$$= \frac{.64}{9.8} + \frac{.64}{7.2} + \frac{.64}{9.2} + \frac{.64}{6.8}$$
$$= .065 + .089 + .070 + .094 = .318$$

The formula for degrees of freedom in a table with four or more cells is:

$$d.f. = (r - 1)(c - 1)$$

where r stands for the number of rows in the table and c for the number of columns. In our fourfold table there are 2 rows and 2 columns, so $d.f. = 1 \times 1 = 1$. Thus we go into the χ^2 table on the first row, where the degree of freedom is 1. We find that our χ^2 value of .318 is much less than 1.64, the smallest value given. Therefore, we conclude that there is more than 1 chance in 5 ($p > .20$) that the results could be caused by chance. Thus we would not have much confidence in a finding that Democrats differed from Republicans in their responses.

Degrees of Freedom

We did the preceding calculation mechanically. It refers to the number of values in the table which are free to vary, once the marginal totals are given. To take our original example:

$$a + b = 17$$
$$+ \quad +$$
$$\underline{c + d = 16}$$
$$19 \quad 14$$

Replace a with any number you wish between 1 and 17. What must b now be if $a + b = 17$? _____ What must c be if $a + c = 19$? _____ And what must d be if $c + d = 16$ and $b + d = 14$? _____ Thus you see that, given the marginals, you had freedom to fill in only one number. Once this is done, all the rest are determined.

Insert any marginals you wish in the following table, remembering that the row and column marginals must add up to the same number, which is N for the table.

	Low	Medium	High	
Yes				____
No				____
	____	____	____	= N

Now confirm that a 2 × 3 table, according to the formula $d.f. = (r - 1)(c - 1)$, has two degrees of freedom by calculating by subtraction all the remaining cell frequencies after you have put in the first two.

A Tricky Example

Where the percentage difference test concentrates on particular pairs of percentages, *chi square* tells you whether your table *as a whole* departs significantly from the cell values that would be expected by chance. This puts upon you the burden of genuinely understanding your table and what there is about it that is unexpected. Suppose you are interested in testing the proposition that Republicans tend to be conservative and Democrats liberal. Here are the data (hypothetical) and the χ^2 calculations.

	Republican	Democratic	Independent	Total
Conservative	20	40	5	65
Liberal	35	70	5	110
Neither	10	10	30	50
Total	65	120	40	225

Row	Col.	O		E	O − E	$(O − E)^2/E$	χ^2
1	1	20	65 × 65/225	= 18.8	1.2	1.4/18.8	= .1
1	2	40	65 × 120/225	= 34.7	5.3	28.4/34.7	= .8
1	3	5	65 × 40/225	= 11.5	− 6.5	43.0/11.5	= 3.7
2	1	35	65 × 110/225	= 31.8	3.2	10.4/31.8	= .3
2	2	70	120 × 110/225	= 58.7	11.3	128.4/58.7	= 2.2
2	3	5	110 × 40/225	= 19.6	−14.6	213.2/19.6	= 10.9
3	1	10	65 × 50/225	= 14.4	− 4.4	19.7/14.4	= 1.4
3	2	10	50 × 120/225	= 26.7	−16.7	277.8/26.7	= 10.4
3	3	30	50 × 40/225	= 8.9	−21.1	445.7/8.9	= 50.1
		225		225.1			79.9

.29 (handwritten)

What is *d.f.*? _____4_____ The table is clearly significant at $p <$ __.001__ . Is the hypothesis supported? _____ Explain. _____

_____

Although the data are contrived, the point they make is important: It is the meaning of the table in light of the hypothesis that is relevant, not merely the value of *chi square* or the level of significance. You need to see which cells contain the departure from expectation and whether they differ in the direction of your hypothesis or in some other direction. The total *chi square* value will not reveal this if it has been calculated by computer, but you can always assess the meaning of the table by looking at percentage differences.

One- and Two-Tailed Tests

The table of *chi square* is calculated for testing non-directional (two-tailed) hypotheses. If the direction is specified in the hypothesis (a one-tailed test), the probabilities given at the head of the columns may be halved. Let us now look at our three examples to determine which way to approach the table.

Governor Ribicoff's policy was designed to reduce, not increase, traffic fatalities. This amounts to a directional hypothesis. Therefore we may halve the values and say that for a one-tailed test the odds are between .10 and .05 that the program had an impact, rather than between .20 and .10.

In the second example, we merely speculated that party would have some effect on the yes/no responses, but we did not specify whether Democrats or Republicans were more likely to respond with a "yes". Thus the two-tailed test is appropriate.

In the third example, if the meaning of the data had not forestalled a significance test, we would have wanted a one-tailed one.

The *chi square* test of significance will work with tables of any size, although the calculations get cumbersome if the table is very large. However, it is perfectly permissible to combine adjacent rows or columns to reduce the size of the table, so long as the meaning of the categories makes this a sensible operation. In fact, if the expected frequency (E) in any cell is less than 5, it *must* be combined with an adjacent cell by combining row or column categories.[2] For example, if respondents were originally divided into Low, Medium, and High participation groups, and there were too few cases in the High group, they could be combined with the Medium group to make a two-level rather than a three-level scale.

A Priori Expectations

Chi square may be used either with expected frequencies derived from the marginals, as in the last example, or with expected frequencies determined by external logic, or *a priori* reasoning. Suppose we had court statistics for a town in which one-fifth of the population belonged to a minority group. Out of 110 convictions last year, 33 of the persons convicted were members of the minority group. Is this a larger proportion than chance would indicate? The expected frequen-

[2]There is an alternative formula for χ^2 where expected frequencies are below 5. It is given in footnote 12 of the Davies article (p. 53).

cies come from the population; one-fifth of 110 is 22. Hence:

	Observed	Expected	$(O-E)$	$(O-E)^2$	$(O-E)^2/E$
Minority group	33	22	11	121	5.5
Others	77	88	−11	121	1.375
				χ^2 =	6.875

Since there are only two cells (Minority group and Others) in our contingency table, the insertion of any number in one would determine the other, so we have 1 degree of freedom. (The $(r-1) \times (c-1)$ formula does not work for two-cell tables.) Our value of 6.875 is significant at .01 according to the table on p. 127. But we hypothesized that a larger proportion of minority members were being convicted, a one-tailed hypothesis. Hence we may say that the probability is .005 or only 5 in 1,000, that this many convictions would have occurred by chance. These numbers, of course, do not reveal whether the minority group commits more crimes, is more likely to be arrested, or is more likely to be convicted.

In this example, the expected frequencies were determined in advance by the population figures. In the Connecticut speeding study, the expected frequency was based upon the death toll in the year prior to the crackdown. Use of *chi square* with *a priori* probabilities such as these is particularly appropriate for public policy evaluation, to see whether a change in some variable can be attributed to an action taken by the government, or instead could easily be the result of chance fluctuation. These are usually one-tailed tests.

The other major use of *chi square* is in testing hypotheses about the relation between two variables, where the data come from surveys or other sampling operations. Here the frequencies are determined by the marginals, and the test will be one- or two-tailed depending on whether the hypothesis specifies direction.

Cramér's *V* and Other Measures of Association

Chi square increases with the number of cases and the strength of the relationship. If we can remove the effect of *N,* we are left with a measure of association or correlation between the two variables. The trouble is that statisticians have found no one best way of doing this. Alternatives are the contingency coefficient *C,* Tschuprow's *T,* ϕ, and ϕ^2. Although you may find any of these used in journal articles, the current favorite is Cramér's V (sometimes called Cramér's ϕ) for which the formula is:

$$V = \sqrt{\frac{\chi^2}{mN}}$$

where $m = (r-1)$ or $(c-1)$, whichever is smaller.

For the example on p. 127

$$V = \sqrt{\frac{79.9}{(3-1)225}} = \sqrt{\frac{79.9}{450}} = \sqrt{.1776} = .42$$

V measures the departures of observed from expected frequencies wherever they may occur, on a scale running from zero where $O = E$ for every cell and hence there is no relationship between the variables, up to +1 where the observed frequencies differ as far as possible from those expected under the null hypothesis. This means a strong relationship between the two variables, but what sort of a relationship it is can be discovered only by a close look at the table to determine the location, size, and direction of the differences between observed and expected frequencies.

Limitations on Statistical Tests

There are numerous statistical tests, each appropriate for different measures of different kinds of data in different problems of analysis. This discussion is designed to enable you to understand what such tests do and to interpret them when they appear in articles. We have not mentioned many complications, qualifications, and assumptions having to do with the choice of appropriate tests. These are set forth in the statistics texts, and before you go beyond a *tentative* reliance on tests in your research, you should get to know more about the particular circumstances under which each test is reliable.

There are some general qualifications that have been made about statistical tests of significance that we should examine briefly:

1. Probability calculations depend upon the assumption of random sampling. Pure randomness, of the sort achieved by spinning a wheel, throwing dice, or flipping coins, is usually impossible or prohibitively costly in political and social research. One would need a complete listing of the population, and even the United States Census does not achieve this. We assume randomness when we apply statistical tests, even though we know our surveys fall somewhat short of it.

In any survey a few persons refuse to cooperate and a few cannot be found to be interviewed, even after repeated calls at their residence; they have moved, are in the hospital, or are on extended vacation. We have no way of estimating the bias caused by omitting them, although their absence seriously limits the assumption of random sampling.

2. If we test only one hypothesis, we may accept the odds quoted by the mathematician. But if we test 20 hypotheses in the course of a study, and we apply the .05 level of significance, we may expect to get 1 of the 20 substantiated by the very rule of chance that we are using to eliminate random results. The best protection against this fallacy is not to scan large numbers of tables and draw conclusions about those found to be significant, but rather to test only those hypotheses that are clearly derived from some coherent body of theory.

3. Significance tests cannot be relied upon in a mindless, mechanical fashion. In the example on p. 127 we would have been foolish to let a highly significant χ^2 value mislead us into believing we had evidence that Republicans were conservative. We must rely upon percentages and measures of association to describe what the relationship is before we ask whether it is significant.

4. The statistical test tells us only the probability that our data are representative of some larger universe or population. Suppose, however, we are studying all the United States senators in a particular Congress, or all the nations in the world in a given year. Are statistical tests appropriate? Of what population of senators or nations is our sample representative? Or suppose we sample the citizens of Detroit and find some interesting and significant generalizations. The statistician would tell us that the universe to which these observations are applicable consists of the citizenry of Detroit, Michigan, in whatever year the study was done. But if this is strictly true, no political scientist outside of Detroit would be interested in the findings. In fact, we implicitly generalize the findings made in Detroit, or New Haven, or Elmira to the population of the United States. We do so, but without statistical justification. We even, on occasion, generalize from some rather crude observations made by Aristotle around 500 B.C. to the behavior of Americans in the twentieth century. And every day, of necessity, we sample the world of experience about us and draw conclusions by methods that would send any statistician into convulsions. A business executive concludes a negotiation with a Japanese manufacturer and becomes an authority on "Orientals." We make generalizations about "African character" after observing the behavior of two homesick exchange students from Kenya. We speak glibly about the nature of "politicians" on the basis of our casual observations of the Jackson County Board of Supervisors.

In sum, the statistical test is a diagnostic tool, like a polygraph, a barometer, a compass, or a geiger counter. It has to be used with some skill, not indiscriminately, and its showing must be accepted in the light of other evidence drawn from the theory, the sampling scheme, and the objective of the research.

9 / New Approaches to Research

If we transgress our proper boundaries,
go into provinces not belonging to us, and
open a door of communication to the dreary
world of politics, that instant will the
foul Deamon of discord find his way into
our Eden of philosophy.
ADAM SEDGWICK
addressing the British Association
for the Advancement of Science, 1833

You know now that with a formula, a table, and a pocket calculator you can compute measures of association and tests of statistical significance. In this chapter we put aside arithmetic for the moment and pursue instead the more important matter of when, whether, and why you might choose to calculate these statistics. We shall also examine how one reaches conclusions (a) in the search for "truth" and (b) in the choice of public policy alternatives.

Basic and Applied Social Research

There is a difference between physics and engineering, between biology and medicine, between economics and business administration, between political science and public administration. This is the difference between basic and applied research. Davies' article is a good example of basic research: it is concerned with *learning* about charisma rather than doing something about it. The hypothesis test is the logical process underlying basic research in the social sciences.

In the last two decades, the same process has been adapted to applied research on problems of education, health, crime, unemployment, and welfare. Policy-makers have asked—and sometimes answered—such questions as:

Do schoolchildren learn more in small classes than large ones?
How frequently do drivers use seat belts? Do seat belts prevent injury?

135

Do long sentences deter criminals?

Does pre-school training improve the academic ability of deprived children?

Is a negative income tax a disincentive to employment?

How did the European public react to President Richard Nixon's visit to China?

What decrease in gasoline consumption will result from a given price increase?

Although its underlying logic is the same as in basic research, the purpose of applied research—ameliorating a condition or solving a problem by using what we know (or think we know)—leads to differences in form or context:

1. Applied research is more inductive than deductive. Problem-solving falls more naturally into the form of questions than of hypotheses.

2. Value judgments are more entangled in applied research. Groups or segments of the population gain or lose from decisions based upon the research.

3. Data are not usually specified in advance and then collected to correspond with operational definitions; they emerge from observing what people have done under everyday circumstances.

These tendencies will become clearer as we examine four general forms that research takes and differences in the way controls are applied, significance tests employed, and conclusions drawn in each of the four approaches.

Approach 1: The Laboratory Experiment

This is the standard method of basic research in biology and psychology. A "treatment," which might be exposure to a drug, a stimulus, or a particular environment, is administered as the independent variable to one group of subjects (human or animal). This is the *experimental* group. Another group, drawn from the same population by some random process that makes it as much like the experimental group as possible, is the *control* group. Behavior of the two groups is observed with respect to the dependent variable. Because the samples are alike in every respect except that the experimental group has been exposed to the treatment and the control group has not, any difference in behavior may be attributed to the effect of the independent variable (assuming that a significance test indicates that the difference is so large that it cannot be attributed to chance variation among individuals). The researcher then concludes that a similar difference would be found in the population from which the groups were drawn.

Though it is infrequently done, this technique may be adapted to political research. Some Northwestern and Western states provide for initiative and referendum measures, wherein citizens vote for or against proposed laws as well as candidates. The Washington state voting law limited the time a citizen may spend in the polling booth to two minutes, regardless of the number or complexity of issues on the ballot. Several years ago, a Washington psychologist was evicted from the booth before finishing his selections. This set him to pondering whether the outcome of such hurried choices might be different from more considered ones. A survey of the literature suggested that while people use information in making decisions, there is a point at which too much information and too little time to absorb it produces "information overload," which confuses more than it clarifies. Other research suggested that conservatives prefer "cognitive simplicity" and avoid novel or complex stimuli. Thus the psychologist hypothesized that voters under pressure would appraise a ballot proposal as simply "liberal" or "conservative" in intent, rather than exploring its ramifications, and they would tend to approve conservative and disapprove liberal proposals.

At this point, a sociologist might have surveyed a cross-section of voters asking if they had ever felt pressed and how they voted. A political scientist might have looked at other states, their legal time limits and whether conservative proposals won or lost, and by how many votes. What might a political activist have done? _____

_____

Being a psychologist, this researcher decided that a laboratory experiment was appropriate. He and his colleagues then selected from summaries of bills introduced in the legislature 10 that were judged to be conservative and 10 judged to be liberal in their intent. Four sections of a psychology class—the control group—were given all the time they needed to "vote" for or against the bills. The other four—the experimental group—were limited to two minutes. Members of the experimental group were found to be more conservative in their choices.[1]

This example exhibits both the strengths and weaknesses of the experimental approach to political research. Great care was taken in constructing the test, judging the items, assuring the likeness of the two groups, and enforcing the time limit and other experimental conditions. It was improbable that other variables influenced the outcome, while the significance test showed the difference unlikely to be due to chance. But these were students, not run-of-the-mill voters; they were in a laboratory situation, not a voting booth. May one generalize from a tightly controlled laboratory situation to the variegated reality of life in the outside world? And what population is being sampled: student voters? Washington voters? voters in all states with referenda provisions and time limits?

[1] Robert O. Hansson, John P. Keating, and Carmen Terry, "The Effects of Mandatory Time Limits in the Voting Booth on Liberal-Conservative Voting Patterns," *Journal of Applied Social Psychology* (1974), 336–342. The research design was actually more complex than this summary of it.

Approach 2: The Social Survey

The prototype for this method was the public opinion poll, introduced in the 1930s and familiar to newspaper readers of Gallup, Harris, and others. When pollsters report that 56% will vote for some presidential candidate, or that 39% will take one side of an issue, there is no control group for comparison (unless they cite an earlier poll or election). The population from which the sample is drawn is well defined, and statistical tests show the probability of error. Comparison with actual election results shows polling to be accurate within a few percentage points in normal election situations.

Academic social surveys use the same methods in basic research, though academic researchers may be somewhat more rigorous in their sampling and interviewing methods. In surveys "control" has a different meaning than in experimental research. Male respondents are compared to women, young respondents to old, white-collar to blue-collar workers. Though this is analogous to the comparison of experimental and control groups in the previous example, we cannot be assured in the survey that the two groups being compared are alike in every other respect. Indeed, we know they are not alike. For example, white-collar and blue-collar workers may also differ in education, income, and other variables.

To cope with this problem, survey samples are much larger than experimental ones, and controls are instituted in another way, called "statistical controls." For example, if the hypothesis calls for white-collar respondents to have a higher proportion giving some answer, the researcher "controls for education," that is, tabulates to see whether college-educated white-collar workers give that answer in a higher proportion than college-educated blue-collar workers. Then he or she does the same for high-school-educated white- and blue-collar respondents, and then does it again with those with grammer-school education or less. In this way the contaminating effects of education are "held constant."

Probability theory holds that tests of significance are appropriate only when the sample is selected at random from the population, as in drawing marbles from an urn. With human populations the randomness criterion is impossible to meet; it can only be approximated. But significance tests are applied nevertheless, for they indicate the amount of error that could be attributed to sample size if the sample were random. Surveys have another weakness. In general they elicit only *verbal* behavior—descriptions by the respondents of what they think or what they have done, or how they plan to vote. Notwithstanding these defects, we have learned from survey research a great deal about political behavior that could not have been discovered by any other method. An authority on survey sampling sums it up this way: "Experiments are strong on control through randomization; but they are weak on representation (and sometimes on 'naturalism' of measurement). Surveys are strong on representation, but they are often weak on control."[2]

Approach 3: Aggregate Analysis

Now we turn to methods that have been used more frequently in applied than in basic social research. Aggregate analysis generally relies on data that have been collected previously, often for purposes other than the research at hand. It seeks relationships among variables in substantially the same fashion as survey research, but more often it studies entire populations rather than samples. For example, we may examine turnout or the Democratic vote in those precincts of a city with large black populations, comparing them to precincts populated largely by whites to discover racial differences in voting patterns. The Census Bureau cross-tabulates individual or family income by education, sex, race, etc., to reveal correlations. Persons are not the only units of analysis: characteristics of state, county, or municipal governments are also cross-tabulated to reveal correlates of expenditures, crime rates, or fire losses. You have already performed aggregate analysis of the Banks-Textor data on national political characteristics. As another example, achievement test score averages in schools with high teacher-to-pupil ratios may be compared to those of schools with low ratios. What sort of correlation would you expect to find? _____

_____

Aggregate analysis has become more important as the amount and quality of information collected by governmental units have grown in recent years. Where the data exist in the form of punch cards or magnetic tapes, the computer can search through large numbers of variables looking for correlations.

There are problems in aggregate analysis. As we have seen (p. 131), if a person or a computer operates entirely inductively, combs through many relationships between variables, and selects those that are statistically significant, he, she, or it will come to some dubious conclusions. There is also the problem of the "ecological fallacy." For example, if we find that Southern counties with large black populations tended to have higher votes for Republican candidates for president (as was the case in some states in the 1950s), may we infer that blacks were voting Republican? Not necessarily. It may be that whites in those counties were voting Republican, while the few blacks who voted were voting Democratic. Another example is the correlation between cities with large foreign-born populations and those with high levels of education. It turns out that immi-

[2]Leslie Kish, "Some Statistical Problems in Research Design," *American Sociological Review,* 24 (1959), 328–338.

grants are not better educated than native Americans, but that they settle in seaboard cities where the education level is high.[3] Finally, there is the issue of the appropriateness of statistical tests, but this will be considered later.

An important advantage of aggregate analysis is the low cost of data collection. Much useful material can be taken from published volumes, punched onto cards, and cross-tabulated by computer. The U.S. Census Bureau is a major source of such data. It publishes *Historical Statistics,* which go back to the American Revolution, the annual *Statistical Abstract of the United States,* the *County and City Data Book,* and *Congressional District Data Book.* County-by-county voting returns appear in the *America Votes* series. Congressional roll calls appear in *Congressional Quarterly Weekly Reports,* and much information about congressmen and senators and their constituencies will be found in the *Almanac of American Politics,* published in election years. More than 100 economic indicators are collected in *Business Conditions Digest,* published monthly by the Department of Commerce. Charles Taylor and Michael Hudson, *World Handbook of Political and Social Indicators* (New Haven, Conn.: Yale University Press, 1972), and the publications of the Organization for Economic Development and Cooperation, particularly *Main Economic Indicators,* are sources of descriptors of the nations of the world. All of these should be available in any college library.

Approach 4: The Quasi-Experiment

This is a term recently applied by Donald T. Campbell to a technique that is particularly relevant to policy-making.[4] It has some of the characteristics of experimentation and some of aggregate analysis. Although the term is new, the method itself is one of the earliest recorded, and can be illustrated by the work of Edwin Chadwick in England in 1842. His theory was that "miasmas"—the odorous fogs that arose from stagnant water—were a cause of death. He collected church records of baptisms and funerals in the community of Wisbeck after the fens (swamps) had been drained. The figures were:[5]

	Baptisms	Burials	Population at Mid-point
1796–1805	1627	1535	4,710 (in 1801)
1806–1815	1654	1313	5,209 (in 1811)
1816–1825	2165	1390	6,515 (in 1821)

[3]W. S. Robinson, "Ecological Correlations and the Behavior of Individuals," *American Sociological Review,* 15 (1950), 351–357.

[4]Donald T. Campbell, "Reforms as Experiments," in *Handbook of Evaluation Research,* E. L. Struening and Marcia Guttentag, eds. (Beverly Hills, Calif.: Sage Publications, 1975) pp. 71–100.

[5]M. Slusser, "Epidemiological Models," *ibid.,* pp. 497–518.

140

Chadwick concluded that "the increased salubrity of the fens produced by drainage is a chief cause of the improvement." Then he hit upon the concept of "control" (as we could call it) and replicated his quasi-experiment. He located two similar communities—Beccles, which had been drained, and Bungay, which had not. This time he computed the death rates, as follows:

	Beccles	*Bungay*
1811–1821	1 in 67	1 in 69
1821–1831	1 in 72	1 in 67
1831–1841	1 in 71	1 in 59

In observing that the declining death rate was due to drainage, Chadwick, a true scientist, pointed to other variables that might have affected his table. A factory established in Bungay could have brought in immigrants to inflate the population. And the Church of England parish records of deaths probably did not include the statistics on "Catholics and Independents."

Finally, we should note that Chadwick's evidence of the relationship between poor drainage and death was correct, but his theory about the connecting link—miasmas—was wrong, as germ theory was to show several decades afterwards.

A quasi-experiment, sometimes called a "natural experiment," is a situation in which some treatment has been applied, deliberately or inadvertently, in a natural setting rather than in a laboratory, and conclusions are subsequently drawn. Examples are comparisons of voting rates in a state before and after the abolition of the poll tax, or comparisons of voter turnout in two similar states, one with rigorous and the other with lenient voter-registration requirements, or comparison of murder rates in states or nations with and without the death penalty.

The problem, of course, is that researchers cannot manipulate the independent variable or assign subjects randomly, as in the true laboratory experiment. They can, however, examine possible contaminating effects of other variables, as Chadwick did, and assess them in a logical, if not a statistical, fashion. Campbell discusses more than a dozen possible contaminating factors, among them the following:

History: All events other than the "treatment" which intervene between "before" and "after" measurements and which might account for the difference.

Maturation: The subjects grow older or more tired or shrewd or better informed between pre- and post-test measurements.

Testing: Administration of the pre-test alerts subjects to the experiment. This, rather than the treatment, may produce the effect. For example, publication of a social indicator, such as the inflation index, may cause the public to act on its own at the very same time the government is instituting new policies in reaction to the same announcement. The spontaneous public action may either enhance or cancel out the policy effect.

Instrumentation: Changes in the measuring instrument. In an experiment, scales may get out of adjustment. Similarly, in a social experiment the police may change their method of reporting crimes, or the Bureau of the Census may alter a question or improve its interviewing system, making results from two time periods incomparable.

Selection: The groups compared are different to begin with. States, cities, and counties differ on a large number of variables besides the one under investigation.

Campbell recommends that researchers systematically go down the list and assess the likelihood that each of these alternative possibilities would explain any difference found. Thus we have three possible explanations of an apparent effect:

1. The difference is due to one or more of these contaminating effects.
2. The difference is due to random fluctuation, which can be estimated statistically by a significance test.
3. The difference is indeed due to the effect of the independent variable.

Evaluation Research

One outgrowth of national policies considered or adopted since the 1950s—policies such as the "war on poverty," school integration and busing, proposals for a negative income tax, and educational enrichment for deprived children—has been an increased emphasis on "evaluation research." (Other terms for research into the effects of policy are "efficiency audits" and "program evaluations.") Agencies are encouraged or required to state the objectives of their programs and to collect information on the results, so that policy-makers can decide whether to continue, revise, or discontinue the activities. Sometimes the agency itself keeps elaborate case records to appraise its accomplishments. Sometimes a university or private research bureau will be employed to monitor a program. Sometimes social indicators such as vital statistics or employment figures are used. If a projected program is likely to be very expensive, a "pilot project" may be undertaken in one or more localities.

Applied research produces findings which may influence policy, rather than simply appear in a journal of limited circulation, as is the case with basic research. This makes a difference in the way it is received. Some bureaucrats anticipate losing their jobs. Others foresee gaining new responsibilities and promotions. Corporations stand to gain or lose contracts. Welfare recipients benefit or suffer losses. Government budgets go up or down—a matter of concern to legislators, executives, and the parties and constituencies they represent. As a consequence, research reports are scrutinized carefully and criticized by experts on the subject, by experts in research methodology, and by politicians who know nothing about either and operate instead from preconceived theories, conservative or liberal. Some academic researchers who eagerly shifted from basic to applied research so that they could have an impact on policy have found their evaluations ignored, attacked, or distorted. Crestfallen, they have then followed Harry Truman's advice: "If you can't stand the heat, get out of the kitchen." For those with political savvy, an understanding of statistics, and asbestos psyches, evaluation research offers the prospect of an exciting career.

One outcome of the concentration on evaluation research in the 1970s has been to reveal the difficulty of demonstrating the effect of social and educational programs, particularly those embarked on with great confidence and optimism during the Johnson administration's "Great Society" days. Henry J. Aaron discusses this phenomenon in *Politics and the Professors* (Washington, D.C.: Brookings Institution, 1978). Edward R. Tufte (ed.), *The Quantitative Analysis of Social Problems* (Reading, Mass.: Addison-Wesley, 1970), collects some early examples of and articles about policy research. Elmer L. Struening and Marcia Guttentag (eds.), *Handbook of Evaluation Research* (Beverly Hills, Calif.: Sage Publications, 1975), is a more technical collection, updated annually in the *Evaluation Studies Review Annual*, also edited by Guttentag and published by Sage. M. S. Shipman, *The Implications of Social Research* (London: Longman Group, 1972), discusses the problem of adjusting the techniques and goals of academic research to the policy area.

When Are Significance Tests Appropriate?

In laboratory experiments, significance probabilities are always calculated and reported. There are dozens of tests, each appropriate to a particular kind of data and research design. The psychological statistics textbook is devoted to their explanation.

In survey research, significance tests were once considered mandatory, but researchers now are using them more selectively. The reason can best be demonstrated with a contrived example, using the Table of Significant Differences (p. 102) for our test. Assume we find a percentage difference of 10% ($D = 45\% - 35\% = 10\%$) between high-income and low-income respondents in a sample of 1,600. The "high" group includes 600 and the "low" group 1,000 persons. The table shows that a difference of 6% or more is significant at $p < .05$, so our 10% difference is quite convincing. Now we decide to control for education to see whether the tendency prevails among grade-school, high-school, and college groups as well. If it does, we will have more confidence that the relationship is really between income and response, and is not being influenced by a relationship between education and income. Miraculously, we discover the same 10% difference in all three educational brackets. But we have divided up our original N of 1,600 among the three groups. The grammar-school group, for example, has 100 high-income and 300 low-income respondents. The table shows that a 12% difference is required with an N of this size, but we have the same 10% as in the overall sample. Are the results now less _____ or more _____ convincing?

Something like this happens whenever we break our original sample into subsamples, but the process of "statistical controls"—examining the effect of several independent variables—is at the very heart of the survey method. A mechanistic application of significance tests would defeat the purpose of the analysis.

Quite a different problem arises with aggregate analysis and quasi-experiments. Here the data cover populations rather than samples. For example, the Banks-Textor list (pp. 72-74) covers all nations for which information was available in 1963. Should a significance test be performed?

One school of thought is that whatever relationship is found—say, between democracy and industrialization—exists in the population. It doesn't matter how weak or how strong it is, or how many nations there were in the world at that date. Therefore they would use only measures of association, such as V, Q, or ϕ, not tests of significance. The 115 nations covered are not a *sample* of some larger population of nation-states. For another example, if we find a tendency for Senate committee chairmen in the 88th Congress to come from Southern states, we have made a descriptive statement about the Senate at that time. The fact that it has 100 members, not 20 or 435, is irrelevant to our conclusion, though it would have a considerable influence on significance tests.

The other school of thought replies that, except for a few historians, no one is interested only in those nations of the world, or only in the customs of the Senate, that existed back in 1963. Instead, we seek enduring generalizations about political systems and infer these generalizations from data available at some recent point in time. The generalizations do apply to a larger population—the nations or the Senates of the past, present, and future. If we base these generalizations on relatively large numbers, they are more stable and less subject to random fluctuation than if they are based on small numbers. The significance test measures the probable effect of such instability, quite properly taking account of the greater stability of large numbers. From this viewpoint, the significance test does not consider whether the sample represents the population but instead addresses the researcher's doubt as to "whether the covariation in his data is so slight as to be haphazard or so great as to be systematic." Phrased this way, the problem is labeled "instability."[6]

The first school replies that significance tests depend upon the assumption of random sampling, and the nations or the senators of 1963 are far from random samples of those in the past and certainly not those of the future. Or they may argue that the 1963 Senate is a sample of one chamber, not 100 members.

These arguments arise among statisticians who know the logic of significance tests. Students have been known to join the first group because they don't understand or don't want to calculate tests of significance. Others fall into the second group because they have spent a year learning statistics and are eager to apply them. It is also possible to join the first group because the tests reject your latest hypothesis and shift to the second when your tests are highly significant. What would be the effect of this?

The Uses of Statistics

The four approaches described here are all serious attempts to understand the human environment—the socio-politico-economic structure in which we live and prosper or decline. Each works a little differently, and each is preferred by a different discipline. But they all involve variables that are measured in numbers and evaluated in terms of probability. And no method has triumphed. The proponents and critics of all four are still arguing, so there is room for tomorrow's scholars to contribute.

The methods developed by scholars are increasingly used in political decision-making. But politicians have still a different approach. As Winston Churchill told an assistant who provided him with more information on infant mortality than he had asked for:

> I gather, young man, that you wish to be a Member of Parliament. The first thing you must learn is that, when I call for statistics about the rate of infant mortality, what I want is proof that fewer babies died when I was prime minister than when anyone else was prime minister. That is a political statistic.[7]

---

[6]Robert F. Winch and Donald T. Campbell, "Proof? No. Evidence? Yes. The Significance of Tests of Significance," *The American Sociologist*, 4 (1969), 140–143. See also Denton E. Morrison and Ramon E. Henkel, "Significance Tests Reconsidered," *ibid.*, 131–139.

[7]Quoted in George F. Will's column, *The Washington Post*, Dec. 29, 1977, A19.

10/Averages and Levels of Measurement

The average golf course has 14.7 holes.
CHARLES PRICE

Two ladies with a penchant for perfumery describe the contents of their dressing tables as follows:

Sheilah's perfumes		Eleanor's perfumes	
	Ounces		*Ounces*
Rose-scented	3	$5 perfumes	1
Lilac-scented	5	$10 perfumes	4
Gardenia-scented	1	$25 perfumes	4

Both tables have one precisely quantifiable element—the number of ounces. But Eleanor's classification scheme has a second such element, the number of dollars for each category. With her data we could calculate total value ($145), average cost per ounce ($16.11), and other statistics. This would permit more sophisticated analysis because we are accurately measuring not just the number of units (ounces) in each category but *the continuum represented by the variable itself,* in this instance dollars. Thus Eleanor is using a "higher" level of measurement.

In this chapter we shall treat four different levels of measurement, starting with the most precise. It turns out that the counting you learned in grammar school is a rather complex form of measurement. Sheilah's classification by flower scents is a form of measurement, too, although you may not have initially considered it as such. At first, we shall not consider relationships be-

149

tween two variables, such as the effect of education on income, as we have been doing. Rather, we shall concentrate on one variable at a time—"univariate analysis." We explore such questions as: how is education measured? how is income measured? It is necessary to understand this because certain statistics are appropriate only for particular levels of measurement.

Levels of Measurement

Here are the levels, or "scales," starting with the most precise and most complex.

Ratio Scales

These are the "highest"—that is, most precise—form of measurement of variables. A ratio scale has precise and equal units of measurement, such as pounds or inches or the digits which are used in counting and arithmetic. A ratio scale also has an absolute zero point, representing the *absence* of some quality. With ratio scale numbers we may add, subtract, multiply, divide, and construct a variety of arithmetic and geometric averages. Length, distance, weight, and amounts of money are susceptible to ratio measurement. Age forms a ratio scale, starting with age zero for a newborn child. Votes are counted on a ratio scale. Each candidate starts with the possibility of receiving no votes at all, should he or she fall ill on election day. There are public works projects which, though authorized by Congress, have so far received appropriations of zero dollars. Since these zero points are absolute, we may apply ratios to such variables: John is twice as old as Edgar and twice as heavy. Only occasionally do we make use of this ratio capacity in political analysis.

Interval Scales

These have precise and equal units of measurement, just as ratio scales do, but they must not be divided or multiplied (only added and subtracted) because they have no absolute zero point. There are several examples from the sciences, the most familiar being measurement of temperature by Fahrenheit and Celsius scales. The zero point is arbitrary: 0° Celsius is equal to 32° Fahrenheit. One degree Fahrenheit is equal to five-ninths of a degree Celsius. To say that a day when the temperature reaches 34° is twice as hot as one when it reaches 17° is meaningless. The statement would not be true if values were converted to the other scale, for the zero is at a different point. But we may subtract 40° from 60° to get 20° on either scale, and, after applying our 5-to-9 conversion rate, the difference will come out correctly on the other scale. The same thing is true of dates, where the zero point depends on whether one uses the Hebrew, Muslim, Gregorian, or Chinese calendar. One may say that the year 2000 is 100 years later than the year 1900, but not that it is 5% later. Physicists use interval rather than ratio measures of energy, we are told, because no principle has been defined which establishes a zero point. The characteristic which interval scales have in common with ratio scales, but not with "lower" levels of measurement, is that adjacent points on the scale are equidistant from one another. This means that the units of measurement are equal; there is the same distance between 6 and 8 as between 13 and 15. This enables us to compute the *mean* as a measure of central tendency.

Any measurement or mathematic process that is appropriate for one level is appropriate for all "higher" levels. Thus we may add and subtract interval *or* ratio scale numbers, although we may multiply and divide only ratio scale numbers. Sometimes the word "cardinal" is applied to interval and ratio level numbers, but here we shall use "interval" to mean "interval or higher" or "at least interval" level, since the distinction between interval and ratio scales is not particularly useful for political measurement.

Ordinal Scales

These are measures in terms of *order* or *rank:* 1st, 2nd, 3rd, 4th, and so on. They are characterized by dividing lines between units of measurement that are *not* an equal distance apart. The order of the winners of a horse race gives no indication of the distance between the horses, whether No. 1 came in by a nose or a length. We resort to ordinal measurement (a) when we cannot discriminate accurately enough to make interval measurements, or (b) when interval measurements could be made, but order is more meaningful than the actual interval values. For example, in Congress, where committee assignments are governed by seniority, it makes no difference whether Jones took office two days before Smith or two years; it is the rank order that counts. The same principle applies in a factory where union members are being laid off.

Leather and lumber are graded on ordinal scales. For a century geologists used an ordinal scale for measuring the hardness of minerals. This was the Mohs scale: 1 for talc, 2 for gypsum, 3 for calcite, and so on, up to 8 for topaz, 9 for sapphire, and 10 for diamond. This is the order in which each substance will cut or scratch another: a diamond is harder than a sapphire and will cut it; a sapphire will scratch a topaz, and so on.

Thus if you were handed an unidentifiable substance and asked to rate its hardness, and you discovered it would cut gypsum, but that calcite would cut it, you would rate it between 2 and 3 in hardness. Obviously you would not need to try it with a topaz or diamond.

It is *not* true, however, that a sapphire is as much harder than a topaz as a diamond is harder than a sapphire. One may subtract 8 from 10 and get 2; one may subtract 1 from 3 and get 2. But one may not say that the difference in hardness between a diamond (10) and a topaz (8) is the same as the difference in hardness between calcite (3) and talc (1). Thus with ordinal measures one may not add or subtract, because the units of measurement are not the same. Some intervals are wider than others. We do not know, or cannot express, the gradation between any two steps; if we could, we would go to interval measurement.

An example of the use of ordinal measurements is the Ringelmann Chart for measuring smoke pollution used by the Bureau of Mines.

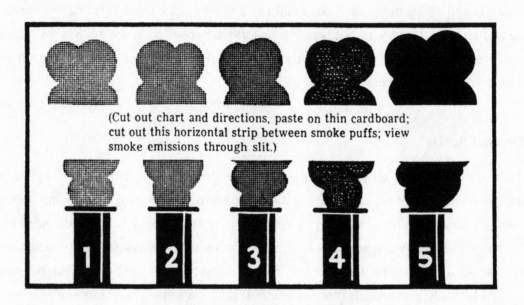

(Cut out chart and directions, paste on thin cardboard; cut out this horizontal strip between smoke puffs; view smoke emissions through slit.)

Directions for using the Ringelmann Chart

1. Find out what Ringelmann ratings industries may have under your county's sanitary code.
2. Stand about 100 feet from source of smoke or at a location with a clear view of the stack and background.
3. Make sure the sun is at your back. Holding the chart at arm's length, aim it at the smoke stack.
4. Readings should be made by looking at right angles to the smoke plume. Concentrate on the densest part of the plume at a point about two feet above the top of the stack.
5. Make observations for five minutes at a time. The more observations, the better. Change your location and compare readings.
6. Note time of day, wind direction, name of plant, and exactly which stack is emitting the smoke.

Source: Adapted from U.S. Bureau of Mines Ringelmann Chart. Courtesy of the *Environmental Action Bulletin*, Emmaus, Pa.

Ordinal measures are often used in studying human perceptions of loudness, brightness, weight, and electric shock. These may also be measured mechanically with interval scales. It was the efforts of psychologists in the 1930s to establish relations between the two kinds of measures that led to an understanding of the nature of ordinal scales. In political science and sociology there are important variables that are based entirely upon human perception, and we usually treat these as having no more than ordinal precision. Some examples are:

1. Ranking of preferences of political candidates during the primary season. The polls do this by a "trial heat" question in which respondents are asked to indicate their preferences among various pairs of aspirants, just as subjects in psychological experiments are asked to decide which of two weights is heavier.

2. Respondents' classification of their party identification as Strong Democrat, Weak Democrat, Independent, Weak Republican, or Strong Republican.

3. Ordering people, either by their own self-estimates or by the observations of sociologists, into Upper class, Upper-Middle, Middle, Lower-Middle, Working, and Lower class. However fine we make these distinctions, we cannot safely assume that the class boundaries are the same distance apart unless we resort to interval level standards, such as income or years of education.

4. Attitudes on public issues measured by responses to such a statement as "The United States should withdraw from the United Nations," in which the respondent says he or she agrees strongly, merely agrees, is undecided or neutral, disagrees, or disagrees strongly. Again we are not justified in assuming that the distance between the first two responses is the same as between some other adjacent pair.

5. Aristotle's original typology of governments: rule by the one, the few, and the many.

Since we cannot assume that the units are all the same, we cannot add values and divide to obtain a mean. The proper measure of the average with ordinal measures is the *median*—the point at which as many cases are ranked above it as below it.

Nominal Scales

These are the simplest scales of all, so primitive that we often do not think of them as measurement with numbers at all, but rather as qualitative distinctions. "Nominal" means "naming." There are two kinds of nominal scales: *polytomies* ("many slices") and *dichotomies* ("sliced in two").

Polytomies. These are multidimensional nominal scales. Examples are Sheilah's perfumes, the regions of the United States, religions (Catholic, Protestant, Jewish, and "other"), and branches of government (legislative, executive, and judicial). Polytomies have more than two positions, but they are nominal and not ordinal scales because we cannot rank positions in order according to some criterion. The party identification scale is ordinal because Independents are more "Republican" than are Democrats. But Catholics are no more "Protestant" than are Jews, nor can we rank the three faiths in any other intrinsically meaningful numerical order that would permit us to calculate the "median religion" in the nation.

Dichotomies. These are scales with only two categories. They may be qualitatively different, e.g., men and women, autocracies and democracies, or Democrats and Republicans. They may also be categories such as "old" and "young" where an interval variable, age, is cut at a convenient point, say 30 years of age. In dealing with dichotomies, we may assign a value of 1 to cases having some characteristic, e.g., "femaleness," and 0 to cases not having it. For this reason, it is mathematically appropriate to treat a dichotomy as a two-number interval scale. And since women have more of this quality of femaleness, we may also consider a dichotomy to be an ordinal variable.

In working with polytomies, we sometimes assign numbers to individuals or classes for convenience. This process is literally "nominal"; the number is used as a name, as in an automobile license, telephone number, football jersey, or clause in an act (e.g., Title I funds). Adding, subtracting, or averaging these numbers is nonsensical. We often attach such numbers to categories for processing through punch-card machines and computers, since these machines have numbers assigned to the holes that register information, but we must remember that these numbers are merely names, as was the case with the Banks-Textor classification of national attributes.

Shifting Levels

We may at any stage move "downward" from a more precise to a less precise level of measurement, from interval down to ordinal, or from ordinal down to nominal. This may be done either for convenience or to gain additional insight into the data. A familiar example of the way measurement levels are shifted is in evaluating academic performance. The mark a student receives in a course may range from 0 to 100 if the grading is done on the basis of the percentage of examination questions answered correctly. This is interval measurement. If there are 100 questions, the student gets a point for each—just as much for getting Question 17 right as for getting Question 93 right. (You may wish to contemplate in passing the observation that the grade assigned is an instructor's "operational definition" of a variable, to which the corresponding "conceptual definition" is the student's "knowledge of the subject matter of the course." Students who complain that an exam is "unfair" are pointing out that operational and conceptual definitions do not coincide.)

Many instructors grade in letters rather than numbers because they feel that answers to essay questions cannot be measured precisely enough for interval level grades. Others transform numerical grades into an ordinal scale. One institution used the following scheme: A = 95–100; B = 88–94; C = 81–87; D = 75–80; F = less than 75. Some brackets are 6 points wide, others 7, and the bottom one is 75 points wide. This is entirely proper in an ordinal scale.[1]

At the end of a high-school or college career, cumulative grades may be turned into ordinal rankings. Those evaluating transcripts as an indication of students' potential ability know that some institutions are generous with As, while others are stingy with them. Admissions officers rely more on class rankings—whether a student is in the top 5% or the top quarter of the class—than upon the average. Finally, the ordinal or interval scales are usually transformed into nominal scales—diploma or no diploma. If a college or graduate school refuses to take any student not in the top third of the class, then ordinal ranks have been transformed into nominal ones—Accept or Don't Accept.

In the non-academic world as well, interval and ordinal measures are transferred into nominal scales when important decisions are made. The price of a car is Too High or All Right. The Dodgers Win the pennant or they Lose. The candidate Wins or Loses the election. The Nielsen rating determines whether a TV show is Continued or Canceled.

Grouped Data

When dealing with a small number of cases, we may use the exact *value* of each case if using interval scales or the *rank* of each case if ordinal. With large numbers of cases and interval level measurement, we customarily group data into brackets or "class intervals" to ease computation.

[1] But in this registrar's office, the letter grades were shifted back to an interval scale, with A = 4; B = 3; C = 2; D = 1; F = 0. The effect of this disregard of scaling rules may be seen in the case of a fictitious student who received a numerical grade in each subject that coincided with the midpoint of each bracket (so that there is no error attributable to grouping):

Subject	Interval grade	Ordinal grade	Reconverted to interval
English	97.5	A	4
History	91	B	3
Math	84	C	2
Language	77.5	D	1
Science	37.5	F	0
Average (Mean)	77.5 = D		2.0 = C

Though mathematically inappropriate, few students objected to the system, for obvious reasons.

If the brackets are of equal width, the data maintain their interval quality. This is like shifting our scale from feet to yards in the measurement of distance. If the brackets are of unequal width—for example, when the last category contains all values above a certain point—we have downgraded the level of measurement from interval to ordinal. Age may be treated in either way, as Table 10.1 shows.

TABLE 10.1

City Population		Electorate	
Age Bracket	Number of Cases	Age Bracket	Number of Cases
0–9	350	18–19	11
10–19	318	20–29	75
20–29	294	30–39	83
30–39	301	40–49	90
40–49	275	50–59	87
50–59	243	60–69	51
60–69	185	70 and up	31
70–79	72	Total (N)	428
80–89	27		
90–99	8		
100–109	2		
Total (N)	2075		

In the first instance, on the left, the brackets are all 10 years in width, so in effect we are measuring age in decades rather than years. Thus we may legitimately compute the mean by multiplying the number of cases in each bracket by the midpoint for the bracket (in this instance, 5, 15, 25, etc.) and then dividing by the total N of 2,075. This would give us approximately the same mean we would get if we added up each individual age in years and divided by the number of cases.[2] We could also compute the median by counting up 1,037 (one-half of N) cases from the bottom or 1,037 cases down from the top. This would put us about a fourth of the way through the 30–39 bracket, giving a median age of about 32.

With the second set of data we cannot compute the mean. The first bracket is only 2 years in width instead of 10 and the last bracket does not have any top limit; hence we cannot find its midpoint. It is nevertheless quite proper to calculate the median by counting down (or up) 214 cases to the halfway point, which puts us in the middle of the 40–49 bracket and gives us a me-

---

[2]Whether or not the mean age, once computed, gives us useful information is another matter.

156

dian age for registrants of 45. If we had the figures for registrants in another city, we might compare the two and draw justifiable conclusions about the difference in average (median) age.

By the way, it makes no difference in assigning ranks to political measurements whether you start at the top and rank the highest value as 1 or start at the bottom and give the lowest value a rank of 1. It is strictly a matter of convenience.

If you plan to make much use of grouped data, you should remember that the number 8 may be either a discrete value, such as 8 persons, or the mid-point on a continuum, such as any length between 7.5 and 8.49 centimeters. Statistics books give rules for coping with this in grouping data.

Measures of Central Tendency

The word "average" refers to any one of several "measures of central tendency." These sum up in one figure a whole series of values that may run into the dozens, or for that matter millions. An average, as we use it every day, abstracts and summarizes the essential features of a complex reality so that we can deal with it.

The most elementary average is the *mode.* It is simply the most frequent class, category, bracket, or number. The modal American is a Protestant. The modal number of meals eaten per day is three. The mode is the only way to summarize a polytomy, even though it is not very meaningful. It is occasionally used at higher levels of measurement.

The *median* is the value which is halfway down a list of values when they are ranked from largest to smallest. Half the values have a higher value and half have a lower value. Thus it is the most appropriate measure for summarizing ordinal data, as well as for interval data such as income, where a few millionaires would inflate the mean.

The *arithmetic mean* (which is what we usually refer to when we speak colloquially of the "average") is computed by taking a series of interval values, summing them, then dividing by the number of values. Where X represents each individual value, and $\overline{X}$ (called "X-bar") represents the mean, the formula is:

$$\overline{X} = \frac{\Sigma X}{N}$$

This is the most widely used measure for summarizing interval data, although there are other means, harmonic and geometric for example, that are computed by different formulae and give different summary values for the same series of numbers. In dealing with grouped interval data, we calculate the mid-point of each bracket and multiply it by the number of cases in that bracket to get a close approximation of the mean. Thus:

$$\overline{X} = \frac{\Sigma fm}{N}$$ where f is the frequency of cases and m is the mid-point of the bracket.

Most of us make appropriate use of these three measures without giving much thought to the matter. The manufacturer of power mowers takes into account when locating the control lever that the modal owner is right-handed, not left-handed or ambidextrous, without consciously considering that the mode is the correct summary measure for a polytomy. A legislature may allocate relief funds to counties on the basis of the median income, because that is the figure the Census

Bureau presents. The Census statisticians know that the mean income would be inappropriate, since it would be inflated by one or two very wealthy citizens. When you trade in your old car, you may look in the *Blue Book* to find its value. This is the mean price at which cars of this make, model, and year have changed hands in the last few months.

Failure to understand measures of central tendency is widespread and is referred to as "the fallacy of averages." We have all heard of the lady who drowned in a pond that averaged 9 inches deep. But we are often startled to learn of the average income of our classmates, or the average amount given to our favorite charity, until we recall the effect of one or two large values upon the mean. The median also can be tricky. One union representative complained to management that half the workers were getting less than the median wage for the plant. And Senator Jacob Javits in the 1975 bond crisis in New York pleaded: "let us remember that in New York, about half the people have less than the median national income."

The rule that lower-level measures are appropriate for higher-level data in certain circumstances, but not the other way around, applies to central tendency. One may use the mode, the median, or the mean with interval data; the median or the mode with ordinal data; but only the mode with nominal polytomies. The *proportion* falling in one class is an appropriate summary measure of a nominal dichotomy and is in some respects statistically equivalent to the mean.

Almost everyone uses averages as a *predictive device.* Going to an unfamiliar region for a few days, you inquire as to the average temperature there during that month, and you decide what clothes to take. You know that unusual weather may make your decision turn out to be a poor one, but you can make a better decision knowing the average than not knowing it. Colleges and graduate schools decide whether they will admit an applicant on the basis of average grade, which sums up the previous academic career in a single statistic. The universities keep out a few students who could graduate, and they admit a few students who flunk out, but they do better using the average as a predictive device than they would by flipping a coin

Measures of Dispersion: Making the Best Guess

Measures of dispersion are statistics that tell us how good a measure the average is, how well it represents all the values it purports to summarize. The simplest of these measures for interval-level values is the *range*—the difference between the highest and lowest values in the array. But the range is not very stable. Assume that the incomes in your county vary from $2,000 for the poorest citizen to $202,000 for the richest—a range of $200,000. Then the richest man dies. The second wealthiest person has an income of $92,000. Overnight the range has become $90,000, yet no one else's income has changed.

Better measures are the *average deviation*—the average of the differences between each value and the mean—and the *standard deviation,* a measure to be treated in some detail. But first, a detour that illustrates the purpose of measures of dispersion.

For the sake of explanation, we shall examine a simple game in which you are promised a reward for guessing the age of the person in the next room, about whom you know nothing. The closer your prediction, the larger will be your payoff. In principle this is no different from dozens of games we play with fate every day: take the umbrella or leave it? walk crosstown or look for a cab? how early should we get to the theatre? can we make the light before it turns red? In this particular guessing game, you have an opportunity to gather some advance information. You discover that the modal age category in the United States this year is 3 years of age. The guess that the person in the next room is 3 years old would give you the maximum chance of being right but a poor chance of winning the smaller prize for coming close. You then look up the median and find it is 28 years of age. With half the people below that and half above, this is not a bad strategy for coming as close as you can. You look for the mean age and find it is seldom calculated: what sense is a measure that counts one nonagenarian as the equivalent of ninety infants?

Suppose you are told reliably that the person in the next room is one of three whose mean age is 21. Should you use this additional information and guess 21 years instead of 28? Here are two of an almost infinite number of possible combinations of ages of three persons; the first would be very profitable for you if you guessed 21, the second not at all profitable.

First Group		Second Group	
Actual Age	*Deviation or Error from Guess of 21*	*Actual Age*	*Deviation or Error from Guess of 21*
18 years	3 years	5 years	16 years
20	1	10	11
24	3	47	26
62 = ΣX	7	62 = ΣX	53

Mean = $\overline{X}$ = $\dfrac{\Sigma X}{N}$ = $\dfrac{62}{3}$ = 21 for either group.

The average age in the two groups is the same, but only in one group is it a help in guessing. Is there a statistic you could seek that would tell you whether or not you should base your guess on the average, or better still, how bad your guess might be if you based it on the average?

163

In this instance you might use the total error—7 for the first group and 53 for the second—as a measure of the likelihood of error. Or better, you might divide these numbers by N, which is 3. This would give you an *average deviation* from the mean.

$$AD = \frac{\Sigma|X - \bar{X}|}{N}$$

It would be equally applicable as a measure of dispersion or probable error for any group, regardless of size. In this case it would be 2.3 for the first group and 17.7 for the second.

If you were told in advance not only the mean but the average deviation as well, you might make a handsome profit at this guessing game, for you would know when to guess the mean and when not to.

Let us take another, more realistic, instance in which mean and average deviation are employed for the same purpose. Suppose you have been offered $960 for your old car and are trying to decide whether to take the offer or wait for another, better offer. Your car is in normal condition with the mileage on it one would expect for a car of its vintage. You find the mean *Blue Book* value for that model is $950. Comparing the offer of $960 with the mean tells you: Take it! Now if you also learned that the average deviation around the mean is $5, would you be more or less likely to take the offer? _____

If you found the AD was $25 would you be more or less likely to take the offer than if AD was $5? _____

Standard Deviation

There is another measure of variability about the mean that, for statistical purposes, has so many advantages that it has supplanted the average deviation. It is the *standard deviation.* The difference between each value and the mean is found by subtraction. This is represented by the term $(X - \bar{X})$. Each of these values is squared to give $(X - \bar{X})^2$. (The squaring, incidentally, disposes of the minus signs, for the product of two negative values, you remember, is positive. Thus both $(5)(5)$ and $(-5)(-5)$ are equal to +25.) Then you add up the squared values to get $\Sigma (X - \bar{X})^2$. You divide this by N, just as with the average deviation, then take the square root of the result. The formula for $s (\bar{X})$, the standard deviation of the mean, is:

$$s(\bar{X}) = \sqrt{\frac{\Sigma(X - \bar{X})^2}{N}}$$

164

Standard deviation is also designated as s or σ (*sigma*). Hereafter we shall call it s. In squaring the numbers we march up the hill and in later taking the square root we march back down again, so we wind up with a value that measures about the same quality as AD but does not give the same figure. In the preceding example, s for the first group of ages is 2.5 where AD was 2.3. For the second group, s is 18.7 where AD was 17.7. This demonstrates an essential quality of s: it is more sensitive to extreme values than AD. Both measures may be thought of as "averages" of the deviation of the values about their mid-point and are called "measures of dispersion." If you are in the habit of thinking of the arithmetic mean as the "right" measure for averaging values, this may be disconcerting. However, we have already treated other average measures—median and mode—that are more useful for certain purposes, and this is just another example of the same point.

This squaring and unsquaring gives s other important properties that make it worth the trouble. If the distribution of values about the mean is "normal" (that is, if it resembled those curves shown on pp. 109 and 110 in connection with the discussion of the null hypothesis), then about two-thirds of the values will fall within plus or minus 1 standard deviation of the mean, and about 95% will fall within $2\,s$ of the mean. To see the utility of this, go back to the used car example. If the mean price had been $950 and s had been $10, you would now know that two-thirds of the cars had changed hands between $940 and $960 and 95% of them between $930 and $970. Your prediction as to whether you should hold out for a better offer will be even sounder. Thus s compresses a great deal of information into a single figure. When you know $\overline{X}$ and s of a series of numbers, you have wrung out of them most of the information that is relevant. These two figures are usually more useful than the numbers themselves, particularly if the series is a long one. The widespread use of averages and measures of dispersion is a necessity in complex societies and economies. None of us can cope with large arrays of figures. Use of averages makes it possible to understand the world about us by reducing complexity to its bare essentials, but doing so with some precision. Measures of dispersion enable us to use averages more effectively by telling us just how accurate and meaningful or inaccurate and misleading any average happens to be.

In getting used to standard deviation, it helps to know that s is roughly one-third of the range for very small samples and about one-sixth for very large samples. Whenever you calculate s, you should check this to see that you have not made some egregious error in your calculations.

Notice that in the discussion the differences between the actual values and their mean have been given alternative interpretations: (a) as *deviations* or *variations* from their average, and (b) as *errors* in a guess when one guesses the average as an approximation of a value that is not known. These two concepts, variation and error, are alternative ways of looking at the same phenomena. You should be conscious of them, for they will reappear shortly.

Measuring Equality

The second half of the twentieth century has been called "the age of equality." In the United States policies have been adopted that would spread the distribution of health care, income, education, self-respect, and other things of value more evenly among the population. "Liberals" have generally supported these programs. "Conservatives" have often argued against them on the ground that preserving some inequalities provides an incentive for effort. In such arguments, it is often useful for both sides to have some measure that will indicate *how* equally some good or service is distributed at present, compared with the past, or how equally it is divided among different groups in the population. If the policy has to do with something that can be measured at the interval level, we may use the standard deviation as a measure of inequality. A small *s* indicates a more or less equal distribution, while a large *s* shows that some individuals have a lot of it and others only a little.

Christopher Jencks began his influential study of education in America with an examination of how equally public education policies of the past and the present had distributed "years of formal schooling"—something most people value highly. He calculated that elderly people, those born from 1895 through 1904, who had received most of their schooling before World War I, had a mean of 8.9 years of school. The post-World War II generation, those born from 1940 through 1944, had an average of 12.2 years of schooling. Since the modern school system is providing many more years of education, we would expect the standard deviation to be larger even if the dispersion about the mean were the same. So Jencks corrected for this difference by using the *coefficient of variation, V,* which simply divides each standard deviation by its accompanying mean. For the older group *s* was 3.76. The coefficient of variation is:

$$V = \frac{s}{\overline{X}} = \frac{3.76}{8.90} = .42$$

(Note that this *V* is no relation to Cramér's *V.*)

For the younger group *s* is 2.8 and *V* is .23. Since *V* is a measure of *inequality*, Jencks concludes that contemporary Americans are not only being provided much more education, but that it is much better distributed.[3] For those born from 1940 through 1944, he gives the following values of *V:* males, .24; females, .21; whites, .22; blacks, .25. What would you conclude from

[3]Christopher Jencks: *Inequality: A Reassessment of the Effect of Family and Schooling in America* (New York: Basic Books, 1972), pp. 2–21, 352–353.

this? _____

_____

There are other uses of standard deviation as a measure of variability. For example, investment advisors calculate the variation in prices of stocks, as well as their average values, over a period of time. Since most investors like stability and peace of mind, stocks that have a large standard deviation—i.e., fluctuate wildly—sell for somewhat less than more predictable ones.

But the real importance of standard deviation is its usefulness in creating "unitless measures." This signal contribution to science is credited to Sir Francis Galton and led to the development of regression and correlation in the late nineteenth century. The basic idea is that any series of values may be expressed in terms of its own standard deviation simply by dividing each value by s for the series. One may then compare it to other variables expressed in terms of *their* standard deviations and subject these values to other mathematical operations. Thus one may compare apples and oranges, dollars and votes, or incomes and IQs.

The Relevance of Measurement Levels

Anyone who seeks to understand the complexities of government must rely to some extent on measurement. There are sometimes choices of measurement level that involve tradeoffs: the lower levels are easier to understand, but the higher ones are more precise and give us more information. Choices depend upon:

1. *Nature of the data.* With polytomies, such as race and religion, we are forced to work at the nominal level. With some variables that are potentially interval, such as age, we may choose to reduce them to nominal (young *vs.* old) or ordinal (young, middle-aged, and old) for the sake of convenience, sacrificing some accuracy in the process.

In policy-making the costs and benefits of several options may be calculated in terms of dollars (interval level). But then they are reduced to ordinal ranks: preferable, acceptable, questionable, unacceptable. And there are some policy considerations that can be assessed only at the ordinal level—e.g., the beauty of an environment, the cultural offerings of cities, the satisfaction of workers. Whether consumers and policy-makers follow the same rules as mathematicians when they move from one level to another has been the subject of research by economists.[4]

2. *Search for meaning.* We generally use an ordinal measure, the median, to summarize age, education, and income figures instead of the mean, although the latter is appropriate,

[4]See Donald W. Taylor, "Decision-Making and Problem-Solving," in *Handbook of Organizations,* James C. March, ed. (Chicago: Rand McNally & Co., 1965), pp. 48–86; David Braybrooke and Charles E. Lindblom, *A Strategy for Decision* (New York: The Free Press, 1963).

since these variables can be considered interval. The median eliminates the effect of extreme values; hence it is more meaningful. We may also reduce interval-level fiscal and budgetary data on state governments to a ranking of states because we are more interested in comparison than in precise differences between any two states.

3. *Appropriateness of statistics.* In subsequent chapters we shall encounter several measures of association, correlation, and significance that are correct for one level of measurement but misleading if calculated for another level. Interval-level statistics are particularly tricky, since they depend upon several assumptions about the data which we may not be willing to make.[5] In this case, we may choose to drop back to a lower level of measurement.

Levels of measurement other than those treated here have been suggested, and the subject is a little more complex than this treatment suggests. For further reading, start with Fred N. Kerlinger, *Foundations of Behavioral Research* (New York: Holt, Rinehart and Winston, 1965), Ch. 23, or Linton C. Freeman, *Elementary Applied Statistics* (New York: Wiley, 1965). Then read Clyde H. Coombs, "Theory and Methods of Social Measurement," in *Research Methods in the Behavioral Sciences,* Leon Festinger and Daniel Katz, eds. (New York: Holt, Rinehart and Winston, 1953), pp. 471−535. Finally, read S. S. Stevens, "Measurement, Psychophysics and Utility," in *Measurement: Definitions and Theories,* C. West Churchman and Philburn Ratoosh, eds. (New York: Wiley, 1959), pp. 18−63, for the psychological problems which gave rise to the development of the concept.

[5]What these assumptions are will be found in most statistics books. For a very intelligible discussion of the principles involved in choosing statistical tests, see Sidney Siegel, *Non-Parametric Statistics* (New York: McGraw-Hill, 1956), Ch. 3.

11 / The Development of Scaling Techniques

*Any measurement is an intended ordering of objects within a frame
of reference engendered by some conceptual imagery.*
PAUL F. LAZARSFELD

How is it possible—at any level of measurement—to gauge a person's emotional state, mental ability, or political attitude, none of which can be directly observed? And how is it possible to summarize millions of such mental states into something called "public opinion," which is important to the functioning of democracy?

One technique for describing such an attitudinal dimension—and measuring, at the ordinal level, each person's location on a continuum along that dimension—is called *Guttman scaling*. Its development was the culmination of three centuries of effort to quantify human behavior. A glance at some of the high points in the history of quantification may help in understanding the rationale of scaling as well as other social-psychological measurement.

A good place to start is England in 1672, when William Petty sought to interpret the government of Ireland, proceeding from the notion that government was related to the social and economic structure of the country and that this structure could best be described in terms of "number, weight, and measure." A few years later Gregory King sought to describe the population of England by number of families, rank, occupation, and annual income and made up a table estimating the number of people in each status group.[1] These devotees of "political arithmetick," as it

---

[1] Set forth in William L. Sachse, *English History in the Making,* vol. I (Waltham, Mass.: Blaisdell, 1967), p. 324.

was called in England, had their counterparts on the Continent, notably Hermann Conring, who attempted to describe the characteristics of the German principalities and the relation of their population size and structure to public policy and military potential. Under the term "political statistics," his system was used in training civil servants throughout Germany.[2] The scholarly traditions started by the political arithmeticians and statisticians (the term in its early, and one of its modern, meanings refers to data collected by the *state*) died out after about a century.

The American Founding Fathers made a major contribution when they wrote a data collection requirement into the Constitution in the form of the decennial census, and Madison in 1790 persuaded Congress to go beyond a mere head count and to support the first analytical tabulation into those above and below sixteen years of age. Jefferson, the scholar and scientist, asked in 1800 for a tabulation by age, place of origin, and occupation, but Congress did not go along with this idea until 1820.[3]

The father of modern social statistics was a Belgian astronomer and mathematician, Adolphe Quetelet. He understood probabilities, averages, and distributions, and he was also interested in crime rates, vital statistics, and intellectual and "moral" characteristics of populations. Around 1840 he set in motion ideas that were to bear fruit at the turn of the twentieth century, but there intervened a period when the focus turned to biological measurement.

Those who collected data on the heights and weights of men and animals discovered time after time that the cases were distributed along what now is called a "normal" curve. A large number of cases would be distributed roughly as follows:

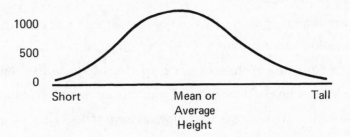

The same distribution was characteristic of the number of heads that would be found if, say, 100 coins were tossed a large number of times. Just as there would be few instances when there were no heads, or 100 heads, and many instances when there were about 50 heads, so there would be a few persons at the two extremes, very short or very tall, and an increasing number as we

[2]Paul F. Lazarsfeld, "Notes on the History of Quantification," in *Quantification*, Harry Woolf, ed. (Indianapolis: Bobbs-Merrill, 1961), pp. 160–161.

[3]*Social Indicators*, R. A. Bauer, ed. (Cambridge, Mass.: The M.I.T. Press, 1966), p. xi.

move toward the center, with the large bulk of people (or giraffes, or whatever) being close to the *mean* or average height for that species. These biological researches were done during the nineteenth century. Along with them, some thoughtful men were beginning to inquire into social and psychological phenomena, such as the distribution of incomes (which turn out to be anything but normally distributed). Better censuses were initiated by the Western European countries, and we began to know more about national and local populations, their number, and a few of their characteristics. Sir Francis Galton undertook to study the hereditary transmission of superior ability (there was hardly a subject about which more had been said and less known than heredity). At the turn of the century, in France, Emile Durkheim made his classic study of suicide and Alfred Binet was seeking some way to distinguish feeble-minded children from the others. These trains of investigation differed from the studies of previous generations in one important respect, which is aptly described by Nathan Glazer:

> Regardless of which route we take, we come back to the same starting point, the first half of the nineteenth century. It was about then that a new way of studying man and society began to develop. . . . [For] great thinkers, over a stretch of two thousand years, the relations between facts and theories in discussing social problems was roughly the same—and completely different from that of contemporary social science. Whether one considers Aristotle or Montesquieu, one will find history and existing social life considered as simply a storehouse of examples to illustrate presumed truths. The notion that it might be possible to survey systematically *all* the facts bearing on some generalization may have been suggested here or there, but it certainly played little or no role in influencing those who concerned themselves with social problems. For two thousand years we will find little change if we consider only *why* certain assertions are made: evidence, if it is presented at all, exists in the form of illustration. . . .
>
> What was truly new was the rise of a belief that the world, the social world around one, was not *known,* and that its reality could not be grasped by reading books, listening to learned men, or reflecting upon the facts of one's experience. . . . We may speak of an age of doubt, affecting not *truths*—these had been doubted since the Renaissance, and before— but *facts,* simple empirical realities. Facts, if previously doubted, had not been considered important enough to matter.[4]

Binet, in his study of children, devised a systematic process whereby a psychologist, teacher, or other skilled practitioner would ask a child to perform a predetermined list of mental tasks and, on the basis of the child's success, reach a quantitative evaluation of the child's reasoning ability, or "intelligence." Translations of his tests into English were eagerly received in the United States, where public education, long recognized to be essential for working democracy, had run into a

[4]Nathan Glazer, "The Rise of Social Research in Europe," in *The Human Meaning of the Social Sciences,* Daniel Lerner, ed. (New York: World Publishing Co., Meridian Books, 1959), pp. 45–47. Copyright © 1959 The World Publishing Company. Reprinted with permission.

serious snag. The prevailing standards of what constituted a "passing" grade had been introduced into a rapidly expanding free public school system, and upon this had been superimposed a system of compulsory attendance laws. A steadily increasing residue of "bad," "lazy," and "stupid" 13- and 14-year-olds had begun to accumulate in the first, second, and third grades. For example, in Birmingham, Alabama, in 1908, a fourth of the boys and a fifth of the girls were three years or more behind in their classes.[5]

In 1916, L. L. Terman at Stanford University made a major revision and adaptation of the French test to the American situation and called it the Stanford-Binet. It still required individual administration to each subject. With the entrance of the United States into World War I, a committee of the American Psychological Association developed the Army Alpha Test, a 40-minute paper-and-pencil version of the Stanford-Binet that could be administered to draftees and soldiers in *groups*. The responses were used to screen out those whose ability was so low that they would be more hindrance than help to the infantry. Another test, the "personal data sheet," weeded out the most serious neurotics.[6]

A consequence of the administration of these tests to a huge and fairly representative cross-section of young American males was confirmation of the fact that "intelligence," like height and weight, was *normally distributed.* For some "humanists" it was a sacrilege to have slide-rule types laying their profane hands on the reasoning ability that God had given man to distinguish him from the "lower" animals, and a shock to discover that these human intellectual and emotional capacities were normally distributed, like the width of acanthus leaves or the length of eels, but for the psychologists of the 1920s it opened up a new vista of the "science of man."

Attitude Measurement Between the Wars

L. L. Thurstone thereupon developed techniques for the more refined measures of attitudes, and E. S. Bogardus, who was concerned about the difficulties of assimilation of immigrant populations, devised a measure of "social distance."[7] It is this device that is of principal interest to us, for it clearly sought to measure a specific attitude on an *ordinal* scale. The respondent was asked: "To which of the following categories would you admit (members of some race or nationality listed, e.g., English, Negro, Chinese, or Turkish):

[5]Florence L. Goodenough, *Mental Testing* (New York: Rinehart, 1949), p. 17.

[6]*Ibid.,* pp. 67, 77, 494–495.

[7]*Immigration and Race Attitudes* (Boston: D. C. Heath, 1928).

"To close kinship by marriage,

"To my club as personal chums,

"To my street as neighbors,

"To employment in my occupation,

"To citizenship in my country,

"As visitors only to my country,

"Would exclude from my country."

For most individuals, this was an ordinal scale. They would start at the bottom and decide they would admit, say, a Turk, as a visitor, as a citizen, and so on. But at some point, say, "to my street," they would stop, and refuse to admit him to any closer distance—to their club or to their family. However, a few persons turned up who (perhaps concerned with property values) would admit persons to their club whom they would exclude from their neighborhood. In effect, such respondents were introducing into the scale another *dimension* of attitude not contemplated by the author.

The variable which a Bogardus scale measured was a clearly understandable one—a social distance—despite occasional tendencies for other dimensions to become entangled in it. But other sociologists and psychologists sought to measure less easily definable variables, such as attitudes toward religion, pacifism, or prohibition. Here the choice of the items which should be included in the scale was not so obvious. The construction of Thurstone scales became quite an elaborate process. To select and weigh the items, panels of "judges" were asked to sort slips with the items on them into ordered piles according to the extremity of the statement. Extreme items were given a heavier weight in the score. The questions devised by Rensis Likert gave five possible reactions to each statement, from "Agree Strongly" to "Disagree Strongly," so that every item was *in itself* an ordinal scale. This allowed a reduction in the overall number of items needed to measure an attitude. It was the practice to word items so that some would require an "agree" response to add to a person's score; others would be reversed, so that a "disagree" response contributed to the score. This guarded against bias resulting from the possibility that some people are confirmed nodders while others are innate head-shakers. The complex weighting schemes, as well as the average and standard deviation measures used, were based upon the assumption that the scales were measuring at the *interval* level.[8]

[8]This is a scanty treatment of the subject of attitude measurement. If you seek a starting place for further understanding of these techniques, see Claire Selltiz et al., *Research Methods in Social Relations,* rev. ed. (New York: Holt, Rinehart and Winston, 1965), Ch. 10, or W. J. Goode and Paul K. Hatt, *Methods in Social Research* (New York: McGraw-Hill, 1952), Ch. 15.

Determining Level of Measurement

Much of the research of the pre-World War II era was done with large batteries of items administered to psychology classes, civic clubs, or other captive audiences. Interval measurement was assumed, which permitted computation of rather complex indices of relationships, such as product-moment coefficients of correlation (which we shall treat later), and tests of significance designed for interval statistics. One such study, for example, found in 1927 that information about Far Eastern affairs correlated highly with favorable attitudes toward the Japanese and that favorable responses toward Orientals in general were correlated with a liking for chow mein.[9]

What is important to realize is that *some* assumptions about measurement underlie *any* attempt to quantify or measure a behavioral, mental, or emotional variable. If you put the items in order, as Bogardus did, you are operating on the assumption that the scale is ordinal and the further assumption that the order you select is "logical"—not only to you but to the mass of interviewees. Even more disconcerting, should you instead compose half a dozen items to measure some quality such as prejudice, intelligence, political adequacy, or alienation from society, and decide to use the simplest possible summary measure, merely adding positive responses to get a score, then you have *implicitly* made the assumption that these items measure a *single* dimension, that they have equal weight, and that they constitute an *interval* scale. Whether such an assumption is mathematically justified, logically justified, pragmatically justified, or not justified at all are matters on which the methodologists continue to argue.[10]

In Exercise 11 in Chapter 10 you may have had trouble deciding whether certain measures were interval or ordinal, ordinal or nominal. One safe rule is to make the minimum assumption about precision of measurement and to consider the *lower* level appropriate. This is conservative in that you eliminate the possibility of "finding" something that is not there, but is merely a figment of arithmetic, an artifact of method, a trick played on you unknowingly by the inappropriate numbers you used. It is as though you had to rely upon a speedometer that might be biased, a tape measure you suspect is stretched, or cheap scales which you think may have a worn spring. Doubting the instrument's ability to measure accurately on an interval level, you decide to accept it at an *ordinal* level. For example, the worn scales tell you that two hams weigh 17½ and 18 pounds, respectively. Though not sure the weights are accurate, you can at least use them to tell

---

[9]Cited in G. Murphy, L. B. Murphy, and T. M. Newcomb, *Experimental Social Psychology* (New York: Harper and Brothers, 1937), pp. 997–1000.

[10]For a discussion of appropriate levels of measurement, see Leon Festinger and Daniel Katz, *Research Methods in the Behavioral Sciences* (New York: Holt, Rinehart and Winston, 1965), Ch. 11.

which ham is heavier. In general, we have confidence that we can measure a number of human social characteristics on an ordinal level, but we are not sure that some of them are susceptible to interval measurement, however easy it may be to compose items and assign interval numbers to them.

Sampling a National Public

Another implicit assumption, which we now consider quite dubious, that lay beneath the studies of the 1920s was that human nature was somehow all of a piece, that if one found a correlation to exist among college sophomores in Psychology 201, one would find about the same tendency among any collection of human beings. As long as the scales were rather elaborate, as the interval assumption both justified and required, it was difficult to work with the mass public. A pioneer student of political behavior, Stuart A. Rice, put his finger on the problems:

> Students may be required, good natured academicians may be cajoled, and sundry needy persons may be paid to sort cards containing propositions into eleven piles. But it is difficult to imagine securing comparable judgments, or satisfactory measurements in the final application, from bricklayers, business men, Italian-Americans, nuns, stevedores and seamstresses.[11]

All social research had to wait for the development of methods of sampling the entire public with some degree of accuracy, and political research particularly needed a sharper concept of "public opinion." The *Literary Digest,* a news magazine, in 1920 mailed 11 million return postcards to members of the public to discover their voting intention. In 1922 it staged a "referendum" on prohibition, in 1924 one on a tax plan, and thereafter it predicted each presidential election with remarkable accuracy—until 1936. The *Digest* sent its cards to whatever lists of persons were easily available, its own subscribers, or lists from telephone books and lists of automobile owners. With a fuzzy concept of sampling, it sought only to balance its mailings geographically, and counted on sheer numbers—well into the millions—to assure accuracy. (See p. 97.)

Systematic sampling of a human population goes back to European censuses of workers and the unemployed around the turn of the century, and was brought to this country in 1932. George Gallup began experimenting with nationwide canvasses on social and political issues in 1934, and by 1936 had devised a sampling scheme utilizing a mere 300,000 questionnaires, compared to the

---

[11] Stuart A. Rice, "Statistical Studies of Social Attitudes and Public Opinion," *Statistics and Social Studies* (Philadelphia: University of Pennsylvania Press, 1930), p. 190.

Digest's millions. Whereas the *Digest* poll, because of its upper-income bias, was in error by more than 17%, Gallup was only 6% in error. He predicted that Roosevelt would win, and, even more impressively, he predicted the figure that the *Digest* would predict, and why it would be wrong.[12]

In 1936, *Public Opinion Quarterly,* an academic journal, was founded. The columns of this publication provided a forum for representatives of several academic disciplines and non-academic occupations to join in attacking the problems of measurement and prediction. With improved sampling methods it was found that the national popular vote could be predicted with samples of 1,500 to 3,000, within the limits of 3% to 5% which the statistical tables (such as we treated in Chapter 6) called for. The *Digest* had shown that there was a universe of attitudes on public issues and candidates. The pollsters had demonstrated that, within limits, we are safe in making generalizations about human behavior and attitudes in the entire country by interviewing only a small proportion of the population.

The pragmatic study of psychological dimensions was advanced during World War II by social psychologists and sociologists examining troop morale and adjustment. One of the products of their research was the Guttman scale, named after Louis Guttman, an ordinal scale, rather like the Bogardus scale but of wider applicability.

Development of "Scaling"

The Army Research branch was interested in measuring an elusive psychological phenomenon, known in World War I as "shell shock" and in World War II as "combat fatigue." It was the tendency of men exposed to repeated danger to build up fears—a perfectly natural and normal response. Some soldiers were, of course, more susceptible to combat fatigue than others. The problem was to measure its level.

The researchers collected a list of all the symptoms of fear that soldiers reported having experienced when they were under fire. They arrayed them in order from the least frequently to the most frequently mentioned. A consistent order established itself except for one item which was experienced by some men who cited the most frequent symptoms but also by other men who cited the infrequent symptoms. The scale, as finally developed, consisted of the following items ranked from the least to the most frequent symptoms (1 being the least frequent):

---

[12]George Gallup and Saul F. Rae, *The Pulse of Democracy* (New York: Simon and Schuster, 1940), p. 35.

1. Uncontrolled urination
2. Losing control of the bowels
3. Vomiting
4. Feeling weak or faint
5. Feeling of stiffness
6. Sick at stomach
7. Shaking and trembling
8. Sinking feeling in stomach
9. Violent pounding of the heart

The item that did not fall on the scale was "cold sweat," and it was eliminated as measuring some other dimension, or at least inaccurately measuring the dimension of combat fatigue.

By a technique to be described later, the researchers established that this scale has a "reproducibility coefficient" of 92%, which is very good for such a long scale. This means, in effect, that a person who is located on the dimension by the fact that he experienced, say, symptom 6 but not symptom 5 should *not* have experienced each of symptoms 1 through 4 but should have experienced each of symptoms 7 through 9. Reproducibility of 92% means that with a large number of men one would be right in about 92% of these individual symptom predictions and wrong in 8%.[13]

The reproducibility of the scale *validates* the fact that the questions measure the dimension *on an ordinal scale* for the population interviewed. The items constitute measurement divisions on an instrument in the same sense that a tape measure which showed a man to be between 6 ft. 1 in. and 6 ft. 2 in. would certainly not measure him as being over 6 ft. 2 in. or under 6 ft. 1 in. Since we are talking about an ordinal scale, a better example would be a stick with irregularly spaced markings on it. The same principle applies: if a person's height fell between two adjacent marks, he would not also be measured as below the lower or above the upper mark.

Mental, emotional, and behavioral characteristics are not as concrete as the visible, touchable dimensions of physical phenomena. Therefore, we settle for somewhat less than perfect accuracy from our scale. If a tape to measure heights made a single error, we would suspect it was made of elastic and would refuse to make further use of it. In measuring combat fatigue, the researchers were willing to accept an instrument that made only 8 errors in 100. Compared with other scales, and with the dubious assumptions underlying interval measures, we consider an ordinal scale that is validated to measure this accurately to be a valuable tool for research.

---

[13]The description of this research and other studies in troop indoctrination, morale, adjustment to army life, and exposure to propaganda may be found in the four-volume study by Samuel L. Stouffer et al., *The American Soldier* (Princeton, N.J.: Princeton University Press, 1949). Vol. 4, *Measurement and Prediction,* tells the story of the Guttman scale. A brief and readable description by Stouffer of the Guttman technique will be found in Marie Jahoda et al., *Research Methods in Social Relations,* vol. 2 (New York: Dryden, 1951) which, confusingly, is an earlier edition of Selltiz.

The Guttman technique provides an empirical solution to several research problems:

1. It selects from a large number of potential items a few—usually 3 to 6—that may easily be incorporated into a mass survey.

2. It provides a standard for selecting these items which insures that they are all points of differentiation on an ordinal scale.

3. It rejects items that measure other variables, leaving those that measure only a *single* dimension. This quality is called "unidimensionality."

4. The standard by which it makes these decisions is the composite logic of the respondents, not the researcher. Thus, after the survey results are in, it tells the researcher whether the variable *exists* as a single dimension in the public being surveyed. This in itself is often a valuable research finding.

A Note on Terminology

Social scientists have sometimes been chided for inventing "gobbledygook" words to make their observations appear mysterious and occult to the uninitiated, when familiar words would do just as well. If they have been guilty of this, it is unfortunate that they did not practice it in this instance. Our understanding would be enhanced if new words had been invented to replace some of the multiple meanings of "scale" and "scaling." Since they have not, you should keep in mind three different ways the term is used:

1. Scale refers to levels of measurement: e.g., ratio, interval, ordinal, and nominal scales.

2. Scale is used (especially in older texts) to refer to any multipart item or battery of items that is designed to measure a variable: e.g., Likert scales, Thurstone scales, and the Bogardus social distance scale.

3. Scale, scaling, and scalability refer to the Guttman or cumulative scale (or scalogram) techniques in a more restricted sense. Thus, when one says "These items do not scale," one generally means that they do not meet the Guttman criterion of reproducibility. "Scale type" is ordinarily, and "perfect scale" always, used in this sense.

The Coefficient of Reproducibility (CR)

Before applying Guttman scaling techniques, we must be able to calculate "reproducibility" to see whether the items we suspect will form a scale actually do so within acceptable limits. To enable you to "see" a scale, the responses to the Bogardus items discussed earlier (p. 174) are arrayed in Table 11.1 in their logical order, with positive responses designated by a + and negative responses by a −.

TABLE 11.1 BOGARDUS SCALE

| | Perfect Scale | | | | | | | | | | | | Imperfect Scale | | | | | | | | | | | |
| | Would Admit to | | | | | | Would Not Admit to | | | | | | | Would Admit to | | | | | | Would Not Admit to | | | | | |
Score	Marriage	Club	Street	Occupat.	Citizen.	Visitor	Marriage	Club	Street	Occupat.	Citizen.	Visitor	Score	Marriage	Club	Street	Occupat.	Citizen.	Visitor	Marriage	Club	Street	Occupat.	Citizen.	Visitor
0	+	+	+	+	+	+	−	−	−	−	−	−	0	+	+	+	+	+	+	−	−	−	−	−	−
1	−	+	+	+	+	+	+	−	−	−	−	−	1	−	+	+	+	+	+	+	−	−	−	−	−
2	−	−	+	+	+	+	+	+	−	−	−	−	1e	−	+	−	+	+	+	+	−	+	−	−	−
3	−	−	−	+	+	+	+	+	+	−	−	−	2	−	−	+	+	+	+	+	+	−	−	−	−
4	−	−	−	−	+	+	+	+	+	+	−	−	3	−	−	−	+	+	+	+	+	+	−	−	−
5	−	−	−	−	−	+	+	+	+	+	+	−	4	−	−	−	−	+	+	+	+	+	+	−	−
6	−	−	−	−	−	−	+	+	+	+	+	+	5	−	−	−	−	−	+	+	+	+	+	+	−
													5e	−	−	+	−	+	−	+	+	−	+	−	+
													6	−	−	−	−	−	−	+	+	+	+	+	+

In the Perfect Scale seven persons, with scores from 0 through 6, are shown. Notice that, because the scale is perfect, we can tell from each person's score not only *how many* items would get a positive response but *which* items. The score indicates in a single number the individual's entire response pattern.

On the right, in the Imperfect Scale, we have added two non-scale or "error types" labeled "1e" and "5e." These are sometimes called "inconsistencies"—a more accurate term than "errors," which implies that perhaps we have recorded the response incorrectly. The scale scores for these persons do not predict accurately which items they gave a positive response to. They break the neat pattern of +s and −s, as shown in the Perfect Scale. However, we would have to change only one sign (under "Street") to change "1e" into a perfect Type 1. Or we could change one sign (under "Club") and turn him into a Type 3. In either case there is only one inconsistent response. As for 5e, we would have to change two signs to turn the person into a perfect Type 2, Type 4, or Type 6. (Which signs?)

Altogether, by changing three signs we could scale these nine persons perfectly. We could then predict 6 responses for each, or 54 responses in all, simply by knowing their scale scores. As it is, we can predict only 51 out of 54. Hence our coefficient reproducibility (*CR*) is 51/54 or

94.5%. The customary standard of acceptability is 90% or better, so our scale meets this standard for these nine persons.

Since the right half of both the Perfect and the Imperfect Scales merely repeats in mirror image the information in the left half, we shall hereafter omit it. Also note that the scale scores could be reversed, counting the +s instead of the −s, and running from 6 down to 0. And note that the items along the top could be reversed, so that they start with "Visitor" and end with "Marriage," making the scale run from lower left to upper right. Such matters are quite arbitrary; the important thing is the regularity of the pattern.

Scaling Legislative Roll Calls

When senators, congressmen, state legislators, or United Nations delegates vote on a series of bills, they are indicating their attitudes in much the same way that respondents to a survey do. From their votes we may ascertain underlying attitude dimensions. Whether these are their own personal attitudes or the positions they feel they should take in representing their constituents is not relevant here, although it is a matter that has received considerable research attention.[14] We may understand these underlying attitudes better if we determine whether each legislator's vote on each bill, amendment, or motion is a separate, independent decision, unrelated to the votes of others, or whether it is made with reference—consciously or unconsciously—to a fundamental, consistent attitude dimension that pervades the chamber. Guttman scaling helps to tell us this.

The best source of information on votes in the United States Senate and House of Representatives is *Congressional Quarterly*, which will be found in most college and many public libraries. *CQ* selects the critical votes, tabulates them, and describes the legislative issue on which they turn, which in parliamentary maneuvering is sometimes obscure. Furthermore it lists "pairs" when two members on opposite sides agree to abstain from voting, thus cancelling out one another (a practice that enables members who must, or wish to, miss the roll call to have the same influence they would have if they were present). *CQ* also asks those members who were absent how they would

---

[14]See Angus Campbell, Philip E. Converse, Warren E. Miller, and Donald E. Stokes, *Elections and the Political Order* (New York: Wiley, 1966), Ch. 11; John C. Wahlke, Heinz Eulau, William Buchanan, and LeRoy Ferguson, *The Legislative System* (New York: Wiley, 1962); Aage R. Clausen, *How Congressmen Decide* (New York, St. Martin's Press, 1973); John W. Kingdon, *Congressmen's Voting Decisions* (New York, Harper & Row, 1973); Morris P. Fiorina, *Representatives, Roll Calls and Constituencies* (Lexington, Mass., Lexington Books, 1974); David R. Mayhew, *Congress, The Electoral Connection* (New Haven, Conn.: Yale University Press, 1974), and Donald R. Matthews and James A. Stimson, *Yeas and Nays: Normal Decision-making in the United States House of Representatives* (New York, Wiley, 1975).

have voted if they had been present, and the replies are useful to analysts, even though they do not affect the legislative outcome.

To illustrate the scaling process, we shall take a series of votes on federal grants to colleges and universities considered by the Senate during October, November, and December of 1963.[15] To simplify your calculations, we shall reduce the Senate to about a third its actual size by selecting a cross-section of senators.[16] Their positions on four roll calls are given in Table 11.2.

The first roll call vote, No. 153 according to *CQ*'s numbering system, is on a motion by Senators Winston Prouty (Rep.-Vt.) and Abraham Ribicoff (Dem.-Conn.) to substitute the House version of the bill for the Senate version, an action which would have broadened the scope of the program. It was defeated, Yeas 33, Nays 49. Those who supported this motion, we anticipate, will be those who wished to go further than the majority was willing to go in providing aid, so they should represent the extreme pro-federal aid position.

The second roll call (No. 155) was an amendment by Senators Sam Ervin (Dem.-N.C.) and John Sherman Cooper (Rep.-Ky.) to permit taxpayer suits against the program. Since both sponsors of the bill voted against it, we may assume that this was intended to weaken the bill. This proposal was accepted, Yeas 45, Nays 33, and it received support from some members who eventually voted for the bill, so we may expect it to draw a line between the more and the less moderate proponents of federal aid.

Roll call No. 158 was on final passage, authorizing $1.9 billion for college education. President John F. Kennedy favored passage, and it received 60 Yeas, to only 19 Nays from hard-core opponents. Roll call No. 211 came two months later; its subject was whether the Senate would accept the conference report (a compromise between House and Senate versions) which cut the authorization to $1.2 billion. The new president, Lyndon B. Johnson, was in favor of the bill, and it passed, 54 to 27.

The first four columns of the table give thirty-four senators' positions on these four issues as reported by *CQ*, according to the following scheme:

Y Voted *Yea* on the motion or bill
√ Paired *For*
‡ Announced or *CQ* Poll *For* (did not vote)
N Voted *Nay* on the motion or bill
X Paired *Against*
− Announced or *CQ* Poll *Against* (did not vote)
? Absent, present but not voting, or "General Pair" (which does not indicate position) and did not announce or answer *CQ* poll to indicate position

[15]These appear in *CQ Weekly Reports* Numbers 42, 43, and 50, for 1963. They were suggested to me by Lawrence K. Pettit.

[16]These senators were selected to represent the maximum number of states and to mirror the total vote as accurately as possible, although, of course, the pairings do not come out even.

TABLE 11.2   ROLL CALL VOTES OF 34 SENATORS ON FEDERAL AID TO COLLEGES, 1963

		153	155	158	211	153	155	211	Score	Errors
Ala.	Hill, D.	N	Y	N	N	−	−	−	0	
Ariz.	Goldwater, R.	Y	Y	N	N	+	−	−	1	1
Ark.	Fulbright, D.	Y	N	Y	Y	+	+	+	3	
Cal.	Kuchel, R.	Y	N	Y	Y	+	+	+	3	
Conn.	Ribicoff, D.	Y	N	Y	Y	+	+	+	3	
Del.	Williams, R.	Y	Y	Y	Y	+	−	+	2	1
Ga.	Russell, D.	N	Y	N	N	−	−	−	0	
Haw.	Fong, R.	Y	N	Y	Y	+	+	+	3	
Ill.	Douglas, D.	Y	Y	Y	Y	+	−	+	2	1
Ind.	Hartke, D.	−	X	‡	Y	−	+	+	2	
Kans.	Carlson, R.	N	Y	Y	Y	−	−	+	1	
Ky.	Cooper, R.	N	Y	N	N	−	−	−	0	
Maine	Muskie, D.	N	Y ·	√	Y	−	−	+	1	
Md.	Beall, R.	Y	N	Y	Y	+	+	+	3	
Mich.	Hart, D.	Y	N	Y	Y	+	+	+	3	
Minn.	McCarthy, D.	N	N	Y	Y	−	+	+	2	
Mo.	Long, D.	−	X	Y	Y	−	+	+	2	
Mont.	Mansfield, D.	N	N	Y	Y	−	+	+	2	
Nev.	Bible, D.	N	Y	Y	N	−	−	−	0	
N.H.	Cotton, R.	Y	N	?	Y	+	+	+	3	
N.M.	Anderson, D.	N	N	Y	Y	−	+	+	2	
N.Y.	Keating, R.	Y	N	Y	√	+	+	+	3	
N.C.	Ervin, D.	N	Y	N	N	−	−	−	0	
Ohio	Lausche, D.	N	Y	X	N	−	−	−	0	
Ore.	Morse, D.	N	N	Y	Y	−	+	+	2	
Penna.	Scott, R.	Y	N	Y	Y	+	+	+	3	
S.C.	Thurmond, D.	N	Y	N	N	−	−	−	0	
S.D.	Mundt, R.	?	?	?	Y	o	o	+(out)		
Tex.	Yarborough, D.	N	Y	Y	Y	−	−	+	1	
Utah	Bennett, R.	Y	Y	N	N	+	−	−	1	1
Va.	Byrd, D.	N	Y	N	N	−	−	−	0	
Wash.	Magnuson, D.	Y	N	√	Y	+	+	+	3	
Wisc.	Nelson, D.	N	Y	Y	Y	−	−	+	1	
Wyo.	Simpson, R.	Y	?	N	N	+	o	−(out)		

Plus (+) score is a: Y N Y Y

Totals: Y, √, ‡ :   15   16   22   23   +: 14   16   22
          N, X, − :   18   16   10   11   −: 18   16   10
          ? :   1   2   2   0

184

The first step in translating these positions into a tentative scale of support or opposition to federal aid to higher education is to eliminate those roll calls which will not give us any useful information. A scanning of the last two columns (158 and 211) indicates that every senator except Bible of Nevada took the same position on these two roll calls. Therefore 158 tells us little that 211 does not tell us. And 158 gives us less information, since Cotton of New Hampshire and Mundt of South Dakota are not recorded. Therefore we shall eliminate 158. Draw a heavy line down the third column of the table to black out the responses.

Senators may register support for a measure in some circumstances by voting *for* the bill or *for* a strengthening amendment. They may register support at other times by voting *against* a crippling amendment or *against* a motion to send the bill back to committee. Thus, depending on the circumstances, a Y vote may be scored either as a + or a −. At the bottom of the table we have made the judgment that a + is equivalent to a Y (and its synonyms, √ and ‡) on all votes except number 155, where + is equivalent to N, X or − in *CQ*'s terminology, for the reasons given on p. 183. With all positions now translated into +, −, or 0, we now transfer our information into the second block. At this point we decide to eliminate Senators Mundt and Simpson because they are not recorded on one or more of these three crucial roll calls.[17] To simplify matters we copy the columns in order of the increasing (or decreasing) number of + responses. Fortunately, 153, 155, and 211 are already in increasing order of +s (15, 16, and 23, respectively), and the second block of columns simply preserves this order.

Now by counting the number of +s, we compute the scale scores, from 0 for opposition to federal aid up to 3 for support on all three of the roll calls. We get the following number of pure scale types and error types.

Number of Senators	Pure Type	Pattern	Number of Senators	Error Type	Pattern
8	0	− − −			
4	1	− − +	2	1e	+ − −
6	2	− + +	2	2e	+ − +
10	3	+ + +			
28			4		

Now to figure reproducibility. Our scale predicts 3 responses for each of 32 remaining senators, or 96 responses in all. The prediction of items from the scale scores resulted in four errors. Each of these four error types could be changed to a pure type by making the + on the left (No.

---

[17]There are various techniques for dealing with missing information of this sort, which we shall not go into here. If you undertake roll call scaling beyond the exercises given here, you should consult a very lucid manual, Lee F. Anderson, Meredith W. Watts, Jr., and Allen B. Wilcox, *Legislative Rollcall Analysis* (Evanston, Ill.: Northwestern University Press, 1966).

153) into a −. Therefore the scale's reproducibility (CR) is 92/96, or 96%, well above the minimum standard of 90%. As a matter of fact, with as few as three items, it is not particularly hard to reach this level. In a scale with five or six items, it often requires two or more sign changes to convert each case that is an error type into a scale type; hence overall reproducibility drops considerably.[18]

What have we accomplished by our scaling operation?

First, we have discovered that there exists an attitudinal dimension within the Senate, which may operationally be defined as "support for college aid." There are four scale positions, from 0 (no support) to 3 (maximum support). If we know only a senator's scale score, we can specify his position on three different roll calls with a minimal (4%) error. We have an *ordinal* measurement scheme and may treat the scale positions as rank orders. This is a considerable improvement in understanding and precision over our previous alternatives, which were either (a) to treat each roll call separately as a different nominal variable, on which each senator was dichotomized into "for" or "against," or (b) to add or summarize the results of the three votes into some arbitrary measure, without knowing whether to treat it as interval or ordinal, and without any assurance that we were not in effect "adding apples and oranges." Thus we have (a) demonstrated "unidimensionality," (b) defined the dimension, and (c) raised our precision of measurement from the nominal to the ordinal level.

We may now use our four-place scale in tabulations against other factors such as party affiliation, support of federal spending for other purposes, or liberal-conservative stands on other issues.

Example : Votes for Aid to Higher Education

By eliminating one of the roll calls (which one?), turn the three-item scale based on Table 11.2 on p. 185 into a perfect two-item scale with 100% reproducibility. Tabulate the resulting scale against party and region in the following table:

Scale Type	Republicans	Southern and Border Democrats	Northern and Western Democrats
0			
1			
2			

[18]Because reproducibility is not a rigorous standard, the more recent literature on scaling suggests other criteria. Since these apply probability methods, they will not be explained here.

What conclusions would you draw about party voting on federal aid to higher education?

_____

_____

The Use of Legislative Roll Call Analysis

It is not too surprising to find from the foregoing analysis that a series of votes on the same act at a single session of Congress form a single dimension. In other circumstances, however, the ability to define and test for an ordinal dimension, to see what votes fall along that dimension and what votes do not, may give considerable insight into the workings of the legislative process. For example, another study of aid-to-education measures considered by the Senate in 1960 and 1961 indicated that the *cost* of various proposals provided a rather neat scale, but that roll calls on matters other than financial outlay did not fall on the scale. The cost-of-federal-aid scale showed some relationship to indices of general conservatism-liberalism and support for the expansion of the scope of federal government.[19]

Duncan MacRae used scaling to analyze the actions of the 81st Congress, elected in 1948, which struggled with management-labor issues, civil rights, the worsening of relations with Russia, and the suspicion that Communists had infiltrated the American government. MacRae found several dimensions that accounted for many of the actions of the congressmen. A Fair Deal scale with eight positions arrayed the Democratic members from conservative to liberal. It incorporated such diverse issues as rent control, social security, public housing, the Taft-Hartley law, the National Science Foundation, creating a new department to deal with health, education and welfare matters (which was accomplished a decade later), and control of Communists and security risks. That these rather diverse items should constitute a single scale is itself a revealing observation with respect to the American party system. Another scale dealing with anti-poll tax legislation, the power of the Rules Committee, fair employment practices, immigration of West Indians and Mexican farm workers, and construction of residential housing near army bases was defined as a Race Relations scale. The Race Relations and Fair Deal scales correlated with one another at a rather high level, although the two sets of items did not form a single scale. Both of them were correlated moderately with an Agriculture scale but not a Foreign Aid scale.

In general, scales that worked for the Democrats did not work for the Republican members, and different bills were included in the Republican scales. There was a Welfare State scale on the

[19]William Buchanan, "Federal Aid to Education on the Conservative-Liberal Scale," *Annals,* 344 (1962), 55–64.

Republican side that correlated rather well with Race Relations but better with Foreign Aid than with agricultural items.[20]

A study of isolationism, covering a longer period, used scales to locate the position of congressmen with respect to foreign aid. It showed the gradual shift of Republicans from their pre-war isolationist stance to a point at the end of the Eisenhower administration when they were substantially more internationalist than the Democrats.[21] Historians have used Guttman scaling to establish dimensions of voting in the British House of Commons in the 1840s, and the United States Congress prior to the Civil War.[22]

H. Douglas Price analyzed the voting behavior of Southern Democratic senators from 1949 to 1956, finding fifty-six scales dealing with such matters as economic reforms, foreign aid, natural gas, and displaced persons. The scales differentiated among those issues—such as cloture and the Electoral College system—where there were sharp cleavages between Southern and non-Southern Democrats; those on which the center of gravity of the Southern bloc was displaced considerably from the Northern Democratic center of gravity; and those where the Southerners were united with the rest of the party against the Republicans. The scaling technique in this instance confirmed in rather precise summary terms what observers of the Senate knew in a general way. The Price study, in which you may also find a discussion of the philosophy and technique of scaling, observes:

> Like mathematics and logic, scaling can tell the omniscient mind absolutely nothing new. The results of such tautological processes are already present, in somewhat less obvious form, in the raw data. If God exists and is omniscient, then He knows all possible deductions, correlations, scale patterns, and all other possible relationships without having to perform any calculations. Hence, as has often been remarked, those who feel on a par with the Deity have no need for logic or mathematics. Those of us with lesser endowments continue to find a considerable advantage in the use of such formal techniques.[23]

Judicial Scaling

Once upon a time it was believed that the principles of the Constitution expounded by the Supreme Court were unchangeable. Then it became accepted that by majority rule the Court altered

[20]Duncan MacRae, Jr., *Dimensions of Congressional Voting* (Berkeley: University of California Press, 1958).

[21]Leroy N. Rieselbach, "The Demography of the Congressional Vote on Foreign Aid, 1939–1958," *American Political Science Review,* 58 (1964), 577–588.

[22]William O. Aydelotte, "Voting Patterns in the British House of Commons in the 1840's," *Comparative Studies in Society and History,* 5 (1963), 134–163; and Joel H. Silbey, *Shrine of Party: Congressional Voting Behavior, 1841–1852* (Pittsburgh, Pa.: University of Pittsburgh Press, 1967).

[23]Douglas Price, "Are Southern Democrats Different?" in *Politics and Social Life,* Nelson W. Polsby, Robert A. Dentler, and Paul A. Smith, eds. (Boston: Houghton Mifflin, 1963), pp. 740–756.

constitutional interpretations to adjust the law to changing times. More recently, irreverent students have suggested that the individual justices perceive the Constitution in highly personal fashion and "vote" for their points of view, rather like congressmen vote on roll calls. Scaling sheds some light on this question. Scale scores of the members of the famous Court of the 1930s that first overturned as unconstitutional the measures passed by New Deal Congresses, but later (when Justices Hughes and Roberts shifted their stance) began to accept similar measures, reveal the relative willingness of each justice to accept new legislation.[24] The scale scores, based upon thirty-five split decisions in the 1936 term, with reproducibility of .98, are:

Stone	35
Cardozo	35
Brandeis	33
Hughes	29
Roberts	27
Van Devanter	13
Sutherland	11
Butler	9
McReynolds	4

A study of civil liberties cases by Sidney Ulmer showed that on twenty-nine such cases the decisions formed a scale pattern with a *CR* of 95%.[25]

Scaling has also been used to analyze the position of justices on cases dealing with the right of indigents accused of crimes in state courts to have a lawyer assigned to defend them.[26]

Among the issues on which scholars of the judicial process are engaged in occasionally acrimonious debate is whether scaling or any other quantitative techniques help us to understand judicial behavior. Those who do not understand the technique condemn it roundly, while those who do understand it differ on what criteria of scalability to use, what meaning should be attached to "unidimensionality" once it is established, and what tests of statistical significance are appropriate.[27]

[24]Glendon Schubert, *Quantitative Analysis of Judicial Behavior* (Glencoe, Ill.: The Free Press, 1959), p. 314.

[25]S. Sidney Ulmer, "The Analysis of Behavior Patterns on the United States Supreme Court," *Journal of Politics,* 22 (1960), 629–653.

[26]Schubert, pp. 322–363. He also gives rules for handling missing data and discusses the rationale for judicial scaling on pp. 280–290.

[27]Schubert's "Ideologies and Attitudes, Academic and Judicial," *Journal of Politics,* 29 (1967), 3–40, and "Academic Ideology and the Study of Adjudication," *American Political Science Review,* 61 (1967), 106–129, give the flavor of the dispute and cite the principal articles involved. A more tempered discussion is Joseph Tanenhaus, "The Cumulative Scaling of Judicial Decisions," *Harvard Law Review,* 79 (1966), 1583–1594. For other quantitative techniques for analyzing the judicial process, see S. Sidney Ulmer, *Introductory Readings in Political Behavior* (Chicago: Rand-McNally, 1961), pp. 238–254 and 276–288.

12 / Scaling Survey Data

Measurement is the assignment of particular mathematical characteristics to conceptual entities in such a way as to permit (1) an unambiguous mathematical description of every situation involving the entity and (2) the arrangement of all occurrences in a quasi-serial order.
PETER CAWS

With legislative roll calls and judicial decisions, the issues on which persons divide are those which legislative demands or personal litigation happen to turn up. There are many such divisions, and scaling technique is used to select meaningful sets of them. When we seek to detect dimensions of attitudes in the public, we must use survey data. The number of questions that may be asked in an interview is limited, and the research must select in advance and put on the questionnaire those items which are expected to cut some attitude continuum in a useful fashion. Until the data are tabulated, the researcher cannot know whether the questions selected in advance actually do form a scale. In testing for the presence of a scalable dimension three criteria are applied:

1. The items must be logically related, dealing with the same topic or concept. Finding several unrelated questions which accidentally formed a scale would be purposeless, since they would not measure any useful variable.
2. They must "cut" the population at a variety of points along the dimension. For example, items with 4%, 10%, and 13% of the population responding positively would not be a very useful scale, since the remaining 87% above the highest cut-off point would fall into one extreme scale type. Several items which split the population approximately in half—say at 50%, 53%, 58%, and 61% positive—would, even if they scaled, be nearly as useless, for half the population would fall below the bottom cut-off at 50%, and 39% above the cut-off at 61%.
3. Reproducibility must be sufficiently high. This has already been treated.

In survey research with large numbers of cases, one cannot conveniently scan columns of 300 to 3,000 +s and −s. A perfect two-item scale has a zero in one of the four cells and gives a Q of 1. Pairs of items that combine in a scale are likely to have high Q values resulting from a low total in one cell. (If you need to review Q, see p. 83.) Cross-tabulation is therefore used as a preliminary step in selecting those items in a survey that are likely to form a scale.

Somewhat lower standards of reproducibility are applied to survey data than to legislative and judicial roll calls. In legislatures and courts the members are taking formal action having considerable import with respect to matters they usually have considered carefully. In surveys the questions are presented unexpectedly, and respondents have only a short time to ponder them. A few persons do not understand the questions, and in a few cases the interviewers misunderstand their responses or record them incorrectly. These circumstances contribute to a somewhat higher proportion of inconsistencies or "error types" in surveys. Legislative and judicial scales normally have CRs of .95 or better; survey scales of public attitudes usually are not much above the minimum of .90.

These criteria are not mechanically applied. Sometimes an item with a relatively low Q association with one or two other items in the scale will be acceptable because it slices the population at a point distant from the other items.

Developing a Scale

In 1970 the research methods class at Washington and Lee University decided to investigate attitudes toward environmental pollution in nearby Virginia towns. The first step was to collect or invent a number of items which might reveal public attitudes. The 12 items selected after some class discussion were then tested on a sample of 57 citizens. The distribution of answers follows. In the margin beside each item, indicate which ones *you* think should be kept in a scale which for various reasons including interview time would have to be reduced to about 6 items. In a word or two, indicate why.

Here are some things people have said about pollution. As I read each of them, please tell me whether you *agree strongly, agree,* are *undecided, disagree,* or *disagree strongly*:

	AS	A	U	D	DS
a. The problem of pollution is *the* major problem facing the nation today.	10	21	11	14	1
b. Each of us contributes to the pollution which exists today.	14	30	5	7	1

	AS	A	U	D	DS	
c. Each of us should take positive action to prevent the environment from being polluted.	17	35	1	2	0	
d. All this concern about pollution is just a passing fad, and isn't really very important.	2	4	7	22	22	R
e. There is no way to prevent pollution under our present system of business and government.	1	12	10	25	9	R
f. We must be prepared to pay more for some products, such as gasoline and beverages, to cover the costs of cleaning up pollution caused by these products.	7	29	2	18	1	
g. Any business or industry that cannot control its pollution should be shut down.	6	17	14	14	6	
h. There should be stricter laws to prevent pollution by the average man.	10	33	6	7	1	
i. We will always be able to draw the resources we need from our environment.	2	12	14	18	11	R
j. Owners of private property should be free to use the plants and natural resources on it pretty much as they are now permitted.	3	19	9	18	7	
k. The pollution problem can be solved by science without government action.	1	7	17	20	12	R
l. If we don't act on the problem of pollution in the next few years, it will be too late to save mankind.	12	21	14	9	1	

Note that most of these items call for those who are concerned about pollution to agree, but several of them call for them to disagree. Put "R" for "reversal" in the right margin by those latter items.

In fact, the items forming the best scale in this pre-test group were *b, c, d, g, h,* and *l.* The remainder were eliminated principally because they failed to correlate with other items, indicating that they measured different dimensions. This eliminated some statements which seemed more meaningful, in our judgment; but the purpose of scaling is to find a dimension that exists in the public mind, not in the mind of the researcher.

Selecting the Cutting Points

The survey was conducted in four industrial towns in Virginia, all of them with pollution problems. The sample consisted of 411 interviews, too many to scale by pencil and paper methods. So the responses to our 6 items were put on punch cards along with the other questionnaire results. The following description indicates how we checked to find whether these items actually scaled in the final survey as they had in the pre-test and how they were ordered, formed into a scale, and used in the analysis.

The object was to construct a measuring instrument for anti-pollution attitudes that will differentiate people along a continuum from those most concerned to those least concerned. For convenience, we needed a label, and we chose "conservationist." Looking at the items one at a time, the *strongest* conservationists, or opponents of pollution, were those who "agreed strongly" with each item (except *d*, where they "disagreed strongly" with the idea that concern about pollution was a passing fad). We labeled them ++. The next most conservationist response, "agree" (or "disagree" to *d*), is labeled +. The undecided responses are 0s, and the responses indicating lack of concern are − and −−. The items are now listed in the order of their apparent difficulty, with those getting the fewest ++ and + responses at the bottom:

	++	+	0	−	−−	++, +/0, −, −−
c	122	273	12	4	0	(395/16)
d	137	214	33	22	5	(351/60)
b	84	247	33	44	3	(331/80)
h	63	262	39	46	1	(325/86)
l	52	194	78	82	5	(246/165)
g	33	94	97	141	46	(127/284)

Each item has five possible responses, forming a potential scale in itself. Before we can combine the items into a Guttman scale, which we hope will be more meaningful than any one item, we need to dichotomize each of them into a single + group and a single − group. We may do this at any point, so for our first trial we shall "cut" each item at ++, +/0, −, −−. The resulting distributions are given in parentheses on the right in the preceding list.

Since a Guttman scale is an ordinal measuring device, we may think of it as a stick on which we cut notches. Even though the notches are not an equal distance apart, we could measure the height of a man as "between the third and fourth notch from the bottom" and know that he was taller than those who did not come up to the third notch but shorter than those whose heads rose above the fourth notch. It is just such a measuring stick for conservationist attitude that we are shaping. Using the "cuts" listed in the preceding parentheses and lining up our survey population with conservationists on the right, our stick would look like this:

c	d	b h	l	g
+395	+351	+331 +325	+246	+127
−16	−60	−80 −86	−165	−284

It is obvious that because so many people profess conservationist views we are discriminating with some accuracy among the hard cases on the left end but not toward the conservationist right end of the stick. We could remedy this to some extent by making our item cuts at different places. First, we decided to cut item *g* between ++ and +, rather than between + and 0. Referring to the list, you will see that this changes the number in parentheses from (127/284) to (33/378), thus moving it to the right end of the stick. But we then need an item to fill in the long space between *l* and *g*. Items *d, b* and *h* are the candidates, and of them, *d* is the one that comes closest to splitting that space in half; therefore cut between ++ and + (137/274). The new scale (bottom) is a much better measuring stick.

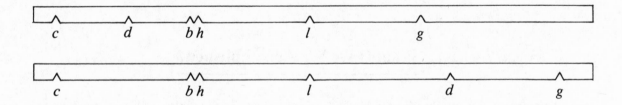

Calculating *CR*

At this stage we decided not to try to refine the scale any more (even though *b* and *h* were too close to do us much good) but to sort the cards and see how well they scaled. The order of sorting was that of the last scale: *c, b, h, l, d, g.*

First, the cards were run through the card sorter[1] on item c, and divided into two stacks: those coded ++ or + (labeled +) and those coded 0, − or −− (labeled −). These were kept separate, and each was run on item b. Now we had four stacks marked:

$$cb \quad cb \quad cb \qquad cb$$

$$++, +-, --, \text{ and } -+.$$

The third run, on h, gave us 8 stacks; the next, on l, 16; the next, on d, 32, and the final run, on g, gave 64 possible stacks. Fortunately, not all these combinations appeared, or our reproducibility would have been very low.

The results are shown in Table 12.1.

Calculate the number of errors (several have been done for you as examples) and write them in the Error column. Then calculate the number of predictions, as explained on pp. 181 and 185. Subtract from 100% the proportion of errors as a percentage of predictions, and you have the CR. You should get .94, which is not bad for a 6-item scale.

Note that some of the 1-error types can be corrected by changing either a + or a −, which gives you a choice of which scale type to count them with. For example, + + + + − +, the third error type under 6e, can be made a Type 6 by changing the − or a Type 4 by changing the last +. Some of the 2-error types require even more arbitrary choices. The last 0e type, − + − + − −, can be made into a 0, − − − − − −, as we counted it, or a 2, + + − − − −, or a 4, + + + + − −.

Now look down the columns to see which item is causing the most errors. Draw a line down it, and recalculate CR (remembering you now have only 6 scale types rather than 7). You should have improved reproducibility to .96.

Our class chose not to make this improvement but to retain the 6-item scale, punching the scale values into a blank column.

What Have We Accomplished?

This protracted number-juggling in fact advanced us considerably and saved work in the long run. Our first pre-test contained 12 different possible measures of conservationism, all of them

---

[1]The counting sorter was the original data processing machine, invented in 1889 by Herman Hollerith. When the U.S. Census fell behind in tabulating the 1890 results, they turned to his cards and sorter. Cross-tabulation is now done by computers, which have routines for Guttman scaling. If you have access to a sorter, you should use it, following the process described here, since this gives a better understanding of the steps involved. The computer does it much faster, but you have to imagine what is going on in the computer's memory.

TABLE 12.1

Scale Type	Item						Number	Errors
	c	b	h	l	d	g		
6	+	+	+	+	+	+	18	
6e	+	−	+	+	+	+	2	2
	+	+	+	−	+	+	2	2
	+	+	+	+	−	+	5	5
5	+	+	+	+	+	−	60	
5e	+	−	+	+	+	−	13	
	+	+	−	+	+	−	6	
	+	−	−	+	+	−	1 X 2 = 2	2
4	+	+	+	+	−	−	94	
4e	+	−	+	+	−	−	24	
	+	−	+	+	−	+	2 X 2 = 4	4
3	+	+	+	−	−	−	57	
3e	+	+	+	−	+	−	23	
	+	+	+	−	−	+	3	
	−	+	+	−	−	−	2	
2	+	+	−	−	−	−	32	
2e	+	+	−	+	−	−	14	
	+	+	−	−	+	−	8	
1	+	−	−	−	−	−	8	
1e	+	−	+	−	−	−	16	
	+	−	−	+	−	−	4	
	+	−	−	−	+	−	2	
	+	−	+	−	−	+	1	
0e	−	+	−	−	−	−	3	
	−	−	+	−	−	−	2	
	−	+	−	−	+	−	2	
	−	−	+	+	−	−	1	
	−	+	−	+	−	−	2	
0	−	−	−	−	−	−	4	____
							411	

having some logical claim as an operational definition. There is nothing against multiple operational definitions so long as they are not negatively correlated with one another. They are often used to confirm findings from one cross-tabulation by comparing the result with another. But 12 is far too many for interviewing and analysis, and the items eliminated were those that included some concept or connotation that distracted the members of our pre-test sample and might have done the same for the final survey group.

The 6 items we kept have several useful qualities. They correlate with one another. (Items that do not correlate will not scale.) They provide a measuring stick with 6 notches reasonably well distributed along its length. Since these items all have to do with pollution, we can more confidently label our dimension "conservationism" than we could with only one item. We have clearly identified an attitude dimension that exists in this population and may exist in others. Other researchers may wish to use these items and could reasonably expect them to scale in their populations—although this cannot be guaranteed. One of the items, d, is reversed, providing a partial check on "response-set bias"—the tendency for some people to agree with any item presented to them. An ideal battery would be composed half of items with which "conservationists" would agree and half of reversed items with which they would disagree. Unfortunately, except for d the reversed items fell off the scale, so our scale is less than satisfactory in this respect.

Our scale was used in several ways, to see what educational or economic backgrounds produced conservationists, to see whether hunting, fishing, and other outdoor activities were correlated, and whether the attitudes were derived from the mass media. The following tabulation resulted from our effort to see whether conservationism as we measured it is an attitude which spurs people to engage in activities that might reduce pollution or whether it is purely an intellectual orientation, unrelated to their daily lives. To do this, we cross-tabulated with another series of items based on the respondents' reported activities. Since this dependent variable also happens to be a Guttman scale, it means that those reporting the rarer activities, such as giving time and money, were also those who reported the more frequent ones, like changing brands or discussing pollution. The tabulations are in Table 12.2.

TABLE 12.2 CONSERVATION ACTIVITIES REPORTED BY CONSERVATIONISM SCALE TYPES

Activism Scale	Type 6	5	4	3	2	1	0
Gave time, money, wrote letters	26%	30%	17%	20%	13%	10%	0%
Changed brands*	19	15	21	19	19	23	14
Discussed with friend	33	35	29	29	33	19	7
None of these	22	20	33	32	35	49	79
	100%	100%	100%	100%	100%	100%	100%
N:	27	80	120	85	54	31	14

*The item was: "(Have you) changed to other brands of detergents or gas or other products even though they are more expensive?"

198

The range from the low to the high end of the conservationism scale on the first and last rows indicates a good correlation between the two items. However, there are several "bobbles" in the pattern; Type 6 is out of line and so is Type 3. These could be caused by random sampling, since the discrepancies are below 4% in every case. If the middle lines were transposed, with "Discussed" put above "Changed brands," the pattern would be better—but this shows a flaw in the activism, not the conservationism scale. Thus we conclude that conservationism has a good deal to do with reported activity. How reported activity correlates with actual activity remains to be researched, but it is fairly safe to assume that those who reported *not* engaging in one of these activities indeed did not engage in it.

Scaling and Political Psychology

The Guttman scale, by making the presence of an attitude dimension that goes beyond a single question empirically testable and demonstrable, has made the search for psychological bases of political behavior more precise. Or, at least, it has made more evident the former imprecision in the intuitive delineation of attitudes or the haphazard combination of test items.

This is demonstrated in the research that followed the publication of the classic work of the World War II era—*The Authoritarian Personality*.[2] This massive piece of research was completed too early to incorporate scaling in its design. It delineated a personality type characterized by rigidity, bigotry, distrust, conformity, fear of sex, and extreme social reactionism, and showed how this personality syndrome tended to coincide with authoritarian and reactionary political attitudes. When subsequent researchers sought to scale the "authoritarianism" items, they found technical flaws in the wording and met with mixed success in discovering a single dimension. Three dimensions emerged: "authoritarianism" as originally conceived, which was found to scale under certain circumstances; "alienation," the tendency to withdraw from social and political involvement; and "anomie" (also spelled "anomy" and "anomia"). This last concept was originated by the French sociologist Emile Durkheim at the turn of the century and refers to a sense of "normlessness" or detachment from the rules of society. A fourth concept, "political efficacy," the belief that one can affect or share in the control of one's government, is almost the reverse of these. All of these concepts have been found scalable with various subsets of items at various times and places. They have been found to be related to education, with anomics and alienates

---

[2]T. W. Adorno, Else Frenkel-Brunswik, D. J. Levinson, and R. N. Sanford (New York: Harper and Brothers, 1950).

coming predominantly from those with less education. As one might expect, they are less likely to participate in elections. But authoritarians are more likely to belong to social groups, perhaps due to their sense of conformity. In Nashville, Tennessee, in an election to decide whether the area would adopt a more modern form of urban county government, the anomics who turned out tended to vote against it because of their distrust of government. Although more sophisticated methods of analysis have been used in tracing these dimensions and their correlates, the Guttman technique has provided an indispensable test in differentiating among them and has led to the sharpening of the diffuse theories in *The Authoritarian Personality*.[3]

Guttman Scaling: How to Do It

Our examples have included scales of legislative votes, court decisions, and attitude surveys, but any phenomenon that has characteristics amenable to ordering may be tested for scalability. For example, Wanderer found that urban riots could be scaled for severity, from those where there was only vandalism and interference with firemen to those where the National Guard was called out and officers or civilians were killed.[4]

Lee F. Anderson, Meredith W. Watts, Jr., and Allen B. Wilcox, *Legislative Rollcall Analysis* (Evanston, Ill.: Northwestern University Press, 1966), is the best manual for legislative scaling. G. David Garson, *Handbook of Political Analysis* (Boston: Holbrook, 1971), Ch. 7, is a useful brief description. R. L. Gorden, *Unidimensional Scaling of Social Variables: Concepts and Procedures* (New York: The Free Press, 1977), is a simple explanation of how to do scaling without mechanical or electronic assistance.

[3]The literature on these concepts is fairly extensive. Among the studies most relevant to political behavior are these: Leo Srole, "Social Integration and Certain Corollaries: An Exploratory Study," *American Sociological Review*, 21 (1956), 709–716, which developed the most frequently used anomie scale; Alan H. Roberts and Milton Rokeach, "Anomie, Authoritarianism and Prejudice: A Replication," *American Journal of Sociology*, 61 (1956), 355–368; Edward L. McDill, "Anomie, Authoritarianism, Prejudice and Socio-Economic Status: An Attempt at Clarification," *Social Forces*, 39 (1961), 239–245, which seeks to distinguish the concepts; and Curtis R. Miller and Edgar W. Butler, "Anomia and Eunomia: A Methodological Evaluation of Srole's Anomia Scale," *American Sociological Review*, 31 (1966), 400–406, which contains a good bibliography of anomie studies. Herbert McClosky and John H. Schaar, "Psychological Dimensions of Anomy," *ibid.*, 30 (1965), 14–40, led to a controversy on methods, *ibid.*, 757–776. Relationships between authoritarianism and political behavior are studied in Robert E. Lane, "Political Personality and Electoral Choice," *American Political Science Review*, 49 (1955), 173–190. E. L. McDill and Jeanne Clare Ridley, "Status, Anomia, Political Alienation and Political Participation," *American Journal of Sociology*, 68 (1962), 205–213, describes the Nashville election. Lester W. Milbrath, *Political Participation* (Chicago: Rand-McNally, 1965), pp. 84–85, cites and provides a valuable summary of the major studies on the relation of authoritarianism and anomie to voting behavior. Angus Campbell, Gerald Gurin, and Warren E. Miller, *The Voter Decides* (Evanston, Ill.: Row-Peterson, 1954), pp. 187–194, describes political efficacy and its correlates.

[4]Jules J. Wanderer, "An Index of Riot Severity and Some Correlates," *American Journal of Sociology*, 74 (1969), 500–505.

More comprehensive works are W. S. Torgerson, *Theory and Method of Scaling* (New York: Wiley, 1958), and Matilda White Riley, *Sociological Research*, Vol. I, *A Case Approach*, especially pp. 502–569 and Vol. II, *Exercises and Manual*, especially pp. 56–101 (New York: Harcourt, Brace and World, 1963).

Since the simple CR has been superseded by more sophisticated probability measures of reproducibility which have not been described here, you should consult one of the preceding sources before writing up results for publication.

EXERCISE 13: **Distinguishing Characteristics of Different Nations**

Select four or more items from the Banks-Textor variables beginning on p. 67 which you think might form a scale of cultural development, political liberty, participation in government, unity, or some other quality distinguishing one nation from another. (If you find these items too limited, go to the original study, which has many more variables.)

Choose your cut-off points to give the best spread possible for a measuring instrument, and construct a scale. If *CR* is below .90, drop the weakest item and see if it improves your scale. Write a description of the scale you have developed. Hand in your work sheets along with it.

(If you are using the method in Chapter 11, you may find it easier to do the preliminary steps with 25 or 30 nations, and move up to the entire population when you calculate the *CR*. If you have a counter-sorter available, you may wish to punch up a deck of cards and use the method in Chapter 12. If your university has a computer statistical package such as SPSS with a Guttman scaling program, let it do the work for you.)

13 / Ordinal Measures of Association

Chapters 10 through 12 dealt with univariate measures—the levels, scales, and statistics employed to describe a single variable. Now we return to examining relationships between two variables, independent and dependent, in search of causal patterns. This is what we were doing at the nominal level with D, Q, and ϕ in Chapter 5 and V in Chapter 8. All of these summarized the amount of association between two dichotomies. In this chapter we advance the quality of measurement to the ordinal or ranking level. The measures to be treated are *gamma*, *tau*-b, *tau*-c, d_{yx}, d_{xy}, and R_s.

Keep in mind the distinction between such measures of *association*—which tell us how strong is the relationship between two variables—and tests of significance such as *chi square*, which tell us whether the relationship found in a sample is likely to be found in the population from which it is drawn. With the higher precision of ordinal data we can construct better measures of association, and these will reveal more about behavior in society. For example, it has long been accepted that there is a relationship between education and income, and that it is a positive one. But *how strong* is it? Is it stronger now than in the 1960s? Is it stronger among blacks than among whites? Those are the sorts of questions these measures can answer.

Recall Yule's Q from Chapter 5, which summarizes the relationship between two dichotomies. Its formula is:

$Q = \dfrac{ad - bc}{ad + bc}$ where cell frequencies are

a	b
c	d

Now we shall expand this principle to tables with more than four cells, using a measure re-lated to Q called *gamma*.

Gamma

Gamma (known also as G, γ, and occasionally as *tau-gamma*) is a measure of association between two ordinal variables where the number of cases is large enough for the data to be grouped into classes. It is ideal for survey data, for Guttman scale typologies meet these specifica-tions, as do single survey questions which order individuals into classes. Examples are attitude items scored Agree, Neutral, or Disagree, and party identification, scored Strong Democrat, Weak Democrat, Independent, Weak Republican, Strong Republican. Also, interval measures of age or education scaled down to ordinal level are appropriately used with *gamma*.

For example, suppose you had two scales to which the members of a legislature had respond-ed. One ranked them in terms of their hostility toward interest group lobbyists, the other accord-ing to their professed loyalty to their political party. If the two measures are positively correlated, they permit *prediction* in the following fashion: taking any pair of legislators, and noting that A is higher than B on the interest group hostility scale, you will predict that A is also higher than B on the party loyalty scale. In other words, you can predict their *order*, which is an entirely appro-priate standard for an ordinal scale. In Table 13.1, if you chose two from the same row, or from the same column, or from the same row and column (i.e., from the same cell in the table) obvi-ously the prediction would have to be called off, for they would have the same score on at least one of the variables. Their ranks would be tied.

TABLE 13.1 INTEREST GROUP AND PARTY ORIENTATION

Party Loyalty Scale		Interest Group Attitude Scale		
		Positive (0)	Neutral (1)	Negative (2)
Independent	(0)	3	5	0
Semi-independent	(1)	6	28	1
Usually loyal	(2)	0	31	4
Always loyal	(3)	0	10	12

Taking pairs of legislators at random, noting their order on one variable, and predicting that they would fall in the same order on the other variable, you would be right part of the time and wrong part of the time. But because party loyalty and interest group hostility are positively correlated, your prediction that the legislator who was higher on one would be higher on the other scale would be correct more often than it was wrong.

If this notion of picking pairs of legislators and predicting their order appears to you to be a logical *tour de force,* you are quite right. The statisticians go through the process because it gives a meaningful interpretation to *gamma.* This is the correctness of such a rank-order prediction calculated according to right guesses minus wrong guesses, as a proportion of all guesses. In other words, it is the *proportional reduction in error* in guessing a case's rank on one variable that comes from knowing its value on the other variable. What is important is that if most of the cases are "concordant" pairs falling along the upper-left-to-lower-right diagonal, as in this table, you will make more right than wrong predictions, and *gamma* will have a *high positive* value. If every case were on this diagonal, *gamma* would be +1, for you would be right every time, except where two legislators are in the same cell, in which case they are tied in rank and not counted. If the legislators were evenly distributed among all the cells of the table, you could not predict their order on one variable from the order on the other, right guesses would equal wrong ones, and *gamma* would be zero. And if the cases are "discordant" pairs clustered along the "off" diagonal, from lower left to upper right, you would make more wrong than right guesses and *gamma* would be negative. And if all the cases were on this diagonal, all your guesses would be wrong, your level of correctness would be −100%, and *gamma* would be −1.

With any pair of ordinal variables the researcher chooses whether to rank the cases on each variable from low to high or high to low. In this example, party loyalty might just as well have been arranged with "Always loyal" at the top and "Independent" at the bottom of the scale. If this had been done, the sign of *gamma* would have been − rather than +, but the value would have been the same. So a high negative value implying more "wrong" guesses in the previous context would have been supportive of the same hypothesis. Ordinal measures are constructed to give a positive value if the data cluster along the "main" diagonal (upper left to lower right) and negative if they cluster along the "off" diagonal (lower left to upper right). Obviously the meaning of plus and minus is not intrinsic but is determined by the way the researcher happens to order his ranks.

Look at Table 13.1. If we wanted to drop from the higher (ordinal) level to the lower (nominal) level to permit the calculation of Q, how could we do it? Here are two ways:

$$\begin{array}{c|cc} 3 & 5 & 0 \\ \hline 6 & 28 & 1 \\ 0 & 31 & 4 \\ 0 & 10 & 12 \end{array} \quad \text{reduces to} \quad \begin{array}{c|c} 3 & 5 \\ \hline 6 & 86 \end{array} \qquad Q = \frac{258-30}{258+30} = \frac{228}{288} = .79$$

or

$$\begin{array}{cc|c} 3 & 5 & 0 \\ 6 & 28 & 1 \\ \hline 0 & 31 & 4 \\ 0 & 10 & 12 \end{array} \quad \text{reduces to} \quad \begin{array}{c|c} 42 & 1 \\ \hline 41 & 16 \end{array} \qquad Q = \frac{672-41}{672+41} = \frac{631}{713} = .88$$

Draw lines to indicate four other possible ways of calculating Q.

Gamma is in effect an average of all these Q measures, but there is a more straightforward way of computing it. First we need two interim figures called P_s and P_d. Think of their meanings as:

> P_s = the concordant pairs of cases, with *similar* rankings on the two variables,
> P_d = the discordant pairs, with *different* rankings on the two variables.

To calculate P_s we take each cell in the table and add up the number of cases *below and to the right of it,* then multiply this total by the cell frequency itself. This gives the number of correct predictions, which contributes to the positive coefficient of association. Then we add up these products. Here are the calculations:

$$\begin{array}{c|cc} 3 & & \\ \hline & 28 & 1 \\ & 31 & 4 \\ & 10 & 12 \end{array} \qquad \begin{array}{c|cc} 5 & & \\ \hline & 1 & \\ & 4 & \\ & 12 & \end{array}$$

$$3 \times 86 = 258 \qquad\qquad 5 \times 17 = 85$$

$$\begin{array}{c|cc} 6 & & \\ \hline & 31 & 4 \\ & 10 & 12 \end{array} \qquad \begin{array}{c|cc} 28 & & \\ \hline & 4 & \\ & 12 & \end{array}$$

$$6 \times 57 = 342 \qquad\qquad 28 \times 16 = 448$$

$$\begin{array}{c|cc} 0 & & \\ \hline & 10 & 12 \end{array} \qquad \begin{array}{c|c} 31 & \\ \hline & 12 \end{array}$$

$$0 \times 22 = 0 \qquad\qquad 31 \times 12 = 372$$

$$P_s = 258 + 85 + 342 + 448 + 0 + 372 = 1505$$

Now we calculate P_d by multiplying each cell frequency by the number of cases *below* and to the *left* of it and summing the results as before. Since most of the cases in this table lie along the positive diagonal, the numbers here will be much smaller. Perform these calculations yourself in the space below. You should get $P_d = 111$.

$$5 \times 6 = 30$$
$$1 \times 41 = 41$$
$$4 \times 10 = 40$$
$$\overline{111}$$

Now we turn to the formula for *gamma,* which is:

$$\gamma = \frac{P_s - P_d}{P_s + P_d}$$

In this example,

$$\gamma = \frac{1505 - 111}{1505 + 111} = \frac{1394}{1616} = .86$$

In essence, this is the number of *good* predictions (of the order on one variable, predicted from the order on the other), minus the number of *bad* predictions, taken as a proportion of all possible predictions. By "good" we mean from the standpoint of positive correlation, of course.

Shown below are four tables representing patterns of numbers which will give a *gamma* value of +1. This maximum value is obtained when the data march straight down the diagonal, but it also occurs in a variety of curves, corners, humps, and sags. For this reason it has been called an "undisciplined" measure.

```
┌─────────────┐  ┌─────────────┐  ┌─────────────┐  ┌─────────────┐
│ 1           │  │ 1           │  │ 5           │  │ 2 2 2 2     │
│   3         │  │   1         │  │   3         │  │         2   │
│     2       │  │   1         │  │   1 1       │  │         2   │
│       2     │  │   1 1 1     │  │     1 3     │  │         2   │
│         4   │  │       1 1   │  │         5   │  │         2   │
└─────────────┘  └─────────────┘  └─────────────┘  └─────────────┘
```

Gamma's value will approach zero when the data cluster around *neither* diagonal but assume an amorphous or irregular pattern. It will show plus values when they cluster about the descending diagonal and minus values when they cluster about the ascending diagonal, from lower left to upper right. Here are some examples:

```
┌─────────────┐  ┌─────────────┐  ┌─────────────┐  ┌─────────────┐
│ 6       6   │  │ 2 3 4 5 6   │  │           6 │  │ 1           │
│   3   3     │  │ 3 4 5 6 5   │  │     6       │  │   3 5       │
│     5       │  │ 4 5 6 5 4   │  │   6   6     │  │     5 5     │
│   3   3     │  │ 5 6 5 4 3   │  │ 6   6       │  │       3     │
│ 6       6   │  │ 6 5 4 3 2   │  │ 6           │  │         1   │
└─────────────┘  └─────────────┘  └─────────────┘  └─────────────┘
  Gamma = 0       Gamma = −.25     Gamma = −.65      Gamma = +1
```

Somers' d_{yx}

Some researchers are dissatisfied with *gamma* because of its propensity to give high values for a variety of different patterns. They want a more rigorous standard, a measure that will reach unity only when *all* the cases lie along the diagonal. They want each increase in the independent variable to produce some increase in the dependent variable, and they are not impressed by a curved pattern with humps or sags.

One measure that meets these requirements is Somers' d_{yx}. In a fourfold table it is exactly the value of our old friend, percentage difference D, turned into a proportion and given a sign, as explained on p. 82. In this table:

40%	55%
60	45
100%	100%

210

D is 15% and d_{yx} is $-.15$.

In larger tables the formula is

$$d_{yx} = \frac{P_s - P_d}{\frac{1}{2}(N^2 - \Sigma C^2)}$$

where C refers to the column totals (column marginals).

To calculate it from the data we used with *gamma*:

$$d_{yx} = \frac{1505 - 111}{\frac{1}{2}(100^2 - (9^2 + 74^2 + 17^2))} = \frac{1394}{\frac{1}{2}(10{,}000 - (81 + 5476 + 289))} = \frac{1394}{\frac{1}{2}(10{,}000 - 5846)} =$$

$$\frac{1394}{\frac{1}{2}(4154)} = \frac{1394}{2077} = +.67$$

This value is somewhat below the .86 that we got for *gamma* with the same table. This is because the formula for d_{yx} reduces its value whenever different ranks on the independent variable correspond with the same value on the dependent variable, since it doesn't consider this a good guess. *Gamma* ignores such mediocre guesses, basing its value on only those guesses that are clearly right or clearly wrong.

We observed on p. 82 that one of the defects of D, the percentage difference, is that it has different values depending on whether you percentage on the columns or the rows. Somers copes with this by providing another measure, d_{xy}, which simply substitutes the row marginals R for the column marginals C in the formula above. This is handy when we depart from the custom of making the column variable independent. So d_{yx} is used when the column variable is independent and d_{xy} when the row variable is independent. Thus we say that *gamma*, which has only one value for any table, is *symmetric*, while Somers' d_{yx} and d_{xy} are *asymmetric*.

Kendall's *taus*

Finally we come to Kendall's *tau*-b and *tau*-c (τ_b, τ_c), which are symmetric. They are linear measures, in contrast to *gamma*, and reach their maximum value of +1 and −1 only when the data march in a straight line up or down the diagonal. *Tau*-b is for square tables and *tau*-c for rectangular ones where the number of rows is not the same as the number of columns. It is hard to visualize the diagonals in such a table, but this doesn't seem to bother *tau*-c. The *tau* measures penalize for tied ranks in either direction, where *gamma* ignores them, and the Somers' *d*'s object only if the ties are on the dependent variable.

There are some rather cumbersome formulae for calculating *tau*-b, but the easiest method is to calculate d_{yx} and d_{xy}, multiply them, and take the square root. Thus

$$\tau_b = \sqrt{(d_{yx})(d_{xy})}$$

Tau-c has the same numerator as *gamma* and the *d*s but a different denominator.

$$\tau_c = \frac{P_s - P_d}{\frac{1}{2} N^2 \left[(M-1)/M\right]}$$

where M is the number of rows or columns, whichever is smaller.

The *tau*-b value for our example, though inappropriate for our 4 X 3 table, is .52; and *tau*-c, which is appropriate, is .42. (If you want practice with the formulae, work through the calculations to get these values.)

These measures—*gamma,* Somers' *d*s, and Kendall's *tau*s—can be used only when both variables are at the ordinal level or higher, but this is frequently the case with political variables, whose categories are usually susceptible to a logical rank-ordering. Further, if either variable is a dichotomy, it may be considered a two-level *ordinal* variable. However, if either or both variables are polytomies—purely qualitative categories not susceptible to ranking—then we must fall back on Cramér's *V* (see p. 130) as a measure to summarize the table.

Which Measure?

Now you are in the absurd position of having five different measures to express the same relationship—and you have been spared half a dozen more that the statisticians have invented. Many have the same numerator, $P_s - P_d$, but different denominators, which treat tied ranks differently. How do you choose the correct one for your purpose?

Gamma is the most widely used, perhaps because it is easier to calculate and gives higher values than the others, which is comforting to a discouraged researcher. The asymmetric *d*s force us to decide which is the independent variable and then measure how well it predicts the order of the dependent variable. The *tau*s are even more rigorous, being particularly demanding about the middle ranks. *Tau*-b is not entirely happy (+1) unless the middle ranks fall in line between the high and low ranks, thus:

X		
	X	
		X

So, if your hypothesis merely calls for some relationship, positive or negative, between the two variables, and you don't care about the exact pattern, use *gamma*. If it is important to predict the order of values on the dependent variable Y from the independent variable X, and tied ranks on the dependent variable are considered as failures (though not, of course, as bad as wrong predictions), then you want d_{yx}. (You want d_{xy} only if the row rather than the column variable is independent.) If the intermediate values are important, then you pick *tau*-b or *tau*-c, depending on the shape of your table.

Let's look at a simple example to illustrate all this:

		Income		
Attitude	High	Medium	Low	Total
Positive	4	0	0	4
Neutral	4	0	0	4
Negative	6	2	2	10
Total	14	2	2	18

$P_s - P_d = 32 - 0 = 32,$
which is the numerator of all. The denominators are:

$\gamma \quad : P_s + P_d = 32$

$d_{yx} : \frac{1}{2}(N^2 - \Sigma C^2)$
$\quad\quad \frac{1}{2}[324 - (196 + 4 + 4)] = 60$

$d_{xy} : \frac{1}{2}(N^2 - \Sigma R^2)$
$\quad\quad \frac{1}{2}[324 - (16 + 16 + 100)] = 96$

$\gamma = \frac{32}{32} = +1$

$d_{yx} = \frac{32}{60} = .53$

$d_{xy} = \frac{32}{96} = .33$

$\tau_b = \sqrt{.53 \times .33}$
$\tau_b = .42$

Each coefficient measures something different in the table:

Gamma finds no discordant pairs and gives its maximum value, +1.

Assuming that income is the independent variable, d_{yx} is concerned about the pair of 2s on the bottom row which could not have been predicted from a knowledge of income. So its value is reduced to .53.

Assuming that attitude is the independent variable and predicts income, d_{xy} finds the two 4s in the first column to be even greater failures to predict, so it drops to .33.

Tau-b doesn't like the zero in the central cell, nor the 4, 6, and 2 in the lower left cells. It gives a value between d_{yx} and d_{xy} of .42.

So you pick your coefficient to correspond with your problem and your theory. Since each one summarizes an entire table in a single number, they are particularly useful in comparing one table with another. For example, a sociologist examining the components of social class might want to know whether money made more difference in the 1940s than it does now. Although dollar income has changed, he or she can use income as measured by the Gallup poll as an ordinal variable with four brackets and compare it to respondents' answers to the question asking what social class they think they belong in. The results might be tabulated into tables for the 1940s and the 1970s, each looking about like this:

	Low $\longleftarrow$ Income $\longrightarrow$ High		
Class			
Lower				
Working	X		
Middle		X	
Upper			

In this instance you would want *tau* as a measure because it is the middle brackets (marked *X*) that are important; do "working-class" people fall in lower income brackets than self-styled "middle-class" people? These are the categories in which most Americans perceive themselves; very few think of themselves as "lower" or "upper" class.

To ask another question, does social class influence the vote more in England than in Germany? Given the difference between the two nations in class and party structures, you might prefer the less demanding *gamma*. Suppose you are interested in the effect of union membership on voting in the 1976 presidential election, and you suspect that the effect will be stronger in the Northeast, where unions are strong, than in the South, where they are weaker. In this case prediction is important; you expect union membership to predict vote and not the other way around. So you compare Somers' *d* values for the two regions: d_{yx} if union is the column variable, d_{xy} if it is the row variable.

Another way of looking at the problem is in terms of necessary and sufficient causation, which we examined in connection with Q and ϕ (pp. 85 and 91). If both are required, then obviously *tau* is the preferred measure.

Jere Bruner has tested measures of association on a variety of tables with differing column marginals and found d_{yx} and *gamma* to be the more consistent measures. This is important where one category on the independent variable is much larger than the others, such as whites outnumbering blacks 10 to 1 in the United States.[1]

If all of this still leaves you in doubt, use d_{yx} or d_{xy}.

A question which many students ask and few statisticians answer is: "What level should these measures reach before they are worth paying attention to?" One answer, of course, is statistical significance at $p < .05$. But this involves the number of cases and leads to different conclusions from large as against small studies. Survey researchers are generally quite satisfied with *gamma*s above .30 (*tau*s or *d*s above .20) as indicating a meaningful relationship. Unless there is some theoretical reason for doing so, they do not pay much attention to *gamma*s below .20 (*tau*s and *d*s below .10). On the other hand, if you get very high values (*gamma*s over .70, *tau*s and *d*s over .50), you would be wise to re-examine your variables to be sure that they are not simply different operational definitions of the same concept.

Interpreting Computer Printouts

As we have just seen, it is quite feasible to calculate measures of association with a pocket calculator. To save time, it is advisable to decide in advance which measure is appropriate and stick to that one. However, some institutions make available to students large computers that crosstabulate data in statistical programs like SPSS, SAS, BMD, and OSIRIS. These calculate all the appropriate measures and a number of inappropriate ones. The computer does not know which variables are ordinal and which are polytomies, or which is independent and which is dependent. And it is so eager to do arithmetic that we usually let it calculate all of the measures of association and then ignore the inappropriate ones.

Let's see how you might approach such outputs. Table 13.2 was produced by classifying states according to the median income of their residents and their U.S. senators' ratings by Americans for Democratic Action. The data were coded by a class in the legislative process from *The Almanac of American Politics, 1978*.[2] The researcher hypothesizes that senators from low-income states would vote for bills supported by this liberal-leaning interest group, which favors civil liber-

---

[1] Jere Bruner, "What's the Question to That Answer? Measures and Marginals in Crosstabulation," *American Journal of Political Science*, 20 (1976), 781–804.

[2] Michael Barone, Grant Ujifusa, and Douglas Matthews, *The Almanac of American Politics, 1978* (New York: E. P. Dutton, 1978).

ties, opposes rises in defense spending, and seeks to reduce inequality in American life. Do you think the data will support this proposition? Or do you hypothesize another relationship between these variables, such as _____ _____ ? On what grounds? _____ _____

Note that income is measured at the ordinal level and ADA rating at the interval level. Since both variables are at least ordinal, we have omitted the nominal measures, as well as some others that have not been treated here.

TABLE 13.2 MEDIAN ANNUAL INCOME OF STATE RESIDENTS

Senator's rating by ADA		Under $9,000		$9,000 – $10,999		$11,000 and over	
Low	0–19	41.9%	(18)	14.3%	(4)	18.8%	(3)
	20–39	11.6	(5)	0	(0)	6.3	(1)
	40–59	16.3	(7)	14.3	(4)	12.5	(2)
	60–79	14.0	(6)	21.4	(6)	18.8	(3)
High	80–100	16.3	(7)	50.0	(14)	43.8	(7)
		100.1%	(43)	100%	(28)	100.2%	(16)

Tau-b	= .30974	Significance: .0004
Tau-c	= .31788	
Gamma	= .43825	
d_{yx}	= .34274	
d_{xy}	= .27993	
Chi square	= 16.00910,	d.f. = 8, p = .0423

Note: 13 senators are omitted because they had not been in the Senate long enough to cast enough votes to be rated.

Look over Table 13.2 and decide whether the hypothesis you stated above is confirmed or disconfirmed. _____

Let's go through the output from top to bottom. The percentages show a general tendency for senators from poor states to get a low ADA rating, and senators from middle- and high-income states to get a high rating. The raw data (in parentheses) run generally from upper left to lower right, so our measures of association will be positive.

The first statistic given is *tau*-b, which is only for square tables. Since this is a 5 X 3 table, we ignore it.

Tau-c is appropriate, but our overeager computer has calculated it to five decimal places. We drop the last two numbers and use the third only for rounding. Since our data don't justify this much precision, we would report *tau*-c as .32. Similarly, *gamma* is .44 and d_{yx} is .34. Since the column variable is independent, we have no use for d_{xy}.

Now we come to tests of significance. Here we have two different values. For *chi square,* the computer first calculates it, then figures degrees of freedom, and then gives us the exact probability that this could occur by chance, .0423, rather than telling us, as a *chi square* table would, that it is between .01 and .05. But the other test of significance gives an even more impressive probability of .0004.[3]

Our researcher hypothesized that senators from low-income states would vote with the ADA. To support that hypothesis, *negative* coefficients would have been necessary. For the researcher's purposes, all the figures support the null hypothesis, and the level of significance is unimportant.

But suppose you, remembering that Northern states tend to have liberal senators and higher incomes, hypothesized just the opposite. Since there is no doubt that income is the independent variable and should predict the vote, you would have chosen d_{yx} for your measure of association and could report a respectable .34. Since this is a one-tailed test, you could halve the *chi square* probability and report significance at approximately .02. The significance of .0004 reported for *tau*-b applies to all the other coefficients, since it involves only the numerator, $P_s - P_d$. While *chi square* applies to all the variations from expected cell frequencies in the table, this test takes account only of those variations that cluster around the diagonals, so its probability may be higher or (as in this case) lower than *chi square.* Your hypothesis would be handsomely confirmed.

Spearman's R_s

Spearman's *Rho* or R_s is the rank-difference coefficient of correlation. It is calculated from the data for individual cases (not grouped data, as with *tau* et al.). It is so easy to compute where the number of cases is not large that political scientists used to transform interval measures into ranks in order to use it.

Let us test the hypothesis: in large metropolitan areas, density increases with population. The proposition is not self-evident, for it may be that the largest cities overflow into the suburbs, acquire parks, and in other ways relieve the extreme population pressure. Both population and density (population per square mile) are given in the Census as interval statistics. We must first

---

[3]The formula for this test is not given here. It is unwieldy and is more frequently calculated by computers than by humans. You can find it in Freeman or Malec, cited at the end of the chapter.

reduce them to ranks by assigning the value of 1 to New York, the most populous metropolitan area, 2 to Los Angeles, 3 to Chicago, and so on. Similarly, rank values according to density must be assigned to these same cities. (Note that only *these* cities are ranked from 1 to 10 in density; there may be denser cities that are not in the first ten in population, but they are not relevant to our hypothesis.)

The rank-difference correlation formula is:

$$R_s = 1 - \frac{6\Sigma d^2}{n^3 - n}$$

Table 13.3 gives the rank order of the ten largest cities, as of 1960, and the calculations called for in the formula. The figures are for the Standard Metropolitan Statistical Area, a multi-county unit defined by the Bureau of the Census as including the central city and its suburbs.

TABLE 13.3

SMSA	Rank Pop.	Rank Density	Difference (d)	d^2
New York	1	1	0	0
Los Angeles	2	5	3	9
Chicago	3	4	1	1
Philadelphia	4	7	3	9
Detroit	5	3	2	4
San Francisco	6	8	2	4
Boston	7	2	5	25
Pittsburgh	8	9	1	1
St. Louis	9	10	1	1
Washington	10	6	4	16
				$\overline{70} = \Sigma d^2$

The number of cases, i.e., cities, is 10, so $n = 10$. Thus:

$$R_s = 1 - \frac{6 \times 70}{10^3 - 10} = 1 - \frac{420}{1000 - 10} = 1 - \frac{420}{990} = 1 - .42 = +.58$$

As you can see, if the cities had fallen in exactly the same order in density as in population, the differences would all have been zero, and R_s would have been 1. If they had fallen in reverse order, with New York as 10 in density and Washington in first place, then R_s would have figured out to -1. Our figure of .58, therefore, is on the positive side, confirming the hypothesis. A moderately strong relationship exists between the number of people in a metropolitan area and the density of the population.

218

In this example, we had to know the actual population and density before we could rank them. So a more appropriate measure would have been an interval statistic, the Pearsonian coefficient of correlation (which will be taken up in Ch. 19). If you have a statistical calculator available, there is little reason to use R_s. If you want a quick approximation for a small number of cases and must do your work on the back of an envelope, then R_s will do the job. If one of your variables cannot be put on an interval scale, e.g., the cleanliness or cultural advantages of cities, then you must use R_s.

Where the values are the same for any two cases, their ranks are tied, and both are given their average rank. For example, two cases tied for second rank would be ranked 2.5. Three cases tied for 7th, 8th, and 9th would all be ranked 8. If there are a great many ties, or if the number of cases is large, *tau* and *gamma* are preferable, for they are designed for grouped data.

Herbert Jacob and Kenneth N. Vines, in a study of American state government that has had a substantial impact on comparative political analysis, made considerable use of rank coefficients. Among their findings: turnout in elections correlated .52 with income and also with education.[4] The state's wealth correlated .89 with its expenditures on education. Those states that were spending for their schools in the 1930s were also the ones spending for them in the 1960s (R_s = .91).

The technique is also susceptible to controlling for a third variable. Though party competition in elections correlated .52 with educational spending, the conclusion that parties were competing to please the parents by improving the school system would not be justifiable. This is to some extent a spurious correlation, stemming from the fact that in the wealthy states parties are competitive. When controlled for income, the coefficients were $-.16$ for high-income states, .26 for middle-income states and .32 for poor states.[5]

Sources

There are other measures, such as Somers' d_{sym} and Kendall's *tau*-a, that have not been dealt with here. G. David Garson, *Political Science Methods* (Boston: Holbrook, 1976), treats them. Murray G. Kendall, *Rank Correlation Methods* (New York: Hafner, 1955), is the original source of theory for these measures. Leo A. Goodman and William H. Kruskal, "Measures of Association for Cross-Classifications," *Journal of the American Statistical Association,* 49 (1954), 733–764,

[4]Herbert Jacob and Kenneth N. Vines, *Politics in the American States* (Boston: Little, Brown, 1965), p. 44.
[5]*Ibid.,* p. 353.

is another early work. Both require some mathematics to read. Michael A. Malec, *Essential Statistics for Social Research* (Philadelphia: Lippincott, 1977), and Linton C. Freeman, *Elementary Applied Statistics* (New York: Wiley, 1965), show how to calculate significance of $P_s - P_d$. Hubert M. Blalock, *Social Statistics,* 2nd ed. (New York: McGraw-Hill, 1972), discusses some of the problems of interpretation as well as presenting the measures. Robert H. Somers, "A New Asymmetric Measure of Association for Ordinal Variables," *American Sociological Review,* 27 (1962), 799–811, is the source for d_{yx} and d_{xy}. Among the more recent articles dealing with the use and interpretation of measures of association are Herbert F. Weisberg, "Models of Statistical Relationship," *American Political Science Review,* 68 (1974), 1638–1665; David K. Hildebrand, James D. Laing, and Howard Rosenthal, "Prediction Logic in Political Research," *ibid.,* 70 (1976), 509–535; William Buchanan, "Nominal and Ordinal Bivariate Statistics: The Practitioner's View," *American Journal of Political Science,* 18 (1975), 625–646; Jere Bruner, "What's the Question to That Answer? Measures and Marginals in Crosstabulation," *ibid.,* 20 (1976), 781–804.

14 /Multivariate Relationships

*The plurality of causes is the only reason
why mere number is of any importance.*
JOHN STUART MILL

Historians adjure us to beware of "single factor" explanations, pointing out that social and political events are too complex for that. Up to this point we have dealt with single independent variables as presumptively causal or explanatory, and single dependent variables as consequences or effects of the independent variables. This gives a marvelously clear picture of the world "out there," though one that is vastly oversimplified. Now we seek to add a third variable for a more refined picture of reality.

A preliminary step is to run a series of independent variables against a single dependent variable and appraise in each instance the amount of relationship as an approximation of the extent to which it constitutes one of the "causes." Let us do this with two independent and one dependent variable, using figures which, though invented for this problem, are not unlike what surveys investigating these relationships have turned up. First with sex and then with age as the independent variable, we find:

raw	data		Vote	Sex	
				Men	Women
8	12		Rep.	50%	63%
			Dem.	50	37
8	7			100%	100%
$d_{yx} = -.13$			$N =$	(16)	(19)

223

<table>
<tr><td>raw</td><td>data</td></tr>
<tr><td>9</td><td>11</td></tr>
<tr><td>11</td><td>4</td></tr>
</table>

$d_{yx} = -.28$

		Age	
Vote		Under 50	Over 50
Rep.		45%	73%
Dem.		55	27
		100%	100%
$N =$		(20)	(15)

Now let us "control" for age—that is, *tabulate by sex, holding age constant*. In other words, repeat the sex tabulation for each age group separately. Note that the two raw data tables add up to the cells in the previous sex breakdown.

Age Under 50

raw	data		Men	Women
5	4	Rep.	46%	44%
6	5	Dem.	54	56
			100%	100%

$d_{yx} = +.02$ $N =$ (11) (9)

Age Over 50

raw	data		Men	Women
3	8	Rep.	60%	80%
2	2	Dem.	40	20
			100%	100%

$d_{yx} = -.20$ $N =$ (5) (10)

What has happened to the apparent relationship between sex and vote? For the younger age group it has virtually disappeared, and the d_{yx} value has changed sign in this group. There is no way this could have been predicted or ascertained from the original bivariate tabulation by age and sex separately. The two factors are working upon one another in a peculiar combination. This phenomenon has been observed in several elections: an apparent tendency for women to vote Republican turned out to be a combination of other tendencies; for elderly people to be Republican in orientation and for women to outlive their husbands. But this is only one of a number of things that can happen.

Varieties of Relationships

The possible relationships between three variables are numerous. The problem may be simplified by treating them as one independent variable, one dependent variable, and a third variable, also independent, which is "held constant" or "controlled" because we suspect it may be entangled in some way with the other independent variable that we are interested in.

These relationships have been given names such as "specification," "explanation," and "interaction," but the names seem to confuse more than they clarify, and we shall substitute arrow diagrams to illustrate three results of "control." That word does not mean precisely what it does when a biologist or psychologist compares a group of subjects that have been treated in some way (an *experimental* group) with another group that is alike in every respect except that it has not been treated (a *control* group). Yet the purpose is the same, to find out whether the treatment itself produces a difference, or whether the difference is due to some other variable unavoidably entangled with the treatment variable.

In each case we start off with an example, using contrived data to highlight the effect, and an arrow diagram indicating the relation between the independent variable I, the control variable C, and the dependent variable D.

Think of the independent variable as ideology, with respondents divided into liberals and conservatives. The dependent variable is an opinion item, which liberals in the original table tend to answer "Yes" and conservatives "No." The control variable is residence, whether the respondents live east or west of Main Street.

	Original Table				East			West	
	Lib.	*Con.*			*Lib.*	*Con.*		*Lib.*	*Con.*
Yes	13	7	breaks	Yes	7	4		6	3
			down				+		
No	7	13	into	No	3	7		4	6
	$d_{yx} = .30$				$d_{yx} = .34$			$d_{yx} = .27$	

This is an example of Type $I \xrightarrow{\hspace{2cm}} D$

$ C$

We show C as detached to signify that it doesn't alter the relation appreciably, so we don't care whether it is related independently to either I or D. The d_{yx} values show that the original correlation remains virtually unaltered in the "partial" tables. The correlation between ideology and opinion is a "real" one, unaffected by the control. Whenever we find some relationship that we consider important, we test it by controlling for sex, age, education, and whatever other variables we suspect are relevant. If we get results comparable to these—with the relationship showing at roughly its original strength in the partial tables—we are satisfied that we have uncovered a genuine correlation.

Now let us look at some of the other things that can happen:

	Original Table				East			West	
	Lib.	*Con.*			*Lib.*	*Con.*		*Lib.*	*Con.*
Yes	13	7	breaks	Yes	5	5		8	2
			down						
No	7	13	into	No	5	5		2	8
	$d_{yx} = .30$				$d_{yx} = 0$			$d_{yx} = .60$	

This is Type $I \rightarrow (C) \rightarrow D$.

There is a real enough relationship between the independent and the dependent variable, but it cannot be explained except in terms of the control variable. This outcome is often called "specification" because the only way of stating it is to specify the trivariate situation: in this case, that the relationship of liberalism to the opinion can be understood only when it is recognized that there is a strong relationship west of Main Street and no relationship at all east of Main Street.

Another possibility under this category would be for a weak relationship to break down into a strong *positive* relationship on one category of the control variable and a strong *negative* relationship on the other category.

Now let us look at the third case, a most interesting one:

	Original Table				East			West	
	Lib.	*Con.*			*Lib.*	*Con.*		*Lib.*	*Con.*
Yes	13	7	breaks	Yes	1	4		12	3
			down						
No	7	13	into	No	3	12		4	1
	$d_{yx} = .30$				$d_{yx} = 0$			$d_{yx} = 0$	

When we control on residence, the apparent correlation, which is exactly the same as in our other examples, disappears altogether. For this reason this result is often called "spurious correlation." What has happened is that the control variable is strongly related to both the independent and the dependent variable. Thus we label it

Type
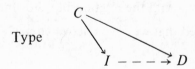

The broken line between *I* and *D* indicates an apparent relationship that does not stand up under control. In our example the people on the west side of town have a strong tendency to say "Yes" to the opinion item and those on the east side to say "No" (perhaps the issue is a west-side playground). It also happens that conservatives tend to live in the east and liberals in the west. But in neither area is there a tendency for liberals to have opinions differing from conservatives, as the d_{yx} values indicate. We can see this if we rearrange the data above into the following table:

	Liberal			Conservative		
	East	West	Total	East	West	Total
Yes	1	12	13	4	3	7
No	3	4	7	12	1	13
	$d_{yx} = -.50$			$d_{yx} = -.50$		

One classic instance of spurious correlation: in some European nations there are a great many more storks in the regions where the birthrate is high. Before concluding that storks deliver babies, it is wise to note that storks prefer rural areas, and rural areas have high birthrates. Another example: there is a high correlation between the number of fire engines and the amount of damage recorded at fires. Should we conclude that the fire department is counter-productive?

A variation, sometimes called "interpretation" has the effects of the control variable occurring after the independent but before those of the dependent variable, thus:

Type $I \dashrightarrow D$
            $\searrow C \nearrow$

The tables would look the same; only the time sequence is different. Here the classic instance is the historic belief that swamps caused fevers. The relationship was real enough, but it was centuries before the intervening variable, the germ-carrying mosquito, was discovered. When the anopheles mosquito (*C*) is present, malaria (*D*) occurs in swamps *or* on high ground. When the mosquito is absent, there is no malaria on high or low ground, and the relationship between swamps (*I*) and malaria (*D*) vanishes.

Thus although there are four Types, when time is taken into account, there are only three possibilities:

1. Coefficients in the partial tables will remain close to the values in the original table, indicating that the independent variable, despite the control, is related to the dependent variable.

2. The partials will go in different directions, one higher than the original and one lower, even to the point of reversing sign. This shows that the effect is confined to one category of the partial, and cannot be explained entirely in terms of the independent variable.

3. Both partials will drop toward zero, indicating that the independent variable does not really correlate with the dependent, but that the control variable correlates with both. Then one looks at their time order to determine whether the control variable is prior or intervening.

Where one has a number of relationships under consideration, it is advisable to look at one independent variable at a time, for the moment considering all the others as possible control variables. Remember that empirical data will probably not show as sharp differences as these "ideal types," and may be a mixture of the tendencies.

Use of Multivariate Analysis

Soule and Clarke interviewed delegates to the 1968 Democratic national convention in Chicago and classified them into amateur, semi-professional, and professional politicians according to the orientation they expressed toward the party.[1] They found that professionals tended to support Hubert Humphrey and amateurs to support Eugene McCarthy and other candidates, with semi-professionals in between. They also classified them according to their ideology, and found that conservatives tended to support Humphrey and others, moderates to support Humphrey, and liberals to support McCarthy and others. Then the question arose: are these two variables *independently* related to candidate choice? A *gamma* coefficient of $-.03$ revealed that there was essentially *no* relationship between amateurism and ideology. Since choice of candidates was a polytomy (Humphrey, McCarthy, others), ordinal measures could not be used, so they selected Cramér's V. The original V of .26 between amateurism and candidate preference, controlled on ideology, broke down into Vs of .41 for conservatives, .31 for moderates, and .33 for liberals.

[1]John W. Soule and James W. Clarke, "Amateurs and Professionals: A Study of Delegates to the 1968 Democratic National Convention," *American Political Science Review,* 64 (1970), 888–898.

Research Strategy

Computers are used in analyzing most survey research results because of the rapidity with which they spew out cross-tabulations, including multivariate control runs, and calculate dozens of statistics, some appropriate, some not. Researchers spend less time in clerical and mathematical drudgery and more in analyzing and interpreting output. The most notable characteristic of the statistical packages that produce these cross-tabs is that they tell you more than you care to know. The customary output gives you the cell frequency ("count")—the raw data for each cell. Then it gives you the row percentages, adding to 100% across the rows, and the column percentages, adding to 100% at the bottom of the column. It gives you both because the computer doesn't know which is your independent variable. You decide which you want to read: row percents if the row variable is independent, column percents if the column is independent. Some programs also give "total" percentages, based on the number of cases in the entire table. These are rarely useful. Then it will give you measures of association for ordinal variables, for nominal variables, for both, or just for the particular measure you specify. Many researchers ask for all statistics and then ignore those that are not appropriate for the particular table they are examining.

The researcher asks the computer first for the bivariate table, then for a series of control tables, each showing the independent and dependent variables in the same format as the bivariate table, but giving the data for only one category of the control variable. Each control table will usually be less significant statistically than the bivariate table. This is because the N is smaller. The original sample in the bivariate table has been divided among the control categories. For this reason, we don't pay as much attention to significance tests on control tables as on the original bivariate table, and pay more attention to the measures of association.

When planning a survey, the researcher must consider not merely the number of cases in the total sample but the kind of complex controls to be made, estimating the probable distribution of cases in the subsamples. If the budget is limited one may have to accept the possibility that conclusions based on multivariate tabulations may not be statistically significant. When analyzing complex patterns with limited resources, researchers are forced to rely on the internal consistency of the findings, for example, on whether the same tendency appears when alternative operational definitions are used. If a series of independent tabulations supports a pattern of behavior that is predicted by a generalized theory, then it is not necessary that every table in the series reach significance.

In choosing the measure of association to use with control runs, it is best to avoid *gamma* if any of the control tables have small Ns; *gamma* gives very high values if the cells in any corner of the table approach zero, and this can be misleading.

To this point, we have equated independent variables with "cause" and dependent variables with "effect." The best test of dependence is time sequence: what comes first is "causal." It was stipulated that this was a cautious and qualified rule. Now we may see why the reservations were necessary. A relationship in a table may be perfectly clear and statistically significant. The time dimension from independent to dependent variable may be entirely in order. A perfectly plausible explanation may suggest itself. Yet, tabulation by a third variable, prior in time to both, may show the correlation to be *spurious*. Or tabulation by an intervening variable may *interpret* the relationship in quite a different way. Similarly, lack of relationship may be only apparent, and a real relationship may appear under *specified* conditions.

We see again why testing hypotheses consists of rejecting the null hypothesis that there is no relationship, and why a relationship that is found to be statistically significant still does not prove the hypothesis. It merely eliminates one possibility—that the apparent relationship is due to chance—and it eliminates that only on a probabilistic basis.

The most readable explanations of trivariate analysis are Hans Zeisel, *Say It With Figures,* 4th ed. (New York: Harper and Bros., 1957), and Theodore R. Anderson and Morris Zelditch, Jr., *A Basic Course in Statistics,* 2nd ed. (New York: Holt, Rinehart and Winston, 1968). The classic article on spurious correlation, interpretation, etc., is Paul F. Lazarsfeld and Patricia W. Kendall, "Problems of Survey Analysis," in *Continuities in Social Research,* Robert K. Merton and Paul F. Lazarsfeld, eds. (Glencoe, Ill.: The Free Press, 1950), and in Lazarsfeld and Morris Rosenberg, *The Language of Social Research* (Glencoe, Ill.: The Free Press, 1955). A fuller development of the topic, containing several examples of each problem, is Herbert Hyman's *Survey Design and Analysis* (Glencoe, Ill.: The Free Press, 1955), Ch. 7. Recent approaches are discussed in Herbert M. Kritzer, "An Introduction to Multivariate Contingency Analysis," *American Journal of Political Science,* 22 (1976), 187-226.

17 TO 29 YEARS OLD

COUNT ROW % COL % TOT %	*Financial Expectations*			*Row total*
	Better	*Same*	*Worse*	*Row %*
	141	106	24	271
Legalize	52.1	39.0	8.9	46.0
marijuana	47.5	44.1	47.1	
	24.0	18.0	4.1	
	53	41	12	105
Neutral	50.5	38.6	11.0	17.9
	17.8	16.9	22.5	
	9.0	6.9	2.0	
	103	94	16	212
Higher	48.6	44.1	7.3	36.1
penalties	34.7	39.0	30.4	
	17.5	15.9	2.6	
Column total	297	240	51	588
Column %	50.6	40.8	8.7	100.0

Chi square = 2.30; $d.f. = 4$
$p = 0.681$

Cramér's $V = 0.044$
Tau-b = 0.020
Tau-c = 0.018
Gamma = 0.034
$d_{yx} = 0.021$
$d_{xy} = 0.019$
  Significance: $p = 0.296$

30 TO 39 YEARS OLD

COUNT ROW % COL % TOT %	*Financial Expectations*			*Row total*
	Better	*Same*	*Worse*	*Row %*
	54	41	7	101
Legalize	53.0	40.1	6.9	28.7
marijuana	36.5	24.8	16.3	
	15.2	11.5	2.0	
	31	27	12	70
Neutral	44.3	38.6	17.1	19.9
	21.2	16.6	27.9	
	8.8	7.7	3.4	
	62	96	24	182
Higher	34.2	52.6	13.2	51.5
penalties	42.3	58.6	55.8	
	17.6	27.1	6.8	
Column total	147	163	43	353
Column %	41.6	46.2	12.2	100.0

√

Chi square = 12.84; $d.f. = 4$
$p = 0.012$

Cramér's $V = 0.135$
Tau-b = 0.145
Tau-c = 0.132
Gamma = 0.236
$d_{yx} = 0.147$
$d_{xy} = 0.143$
  Significance: $p = 0.002$

40 TO 49 YEARS OLD

COUNT ROW % COL % TOT %	Financial Expectations			Row total
	Better	Same	Worse	Row %
Legalize *marijuana*	25 39.7 26.0 9.8	27 42.9 21.9 10.6	11 17.5 30.6 4.3	63 24.7
Neutral	17 35.5 17.2 6.5	21 44.1 16.6 8.0	10 20.4 26.4 3.7	47 18.2
Higher *penalties*	55 37.3 56.8 21.3	76 52.1 61.5 29.7	16 10.6 43.1 6.1	146 57.1
Column total *Column %*	96 37.6	124 48.3	36 14.1	256 100.0

Chi square = 4.20; *d.f.* = 4
   p = 0.380

Cramér's *V* = 0.091
Tau-b = −0.030
Tau-c = −0.026
Gamma = −0.049
d_{yx} = −0.029
d_{xy} = −0.030
   Significance: *p* = 0.301

50 TO 59 YEARS OLD

COUNT ROW % COL % TOT %	Financial Expectations			Row total
	Better	Same	Worse	Row %
Legalize *marijuana*	11 22.3 18.1 3.8	26 55.3 15.3 9.4	11 22.3 21.6 3.8	47 17.0
Neutral	9 18.8 15.5 3.3	31 64.6 18.3 11.2	8 16.7 16.5 2.9	48 17.4
Higher *penalties*	39 21.3 66.4 13.9	113 62.2 66.4 40.8	30 16.6 61.9 10.9	181 65.6
Column total *Column %*	58 21.0	170 61.4	49 17.6	276 100.0

Chi square = 1.27; *d.f.* = 4
   p = 0.866

Cramér's *V* = 0.048
Tau-b = −0.027
Tau-c = −0.021
Gamma = −0.050
d_{yx} = −0.026
d_{xy} = −0.028
   Significance: *p* = 0.316

COUNT ROW % COL % TOT %	*Financial Expectations*			*Row total*
	Better	*Same*	*Worse*	*Row %*
	10	20	3	32
Legalize	29.7	60.9	9.4	8.2
marijuana	17.3	6.9	6.0	
	2.4	5.0	0.8	
	2	46	8	56
Neutral	3.6	82.0	14.4	14.3
	3.6	16.0	16.0	
	0.5	11.7	2.1	
	44	219	39	301
Higher	14.5	72.6	13.0	77.5
penalties	79.1	77.1	78.0	
	11.2	56.2	10.0	
Column total	55	284	50	389
Column %	14.2	73.0	12.9	100.0

Chi square = 11.50; *d.f.* = 4
   p = 0.022

Cramér's V = 0.122
Tau-b = 0.009
Tau-c = 0.005
Gamma = 0.022
d_{yx} = 0.008
d_{xy} = 0.010
   Significance: p = 0.427

237

15/Interval Data and Student's *t*

Errors, like straws, upon the surface flow;
He who would search for pearls must dive below.
JOHN DRYDEN

After the close 1968 presidential election there was widespread discussion of whether the news media, especially TV, had been biased in their coverage of the campaign. Edith Efron taped and analyzed the campaign news broadcasts and found that all three networks were biased against Richard Nixon and in favor of Hubert Humphrey.[1] Vice-President Spiro Agnew made similar charges of slanted news controlled by an Eastern "establishment." Other studies, however, found that the public considered radio and television to be relatively unbiased sources of election news.[2]

Example : Network Bias

As the 1972 election approached, the Washington and Lee class in research methods decided to appraise the extent of bias in the evening news broadcasts of CBS and NBC. (Reception of ABC in the Lexington, Virginia, area was not then strong enough to include that network.)

Theory: We decided that there were two measurable ways that news coverage could be biased: in the newscaster's presentation of events and in the news editor's selection of the events

---

[1] Edith Efron, *The News Twisters* (Los Angeles: Nash Publishing, 1971).

[2] John P. Robinson, "Perceived Media Bias and the '68 Vote: Can the Media Affect Behavior After All?" *Journalism Quarterly*, (1972), 239–245.

to be shown. Examples of the latter would be the choice of an enthusiastic or a dispirited rally, or the choice of a Watergate development *vs.* an encouraging report from Vietnam. Of course, the events themselves are beyond the control of the media and might favor one of the candidates. We hoped to allow for this by sampling the news for a number of days and asking viewers to evaluate the purport of the event covered, independently of their appraisal of the newscaster's treatment of it. It was also recognized that bias itself could not be measured, only people's *perception* of bias.

Operational definitions: We videotaped the 6:30 evening news, alternating between networks. Each story relevant to the campaign was designated for separate evaluation, first for "event bias" and second for "newscaster bias." To get a more representative group than our students, the tapes were replayed before members of Lexington civic clubs, nearby high schools and colleges, and wives of law students. Each group was shown all the political items from one evening news broadcast from each network. (It would have been better research design to show the same day's news from both CBS and NBC, but we had only one video recorder.) Each item was evaluated twice by each viewer, using a scale that looked like this, with an *X* to mark the viewer's perception of bias:

McGovern • _____ • _____ • _____ • _____ • Nixon

As it turned out, there was not much difference between the ratings of "event bias" and "newscaster bias." So, for this example, we shall stick to the "event" data, using about one-tenth of the cases in order to illustrate the use of *t*. Assuming our scale was interval, we scored the viewers' *X*s as follows:

$$-4 \quad -3 \quad -2 \quad -1 \quad 0 \quad +1 \quad +2 \quad +3 \quad +4$$

McGovern • _____ • _____ • _____ • _____ • Nixon

To compare the two networks, all the viewers' scores for all the events they watched were averaged. The hypothesis we shall test is that there is a difference in perceived event bias between CBS and NBC.

Since all of the evaluations are given one of 9 scores between −4 and +4, we multiply each score by the frequency with which it occurs. These calculations are done for the CBS events in Exercise 16. The NBC data are left for you to calculate. The CBS mean, which we label $\overline{X}_1$, turns out to be −.4487, which we round to −.45. The NBC data give $\overline{X}_2 = +.2128$, rounded to .21. The distributions are shown in Figure 15.1.

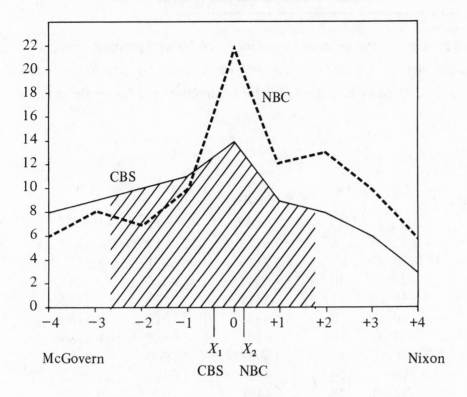

FIGURE 15.1 DISTRIBUTION OF BIAS ESTIMATES

You can see that the CBS mean is slightly to the negative or McGovern side of 0, and NBC slightly to the positive, Nixon, side. Both distributions approximate the normal curve, with the largest single group of judgments at the mid-point, indicating no bias. For both distributions the standard deviations are about 2.2. The area under the curve representing 1 standard deviation on either side of the CBS mean has been shaded. Do the same for NBC and note how much of the shaded areas overlap. This should not be surprising, since we know that two-thirds of the cases fall within +1 s of the mean. Thus we can tell from either the graph or the calculation of s_1 and s_2 that on a substantial number of judgments, NBC was on the *McGovern* side of CBS. And that, of course, is our problem. With so many contradictions, can we trust what our averages tell us: that the viewers saw CBS as leaning slightly more to McGovern than NBC? The answer will be provided by the *t*-test.

Preliminary Calculations for the *t*-Test

There are two ways to calculate the mean and standard deviation with grouped data. The first is more understandable, starting with the multiplication of the scores by their frequencies and adding them up. Ignore the fourth column, headed fX^2, for the moment and follow the calculation of the mean.

CBS Events Scores

(1) Score X	(2) Frequency f	(3) fX	(4) fX^2	(5) $(X - \bar{X})$	(6) $(X - \bar{X})^2$	(7) $f(X - \bar{X})^2$
-4	8	-32	128	-3.5513	12.6117	100.8939
-3	9	-27	81	-2.5513	6.5091	58.5822
-2	10	-20	40	-1.5513	2.4065	24.0653
-1	11	-11	11	$-.5513$	.3039	3.3432
0	14	0	0	.4487	.2013	2.8186
1	9	9	9	1.4487	2.0987	18.8886
2	8	16	32	2.4487	5.9960	47.9690
3	6	18	54	3.4487	11.8935	71.3612
4	3	12	48	4.4487	19.7909	59.3727
	78	-35	403			387.2947

$N_1 = \Sigma f = 78$

$\Sigma fX = -35$

$\bar{X}_1 = \dfrac{\Sigma fX}{N} = \dfrac{-35}{78} = -.4487$

Now we calculate the standard deviation by the regular formula. Subtracting the mean from each score (fifth column), squaring it (sixth column), and then multiplying that by the frequency gives us the values in the last column, which we then sum.

$$s_1 = \sqrt{\frac{\Sigma f(X - \bar{X})^2}{N-1}} = \sqrt{\frac{387.2947}{77}} = \sqrt{5.0298} = 2.2427$$

Is it necessary to carry out the calculations to four decimal places? Certainly not. However, your calculator keeps track of at least this many digits, and at the end of each row you add them into a memory and read off the sum when you have finished. So why not keep them?

If you are calculating means, standard deviations, and *t* values only occasionally, the above method is preferable, since you know what you are doing at each stage and can ask yourself if the resulting figure is sensible. There is a "short-cut" method of calculating s which avoids first calculating $\overline{X}$ and then subtracting it from each score. Instead, you multiply the frequency by the squared value X^2 rather than by the squared deviations from the mean $(X - \overline{X})^2$. This is done in the fourth column. Then you use a derivation of the basic formula.

$$s_1^2 = \sqrt{\frac{\Sigma fX^2 - \frac{(\Sigma fX)^2}{N}}{N-1}} = \sqrt{\frac{403 - \frac{(-35)^2}{78}}{77}} = \sqrt{\frac{403 - 15.70}{77}} = \sqrt{\frac{387.2949}{77}} = \sqrt{5.0298}$$

$s_1 = 2.2427$

Note that the denominator of s in these formulae is $N - 1$ instead of N, as it was introduced on p. 164. When calculating s for a sample rather than a population, using $N - 1$ improves the estimate, for reasons that are made clear in statistics texts. When samples are small, this can make considerable difference, but not with the Ns as large as these.

The Experimental Method

Before we go further, let's look at the TV bias study to see how it differs from the research treated in earlier chapters. The conclusions are expressed as means and standard deviations, which may be calculated only with data of interval quality. Previous tests of significance dealt with percentages and contingency tables, which are appropriate for nominal or ordinal data.

The class exposed a group of viewers to certain stimuli and got them to record their reactions. This is a variation of the classic experiment, a technique only occasionally used by political researchers. It is important to understand the method and the tests it uses for three reasons:

1. They underlie most of the research done in psychology, medicine, and biology.
2. The significance tests (t and F) used in analysis of variance are programed into computer routines for regression and correlation and appear in the printout.
3. Evaluators of governmental programs in education, welfare, mental health, and the like may consider them "quasi-experiments" and apply these tests.

The laboratory experiment in its purest form consists of comparing two groups of subjects (plants, insects, pigeons, rats, monkeys, people) that are alike in every respect except that one group has been exposed to a treatment (fertilizer, drugs, diet, electric shocks, altered environment, propaganda) and the other has not. Or the amount (level) of treatment given to two or more groups may be different. This constitutes the independent variable and is considered a qualitative variable—presence or absence of a certain treatment. Each group of subjects is measured on the dependent variable, which is measurable at the interval level. Then the means of the two groups are compared. The null hypothesis is that the means do not differ: $\overline{X}_1 - \overline{X}_2 = 0$.

In the classic experiment, subjects are assigned to groups on a random basis that assures they are alike in all respects except the treatment. The carefully controlled environment of the laboratory assures that no other factor intervenes. These restrictions are not easily carried over to political research. Voters can't be randomly divided into two groups, one exposed to TV, the other not, and their ballots separated on election day. Even if they could, the environment of the control group would be so unrealistic that the results of the experiment would be dubious. We want to know how voters behave in the real world. There are, however, approximations—such as the TV bias experiment described above. When governments undertake pilot projects—for example, giving one group of schoolchildren or welfare clients the benefit of an experimental program and withholding it from a similar group—this is known as a "quasi-experiment." Sometimes "natural experiments" occur, as when one state or nation abolishes capital punishment and a similar state or nation does not.

The Importance of Standard Deviation

You will remember that statistical testing with *chi square* at the ordinal or nominal level takes into account three factors:

1. The amount or strength of the relationship between the variables.
2. The number of cases in the sample.
3. The degrees of freedom.

As each of these increases there is a higher probability that the results are statistically significant. Now that we are working at the interval level with our dependent variable, we add a fourth factor—the amount of variability in the sample, which is measured by s, the standard deviation, or s^2, known as the *variance*. When these are large, we have less confidence in our results. You can see this by comparing the hypothetical distribution shown in Figure 15.2, which uses the same means for CBS and NBC as in Figure 15.1 but supposes a very small standard deviation. There is very little overlap between the two appraisals.

FIGURE 15.2

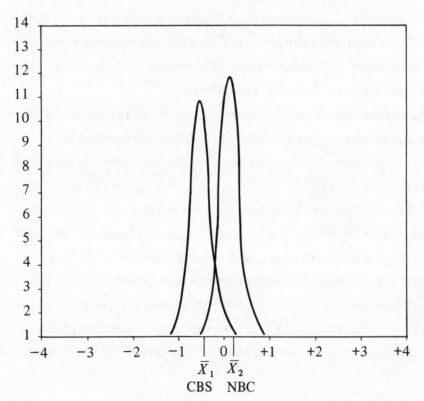

Student's *t*

All four factors are incorporated into a test of significance of the difference between two means called "Student's *t*." The odd name stems from its origin. W. S. Gosset was an early statistician employed at the turn of the century by the Guinness brewery in Dublin to do quality control. Guinness is the manufacturer of a potent, dark, velvety brew called "stout," which was—and is—a staple in the diet of the Irish. He invented the *t* test, but Guinness wouldn't let him publish under his own name, so he described the test in a journal article signed "Student." The basic formula is:

$$t = \frac{\bar{X}_1 - \bar{X}_2}{\sqrt{\dfrac{s_1^2}{N_1 - 1} + \dfrac{s_2^2}{N_2 - 1}}}$$

This is just one of the tests of significance for interval level data, but it is the one you are most likely to encounter, and the only one to be treated here; related tests are *z* and *F*. To understand the circumstances in which each test, and each version of *t* and *F*, is appropriate requires a statistics course. The formula above is the most basic one, and the use illustrated here is typical of what political scientists do with *t*.[3]

Since we have two samples, we distinguish them by subscripts. The numerator, $\bar{X}_1 - \bar{X}_2$, is the difference between the means of our two groups, and the null hypothesis is that the difference is zero. As you can see, a large difference contributes to a large *t* value. It is also apparent that large standard deviations, s_1 and s_2, will increase the size of the denominator and thus reduce the *t* value. But a large number of cases, N_1 and N_2, will diminish the effect of those *s* values, bringing down the size of the denominator and thus increasing the value of *t*. If we get a large *t* value, our difference is more likely to be significant.

---

[3]Other derivations of this formula, which short-cut the need for calculating $\bar{X}$ and then subtracting the individual *X* values from it, are useful if you need to calculate *t* frequently. There are different formulae if you want to compare a sample mean with a population mean or to conduct a before-and-after experiment. There are assumptions that must be met, at least approximately, such as normal distribution and similar standard deviations for both samples. A close relative of *t* is the standard normal distribution of *z* scores, but *z* tests are not as valid as *t* for small samples. If there are three or more groups, then the *F* test is appropriate. Before basing policy on a *t* test, you should consult a statistics text. One that is written at the beginner's level is Joseph B. Thompson and William Buchanan, *Analyzing Psychological Data* (New York: Scribners, 1979).

With CBS values from Exercise 16 as subscript$_1$ and NBC as subscript$_2$ we substitute the values:

$$t = \frac{\overline{X}_1 - \overline{X}_2}{\sqrt{\dfrac{s_1^2}{N_1 - 1} + \dfrac{s_2^2}{N_2 - 1}}} = \frac{-.4487 - .2128}{\sqrt{\dfrac{5.0297}{78-1} + \dfrac{4.8576}{94-1}}}$$

$$= \frac{-.6615}{\sqrt{.0653 + .0523}} = \frac{-.6615}{\sqrt{.1175}} = \frac{-.6615}{.3428} = 1.9297$$

Degrees of freedom for the t test is $N_1 + N_2 - 2$, which in this case is $78 + 94 - 2 = 170$. Since this is higher than the maximum of 120 shown in Table 15.1, an abbreviated table of t, we use the bottom line, labeled infinity (∞).

TABLE 15.1 ABBREVIATED TABLE OF t*

	Level of Significance			
One-tailed	.05	.025	.01	.005
Two-tailed	.10	.05	.02	.01
d.f.				
1	6.314	12.706	31.821	63.657
2	2.920	4.303	6.965	9.925
3	2.353	3.182	4.541	5.841
4	2.132	2.776	3.747	4.604
5	2.015	2.571	3.365	4.032
6	1.943	2.447	3.143	3.707
7	1.895	2.365	2.998	3.499
8	1.860	2.306	2.896	3.355
9	1.833	2.262	2.821	3.250
10	1.812	2.228	2.764	3.169
15	1.753	2.131	2.602	2.947
20	1.725	2.086	2.528	2.845
25	1.708	2.060	2.485	2.787
30	1.697	2.042	2.457	2.750
40	1.684	2.021	2.423	2.704
60	1.671	2.000	2.390	2.660
120	1.658	1.980	2.358	2.617
∞	1.645	1.960	2.326	2.576

*Abridged from Table III of Fisher and Yates: *Statistical Tables for Biological, Agricultural and Medical Research* (London: Longman Group Ltd.; previously published by Oliver & Boyd Ltd., Edinburgh). Used by permission of the authors and publishers.

Our hypothesis was simply that there was a difference between the means for CBS and NBC; it did not specify which mean was larger. Since this is a two-tailed test, we find that the critical value of t is 1.96. Our value of 1.93 (ignore the minus sign) is just short of this, so we cannot reject the null hypothesis. The probability is greater than .05 that the difference is due to chance.

Had we hypothesized that CBS favored McGovern more than NBC, thus specifying the direction, the t value would have been significant with $p < .05$. On the other hand, had we hypothesized that NBC favored McGovern, we would have discovered when we compared the means that our hypothesis was not supported by the data, and we would not have bothered with a significance test.

One assumption underlying the t test is that the sample in the experiment is randomly chosen from the population to which the results are generalized, a dubious assumption in our example. The citizens we persuaded to view our newscasts were representative of neither the local nor the national population, but that difficulty is characteristic of almost every social or political experiment.

If we had included the ABC newscasts, we would have had three means to compare and would have used another test, the F test, in a process called *analysis of variance* (ANOVA), which is too complicated to treat here. It is widely used in agricultural, physiological, and psychological experimentation, where three or more independent variables and several levels of treatment are employed.

In computer programs for multiple correlation and regression, you may find t values reported to indicate significance of relationships between single independent variables and the dependent variable, and F values to appraise the total effect of several independent variables.

These significance tests play an important part in research, but it is essential to remember their limitations. They tell us whether, given the number of cases and the variability of the data, we can safely assume that the outcome was not due to chance. But that is all they tell us. Whether the sample is representative, whether the operational definitions are sound, whether the relevant variables were included in the design, and whether the conclusions are applicable to the future are among the questions they do not answer.

16 / **Prediction**

Don't never prophesy onless ye know.
JAMES RUSSELL LOWELL

The word "prediction" is used in several senses in the study of behavior, all of them worthy of examination. But first, let's dispose of a sense in which it is *not* used. A few people still are misled by a pronouncement that goes something like this: "Human beings are complex individuals, and you never know what they are going to do; therefore you obviously can't predict human behavior and you might as well give up trying." The fallacy in this statement lies in the failure to define such words as "know" and "predict." Within a very narrow definition of the words, meaning 100% accurate knowledge of what a particular individual will do on a specific occasion, the statement is quite true. But with a probabilistic definition, which corresponds with reality, it is false. Most of us do know how our acquaintances will react to most situations they are confronted with; only occasionally do they surprise us (though these may be the occasions we remember best). The probability of our predicting their behavior is quite good. Similarly we know a good deal about how classes or categories of individuals will behave: we know that blacks tend to vote Democratic, that uneducated people are more likely to distrust government, and a host of other facts about political behavior. This does not enable us to predict how a particular black person will vote with certainty, or to predict a person's attitude because we know he left school at the fifth grade. But if we know that relationships between variables exist, we will make more right than wrong guesses when we predict behavior from a correlated variable. So the fallacy of the statement lies in a false dichotomy: that one must be either omniscient or ignorant; if we do not know everything, then we know nothing.

People who are ignorant of statistics can often predict human behavior with some success. For example, a car dealer discovers that men entering his showroom with their wives are more likely to buy a new car than if they come in alone. From this observation, he predicts that future car buyers will behave the same way. Of course, the relationship does not have to be perfect; there are couples who don't buy and men without their wives who do. But the relationship is strong enough that the dealer runs a series of advertisements aimed at bringing both spouses into the showroom and finds it pays off. Another example: a high-school guidance counselor finds that students from broken homes tend to drop out earlier than those from homes where both parents are present. She institutes a program for special help and encouragement to students from broken homes, and it is successful in a number of cases. Again, the earlier discovery of a relationship is used as a basis for action.

In both examples, if the collection of information had been systematized in the first place, a table could have been constructed and a measure of association calculated. And after action had been taken, another table could have been constructed. But the new table would have shown a different relationship, stronger in the case of the auto dealer because more men are bringing their wives and they have been influenced by the ads, weaker in the case of the guidance counselor because fewer children from broken homes are now dropping out of school. Social scientists and policy-makers must realize (a) that studying a phenomenon may change the nature of the phenomenon (known as the "Hawthorne effect") and (b) that acting upon a prediction may also change the nature of the phenomenon. This is not usually the case with natural scientists, although it may occur, as in the Heisenberg principle.

Postdiction

In dealing with d_{yx} and *gamma* in Chapter 13, "prediction" was used in quite a different sense. It meant the improvement in guessing the values on the dependent variable if we knew the values on the independent variable, i.e., the proportionate reduction in error. In the sense of forecasting the future, this isn't prediction at all. We have already gathered the data for our table, so we are merely evaluating an association or correlation between two variables as they existed at that time. This is often referred to as *postdiction.* Of course, if we had not gathered the information and assessed the relationship, we could not use this information to forecast the future or even, by acting on the information, improve the conditions prevailing in the future. So postdiction is a prerequisite for true prediction.

Up to the Interval Level

At the nominal and ordinal levels we have treated measures of association, which told us how strong a relationship is found in a table, and significance tests, which told us the likelihood that the relationship we found was due to chance. As we move to the interval level, with its greater accuracy in measuring our variables, we use the techniques of regression and correlation. We shall be somewhat less concerned with testing the hypothesis that there really is a relationship and that it is positive or negative, and considerably more concerned with defining exactly how strong that relationship is. Linear regression is a technique for predicting the value of a particular case on the dependent variable if we know its exact value on the independent variable. Since we have already gathered the data, this really means postdicting. We shall use methods that are appropriate only with interval data for evaluating how accurate these predictions are.

First, let us look at a natural science, meteorology. It originated in the lore of farmers and sailors, whose intuitive and unsystematized generalizations led to moderately accurate short-range forecasts. Relying on primitive theories about relationships, the meteorologists first developed tentative formulae, taking into account such variables as today's temperature, humidity, barometric pressure, wind velocity, and direction, to produce a prediction of some single variable, say, temperature, tomorrow. But what is a "successful" prediction? If one predicts 83° F and the actual temperature is 80° F, is this a successful or an unsuccessful forecast? One standard of success might be near perfection; unless one predicts temperature to the nearest degree, the forecast is counted a failure. This standard is much too rigorous; the meteorologists would soon have given up the effort. Another standard, similar to the one we used in testing hypotheses, is randomness. If a prediction is closer than we could get by simply picking a two-digit number from a random table, it is a success. This standard is too lenient, for we could do better simply by knowing whether it was winter or summer. The meteorologists have, instead of either, used "persistence" as a standard—the prediction that tomorrow's temperature will be exactly what today's was. If the formula prediction, taking into account several variables, was better than the persistence prediction based upon mere continuity, they concluded that they had a genuine understanding of the variables and their relationships. (An example: if the formula predicts 80°, today's temperature is 81°, and the actual temperature tomorrow is 83°, the prediction is accounted a failure, for it has an error of 3°, compared with 2° for persistence.) The persistence test has also been applied to political prediction. After the 1948 poll failures, a committee of scholars went over all the state vote percentage predictions of the major polling agencies during the 1930s and 1940s. They figured the deviation of the poll prediction from the actual election percentage. Then they did the same thing with a persistence prediction—that the state would have the same Democratic percentage it had in the last election. This revealed the moderate accuracy of the poll predictions and the bias that then existed in favor of the Republican party. What was learned in this study helped to improve the accuracy of polling in the years since.[1]

Given a series of data for past years, whether day-by-day readings of climatic variables or election-by-election results of contests between the two parties, one may use postdiction to develop and test theories inductively. One may develop a dozen formulae, each combining the variables with different weights or in different equations, and compare each prediction with the true outcome, whether it is tomorrow's weather or next fall's election. Finally the successful combinations of variables will be analyzed to find what theories are consistent with them. In this task meteorologists have a considerable advantage over political scientists, for they have daily observations while we usually have elections only biennially.

"As Maine Goes, So Goes the Nation"

This statement was long part of the folklore of American politics. Maine, unlike other states, used to hold its gubernatorial election in September of the year in which presidential elections were held. It established its reputation in 1840 when it elected a Whig as governor, and the nation unexpectedly went for William Henry Harrison, the Whig candidate for president. The reputation persisted for nearly a century, demonstrating the vast attractiveness of sheer nonsense in the field of popular political prognostication. In the twelve elections from 1884 to 1928, Maine elected a Republican governor eight times, and the United States also chose a Republican president. Maine elected a Republican governor in the other four elections, but the United States elected a Democratic president. The state's record was comparable to that of a stopped clock: correct twice every day. Then in 1932 Maine unexpectedly elected a Democratic governor, and the nation subsequently went for Democrat Franklin D. Roosevelt. Maine's reputation was re-established. But not for long. In 1936 the Republican presidential candidate (after taking soundings which showed that the

[1]Fred Mosteller et al., *The Pre-Election Polls of 1948* (New York: Social Science Research Council, 1949).

Maine gubernatorial candidate of his party had a 2-to-1 edge) rushed to Maine to campaign in his behalf and share in the omen of victory. Sure enough, the Republican governor won. And the Republican candidate for president carried Maine. And as Maine went in 1936, so went Vermont. The other 46 states went Democratic. That disposed of Maine's reputation, and soon the state gave up its pre-season gubernatorial election and went on the same election calendar as the rest of the nation.

Predicting the United States Vote

Now let's try several methods of predicting the Democratic *percentage* of the national two-party vote for president (not just which party won). We shall use the 1940–1964 period, after Maine had lost its reputation. First we shall predict *without* using Maine as a guide. Then later we shall use it to get a better prediction. The Maine presidential vote will be employed, rather than its gubernatorial vote. "Predict" is being used in the social science sense of "postdict" in this instance, for everyone now knows how both Maine and the nation went in these elections. The raw data are:

	Winner		Percentage Dem.	
Year	Maine	U.S.	Maine	U.S.
1940	R	D	49%	55%
1944	R	D	47	53
1948	R	D	42	52
1952	R	R	34	45
1956	R	R	29	42
1960	R	D	43	50+*
1964	D	D	69	61

*Since the percentages are rounded to 50%, + or − indicates which party won.

Method 1—Persistence

Since we are predicting the United States vote, we simply hold that it will be the same in each election as in the preceding election. Then we compute a measure of the error of these predictions. The calculations:

Year	Percentage Dem. U.S. Vote	Prediction	Difference	D^2
1940	55%‑ ‑ ‑ ‑ ‑			
1944	53	‑ ‑55%	+2	4
1948	52	53	+1	1
1952	45	52	+7	49
1956	42	45	+3	9
1960	50 ‑ ‑ ‑ ‑	42	−8	64
1964	61	‑ ‑ ‑ 50	−11	121
				248

$$S.E. = \sqrt{\frac{248}{6}} = \sqrt{41.3} = 6.4$$

The measure of error, 6.4, we shall call "squared error," $S.E.$, since it is an estimate of error arrived at by averaging in the same fashion that standard deviation is computed (see p. 164).

Method 2—Mean Prediction

This is the method treated in Chapter 10 in the guessing-game example. We calculate the United States mean for the period, which is 51.1, and predict that each year's result will be the same. The calculations are:

Year	(Y) U.S. Vote	$(\bar{Y})$ Prediction	$(Y - \bar{Y})$ Difference	$(Y - \bar{Y})^2$
1940	55%	51.1	+3.9	15.2
1944	53	51.1	+1.9	3.6
1948	52	51.1	+ .9	.8
1952	45	51.1	−6.1	37.2
1956	42	51.1	−9.1	82.8
1960	50	51.1	−1.1	1.2
1964	61	51.1	+9.9	98.0
			−0.3	238.8

$$S(\bar{Y}) = \sqrt{\frac{238.8}{7}} = \sqrt{34.1} = 5.8$$

(Notice, as a check on your work, that the sum of the differences from the mean, taking account of sign, is zero, except for rounding-off error, which in this case is 0.3.)

The standard deviation, $S(\bar{Y})$, is smaller than the persistence prediction, $S.E.$, so the mean gives a better prediction. Now we shall turn to predictions based on the Maine vote.

Method 3—Nominal Prediction

This is the historical practice of predicting that the party that wins Maine will win the nation. It was not very accurate in the past, and a look at the Winner column in the raw data table (p. 259) shows that for this period it is about as good as flipping a coin—3 correct predictions out of 7 tries. In this method we are taking into account some additional information—the Maine vote—that we did not incorporate in the previous methods, but we are "throwing away" much of this information by dichotomizing on a win-or-lose basis, considering merely whether the state is above or below 50% Democratic.

Before going to Method 4, you may want to check your understanding of these prediction devices by updating the series. The national Democratic percentage of the two-party vote was as follows:

1968	50-
1972	38
1976	51

The $S.E.$ value for the persistence prediction is 8.7, substantially higher than the 6.4 above. The $S(\overline{Y})$ for the variation around the mean of 49.7% turns out to be 6.3, again higher than the 1940–1964 figures. Obviously neither method is as good a predictor when we add in recent elections. What does this tell you about the political system in the United States?

_____

_____

_____

_____

Using Method 3, Maine's record is slightly worse, since it went the same way as the United States only once, giving it a win-lose record of 4 out of 10.

Now we return to the 1940–1964 figures to continue with the most sophisticated method of all.

Method 4—Scattergram and Freehand Regression

Now examine the relation of Maine to the United States at an interval level. In 1948, Louis Bean, a statistician for the Department of Agriculture, whose hobby was studying election returns, called attention to the relation between every state's vote and the national popular vote. He formulated the rule: "As your state goes, so goes the nation." He meant not which party wins, but that the U.S. percentage may be predicted from your state's percentage.[2]

[2]Louis Bean, *How to Predict Elections* (New York: Knopf, 1948), Ch. 10.

You may already have noticed as you looked over the figures that the difference between Maine and the United States is greater when Maine has only a small Democratic vote (1948, 1952, and 1956) than when it has a large one. Thus the larger the Democratic vote in Maine, the less one has to add to it to predict the United States vote. With Maine at its Democratic peak in 1964 one adds an amount so small that it is less than zero, i.e., −8%. We need to incorporate this diminishing difference into our prediction scheme.

One way of doing this is by presenting the data graphically in Figure 16.1. Let us call the Maine percentage X (the independent variable) and the United States percentage Y (the dependent variable) and plot them on a scattergram with X along the bottom of the graph and Y on the left side. Each dot on the graph is the point where the percentage values for a given year intersect. The one in the lower left, for example, is 1956.

FIGURE 16.1

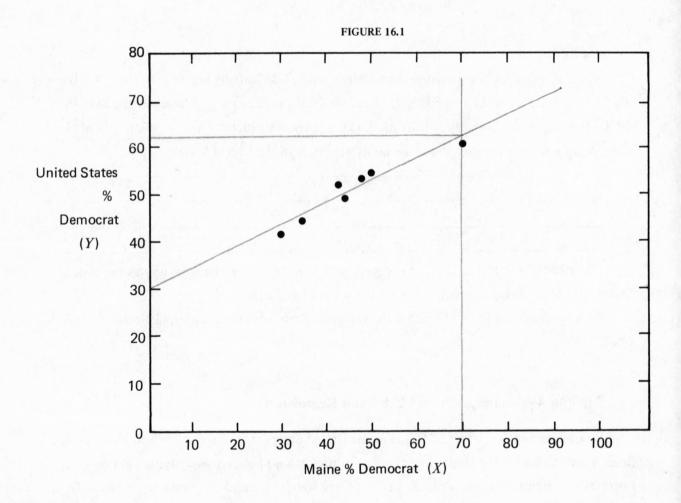

262

Now, on the illustration, pencil a *straight* line that comes as close as possible to all the points. This is approximately the "line of regression." From it you can "predict" how the United States would go in any year. Run a perpendicular line up from 69% Democratic (the 1964 percentage for Maine) until it hits the regression line, then go left from that point until it cuts the left-hand margin of the graph. This is your United States prediction for 1964. It will be in the vicinity of 65% Democratic for the nation. This is a considerable improvement on our previous prediction for 1964, of 50% by persistence and 51.1% by mean prediction methods.

We shall not calculate possible error for this method, since the next method does the same thing more accurately.

Method 5—Regression by Formula

In penciling the approximate regression line you may have discovered that there were several straight lines, with different slopes, that seemed to be equally close to all the points. There is a formula for finding the one "line of best fit" which describes the path of the dots.[3] It is:

$$Y_c = a + bX$$
$$b = \frac{N\Sigma XY - (\Sigma X)(\Sigma Y)}{N\Sigma X^2 - (\Sigma X)^2}$$
$$a = \frac{\Sigma Y - b\Sigma X}{N}$$

$$b = \frac{7(16477) - 112054}{7(14981) - 97969}$$

$$b = \frac{3285}{6898} \quad b = .476$$

Fill in the following table. The first two lines are calculated, to give you a start.

Year	Maine (X)	(X²)	U.S. (Y)	(XY)
1940	49	2401	55	2695
1944	47	2209	53	2491
1948	42	1764	52	2184
1952	34	1156	45	1530
1956	29	841	42	1218
1960	43	1849	50	2150
1964	69	4761	61	4209
	313	14981	358	16477
	(ΣX)	(ΣX²)	(ΣY)	(ΣXY)

(N = 7, the number of cases)

$$a = \frac{358 - .476(313)}{7}$$

$$a = \frac{209.01}{7}$$

$$a = 29.86$$

[3] Actually, this line measures the minimum squared distances in a *vertical* direction. If one should reverse the X and Y axes, another line would be found to fit better for predicting X from a knowledge of Y.

Corr 0.975

Now substitute in the formula to get the value of b. (Remember that ΣX^2 means square before summing; $(\Sigma X)^2$ means sum before squaring.) If you don't get .476, one of us is wrong.

$b =$

Now work out the value of a. You should get 29.86.

$a =$

$Y_c = 29.86 + .476X$

Now, for each value for Maine, multiply by .476 and add 29.86, then round to the nearest percentage point. These are the regression predictions.

The standard error of the regression $S(Y_c)$ tells you how accurate the regression predictions are.

Maine	Me. X .476	Y_c (predicted U.S.)	Y U.S.	$(Y_c - Y)$ Diff.	$(Y_c - Y)^2$ Diff.^{2}
49	23.324 + 29.86 =	53	55	− 2	4
47	22.372 + 29.86 =	52	53	−1	1
42	19.992 + 29.86 =	50	52	−2	4
34	16.184 + 29.86 =	46	45	1	1
29	13.804 + 29.86 =	44	42	2	4
43	20.468 + 29.86 =	50	50	0	0
69	32.844 + 29.86 =	63	61	2	4
					18

$$S(Y_c) = \sqrt{\frac{\Sigma(Y_c - Y)^2}{N}} = \sqrt{\frac{18}{7}}$$

$$S(Y_c) = \sqrt{2.5714} = 1.6036$$

Comparison of Predictions

Leaving a discussion of what regression is and does for the next chapter, let us summarize these methods as predictive techniques in the three instances where there is a comparable estimate of error.

Method 1—Persistence	$S.E.$	$=$	6.4
Method 2—Mean	$S(\overline{Y})$	$=$	5.8
Method 5—Formula regression	$S(Y_c)$	$=$	1.5

Each of these methods of prediction, however primitive, rests on a set of theoretical premises which may be translated into formulae. The persistence prediction assumes that there is minimal change in the United States vote from election to election with possible gradual trends or cycles. The mean prediction assumes that there is a long-term stable level of party voting in the United States, with minor, but erratic alterations from year to year. If there were a constant steady change in the party balance from year to year, the persistence prediction would give a better result than the mean prediction.[4] The regression method assumes that there is a relationship between Maine and the nation, in which the United States has a basic Democratic voting percentage to begin with, and on top of this a conversion rate which is indexed by the Maine vote. The fact that the regression method gives a much lower measure of prediction error indicates that, for this period, the regression "model" is the most accurate of the three.

Let us consider the methodological implications of what we have done in this rather simple-minded excursion into research and theory building. Our method has been inductive in the sense that we proceeded from empirical observation to statement of a relationship—from data to theory, as it were. (Of course, the vague theoretical assumption that there is some stability or continuity to the United States vote and some relationship between the Maine vote and the United States vote underlies the collection and the juxtaposition of these data. No investigation can proceed without a theory as to what data are pertinent.) We tried a series of formulations, testing them against data configurations, and then, when we found the best one, we sought to account for it. The process has been called "brute empiricism" or "barefoot empiricism," and some purists have scorned it. But it has accounted for many advances in knowledge, sometimes through mistakes, sometimes through serendipity. The medical profession made its initial breakthroughs by observ-

---

[4] If these methods seem so obvious that they are hardly worth citing, you may be interested to know that a few years ago there was a political sage in California who was renowned in local circles for his "uncanny" ability to predict state elections. His reputation for political insight was enhanced by a solemn mien, a steady gaze, and occasional vague references to confidential sources of information. His acquaintances testified to the awesome accuracy of his past prophecies, though they could not recall exactly what he had predicted or exactly how accurate it had been. His one forecast which I was able to record was close enough to persistence to suggest that he was using that method. That year it turned out to be a remarkably *bad* forecast.

ing relationships between early symptoms and later illnesses, by trying one remedy after another until one appeared to work the best. For a century aspirin has been relieving headaches, but not until 1972 did anyone profess to know *why*. One of the techniques used by the Weather Bureau is to combine a variety of measurements taken at different places in an elaborate computer search for those that best predict conditions at a particular point. For example, it was discovered that among the sixteen variables that best predicted the weather in Hartford, Connecticut, were the cloud cover in Boston, the temperature in Buffalo, the pressure change in Norfolk and the wind in Oklahoma City.[5]

We may use our own observations of the relation between Maine and the nation to construct a theoretical scheme to account for our findings. First, consider the theory that Maine varies with the national vote because it contributes to it. This cannot survive close examination, for Maine does not supply a large enough proportion of the national electorate to have the effect we found. A more plausible theory is that Down Easters share a common reaction to candidates, issues, and parties with the rest of Americans. This theory squares with the regression results. It might be tested by comparing Maine survey data with national survey data over several elections to discover what these common reactions are.

This is an example of the sort of inductive research in which observation gives rise to a theory. The Nobel laureate Herbert A. Simon describes the process as (a) finding a generalization that approximately agrees with observed data, (b) testing the relationship between generalization and observation under different conditions to refine the generalization, and (c) developing a theory that accounts for the relation between the generalization and the facts.[6] In this example, the question is: "Why should Maine and the United States be expected to vary together?"

This kind of research is often referred to as "model building." Our formulae are primitive mathematical *models* of American voting behavior.

---

[5] Judith M. Tanur, ed., *Statistics: A Guide to the Unknown* (San Francisco: Holden-Day, 1972), p. 377.

[6] H. A. Simon, "On Judging the Plausibility of Theories," in *Studies in Logic and the Foundation of Mathematics*, B. Van Rootselaar and J. F. Staal, eds. (Amsterdam: North-Holland, 1968), pp. 439–459.

EXERCISE 20 :   **Updating U.S. Vote Predictions**

Democratic percentages of the vote in subsequent elections were:

	Maine	*U.S.*	Y_c *(predicted U.S.)*
1968	56	50–	_____
1972	39	38	_____
1976	50–	51	_____

1. Plot these points on the graph below:

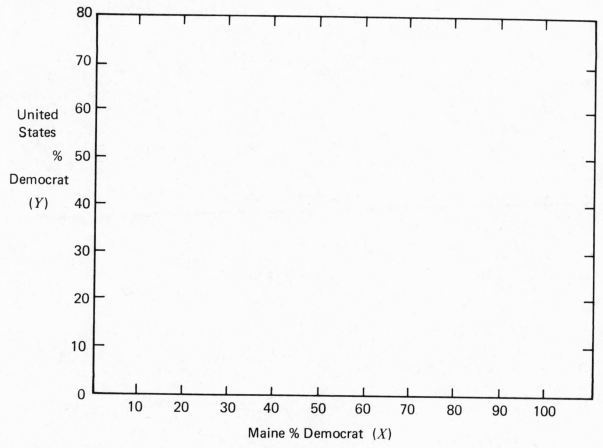

2. Using the previous regression formula, $Y_c = 29.86 + .476X$, predict the U.S. vote from the Maine vote and fill in the blanks above. How good are these predictions? _____

_____

_____

3. Calculate a new regression formula, based on all 10 elections.

$$Y_c = \underline{\hspace{2cm}} + \underline{\hspace{2cm}} X.$$

4. What does comparison of the new value for b and the old value of .476 tell you about Maine's relation to the U.S. political system? _____

_____

_____

_____

17/ **Regression**

*Thus it is easy to prove that the wearing of tall
hats and the carrying of umbrellas enlarges the chest,
prolongs life, and confers comparative immunity from
disease; for the statistics shew that the classes which
use these articles are bigger, healthier, and live
longer than the class which never dreams of possessing
such things.*
GEORGE BERNARD SHAW

The term "regression" used by statisticians has diverged from its original meaning. This same word, as used by psychoanalysts to mean "revert" to a previous state, retains the original meaning. Sir Francis Galton, who applied the technique to data showing that tall fathers tend to have sons somewhat shorter than themselves and brilliant men to have somewhat less able sons, called the process "regression back to mediocrity," but the name stuck to the technique as well as to the finding. It was first extensively employed in genetic, biological, and horticultural research. Regressions between the length of particular bones and the size of the body itself were examined, making it possible to reconstruct the size and stature of a person or an animal from one or two bone fragments. Other scientists tested Darwin's theory by such procedures. Then psychologists used regression to predict skill in performing tasks from test scores, and economists used it to probe the factors underlying business cycles.

Let us return to the Maine example to describe what the technique of linear regression reveals. The basic relationship, you recall, was:

$$Y_c = a + bX$$

The X refers to any value of the independent variable. The b value is the "slope" of the regression line. The a term gives the starting point of the line, the point where the X value is equal to zero, called the "intercept" or "origin."

From Formula to Graph

To draw any regression line, take some convenient X value, multiply it by b, and add a to the product. This gives you the corresponding Y_c value. (Y_c is called "the computed value of Y" or "the Y estimate." It sometimes appears as $\hat{Y}$, called "Y-hat," or Y', called "Y-prime.") Now plot the point on a graph where your X value on the bottom scale and the corresponding Y_c value on the side scale meet. Then take another X value some distance away on the X scale, calculate a second Y_c value and plot another point. A straight line that runs through these two points is the regression line. It will also run through the point where the means of X and Y intersect. (If it doesn't, you've made a mistake.) It will also run through the origin, although that may not appear on your graph. Figure 17.1 gives examples of some regression lines and the $Y_c = a + bX$ formulae they represent. The dotted lines show how the graphic and algebraic computation of the intersection of X and Y_c are equivalent.

FIGURE 17.1

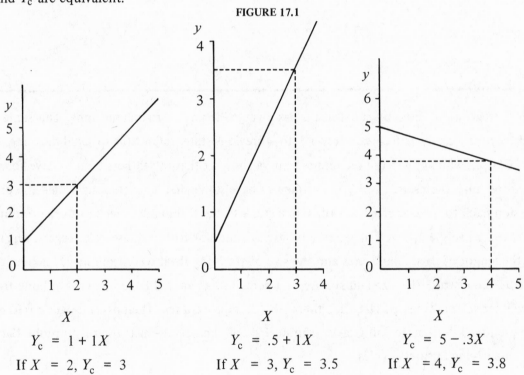

$$Y_c = 1 + 1X$$
If $X = 2$, $Y_c = 3$

$$Y_c = .5 + 1X$$
If $X = 3$, $Y_c = 3.5$

$$Y_c = 5 - .3X$$
If $X = 4$, $Y_c = 3.8$

For the Maine example the value of a is 29.86. This indicates that during the period 1940–1964 if not a single Maine resident voted Democratic, the United States would still be nearly 30% Democratic. Forward from that point, the b value of .476 means that for every 1% of the Maine electorate converted to the Democratic party, slightly less than half of 1% of the American electorate was so converted. Now go back to Figure 16.1 (p. 262) and draw the correct regression line.

How does it compare to the freehand line you drew by looking at the pattern of points?

This is called "the regression of Y on X." For each X value we can predict what Y should be, on the average, and this prediction is called Y_c. With the same raw data, one could solve the equation so that it would predict X_c given the value of Y. But this would involve reversing the variables in the formula, computing different values of a and b, and it would be referred to as "the regression of X on Y."

If the variables are positively related, so that an increase in X produces an increase in Y, then the slope is upward and the b value is positive. If an increase in X is accompanied by a decrease in Y, the b value is negative and the slope is downward. (For example, in the 1960s some Southern states had a negative regression; the more Democratic the United States went, the more Republican these states went.) If there were no relation at all, the line would be perfectly horizontal, and would correspond to the mean value of the Ys. The b value would be 0.

If all the points lay along a straight line, as they would, for example, if X were the various customer balances in a bank's savings accounts and Y were the interest paid on them, we would have a perfect correlation. Then all the points would lie along the line of regression, and the Y values would be the same as the Y_c values.

One of the virtues of linear regression is that it is easily interpretable. It keeps the researcher "close to the data." The answers come out in the same terms the values are put in: dollars, percentages, votes, people. The meaning of it is perfectly straightforward: for every additional unit of X, Y increases by b units.

Limitations and Qualifications

Because the meaning of regression is so clear, we have to be especially self-conscious about our assumptions if we are to use it appropriately. It is particularly susceptible to what computer scientists call the GIGO principle—"garbage in; garbage out." Tack a sheet of graph paper to a barn door, fire a load of birdshot into it, and you can fit a regression line to the holes in the paper, though one without a very steep slope (unless you use a cheap shotgun).

There are some assumptions necessary to the regression method which we shall not treat here, e.g., random variation and normal distribution. One assumption which is critical, however, is that the center of the path of the points is a straight line. If not, we must abandon linear regression or resort to the more complicated formulae for curvilinear regression. The problem, however, goes beyond this. We know only about the values we have observed. Yet the line may be projected forward or backward indefinitely. In the previous example, *a* referred to the U.S. vote that would be expected if Maine had no Democratic voters, which is highly unlikely. In fact, we had no observations below 29% Democratic in Maine, so this is sheer imagination. For all we know, the dots may form a pattern like that in Figure 17.2, in which the white dots represent hypothetical values that would occur if we could measure more extreme elections than are represented by our actual observations, the black dots. You can see that a prediction from the straight regression line would be erroneous for very low or very high Democratic votes in Maine if this were the case.

Another possible regression fallacy is the situation in which the bulk of the points cluster in one corner of the field, but one or two "outliers" are largely responsible for the slope. Figure 17.3 illustrates a situation in which a positive slope could be changed to a negative one by omitting the two outliers.

FIGURE 17.2

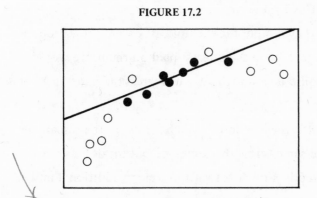

FIGURE 17.3

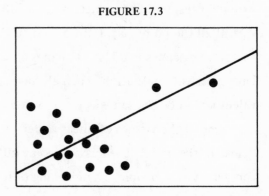

Temptations to misinterpret a regression formula are easier to resist if you plot the values on a scattergram. If the pattern is curving, you will recognize that *linear* regression is a poor representation of their relationship. If the pattern is dependent on a few extreme outliers, ask if they are not so atypical that they represent another population than the one you are studying. Perhaps they should be omitted from your analysis and the regression slope should be calculated without them. It is customary to present your scatter plot to the reader to make the regression easier to interpret.

Improving Prediction by Reducing Unexplained Variation

In both the game of guessing the age of the person in the next room and the game of predicting the United States vote from the Maine vote, we examined the mean as a predictive technique and the standard deviation as a measure of variation around the mean. Thus $S(\overline{Y})$ has a double significance, expressing both the scatter of the values about their average and the error we would make if we predicted, in the absence of any better information, that the value of any given point was the same as the mean value. We used the standard deviation of the regression (p. 264) for the same purpose. It is the (squared) average of the distance of the points from the regression line, the sum of the differences between the Y_c and the actual Y values, and it is also a measure of the error we would make by guessing that every Y value is actually the same as Y_c for the corresponding value of X.

To pursue this meaning a little further, we shall use a new set of data, the median per capita personal income in a state for 1964 and the percentage of persons of voting age there who cast a vote for president in 1964. These data, which are presented in Table 17.1, are from the *Statistical Abstract of the United States, 1966,* Tables 464 and 528. Income has been rounded to the nearest $10. The analysis will be confined to the Southern states, including Maryland.

TABLE 17.1

State	Income	% Turnout		State	Income	% Turnout
Maryland	$2830	57.0		Kentucky	$1890	54.1
Virginia	2270	43.1		Tennessee	1880	51.7
N. Carolina	1920	53.2		Alabama	1780	36.2
S. Carolina	1690	40.1		Florida	2290	54.5
Georgia	2000	44.9		Arkansas	1710	50.4
Mississippi	1490	33.7		Louisiana	1940	47.9

The mean percentage turnout is 47.23. If one had to guess what the turnout was in a Southern state without knowing the name of the state, it's about the best guess one could make. A graphic portrayal of probable errors is shown in the left portion of Figure 17.4, with each state given in the preceding order. The dotted lines between the points and the mean indicate the variation, or errors. The length of these 12 lines, squared, added, and divided by 12, is called the "variance." The square root of the variance is the standard deviation, i.e., $s^2 = V$. Since the variance has this constant relationship to standard deviation, it too is used as a measure of variability.[1] In this instance, $V = 53.62$ and $S(\overline{Y})$, the standard deviation of the mean of the Ys, is 7.32.

In the right portion of Figure 17.4 we take these same vote percentages, Y, and order them

[1]There are some theoretical and computational advantages in using V rather than s as a measure of error. These are explained in statistics books. Solomon Diamond, *Information and Error* (New York: Basic Books, 1959), gives an explanation that is less murky than some. The disadvantage of V for applied analysis is that an answer in squared units of measure is difficult to comprehend.

along the *X* axis according to their incomes. They follow a roughly linear path, though not a very tight one, and we shall assume (somewhat unjustifiably) that we may use linear regression to analyze the relationship. The regression equation in this instance works out to be $Y_c = 21.3\% + .01314X$. To interpret this: if a state's citizens had a median income of \$0 (an obvious absurdity), 21.3% of them would have turned out to vote for Johnson or Goldwater. Above this point, for every dollar added to the average citizen's income, the state turnout increased by slightly over one one-hundredth of 1% (see p. 263 for calculation of *b*).

FIGURE 17.4

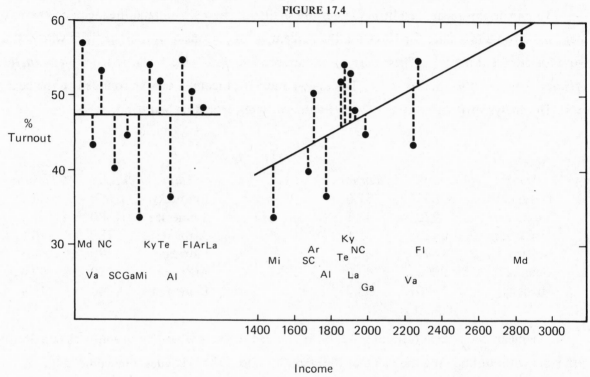

Income

The dashed lines drawn from each point to the regression line on the right side of the figure show how much difference there is between each state's turnout and an estimate of that turnout, Y_c, based upon the regression equation. Now compare this difference—the length of the line—with the difference between that state's turnout and the mean, which is shown on the left side of the figure. In all but two or three states the length of the dotted line is shorter on the right side, and certainly the average of the distances from the regression line is shorter than the distances from the mean. And the shorter the lines, the better the estimate. Thus by taking account of the *X* values—the effect of income on turnout—we have improved our turnout estimates. One measure of this is the reduction in variance. The variance from the mean was 53.63; the variance from the line of regression is 33.35; standard deviation is reduced from 7.32 to 5.78.

Residuals

We started with the variability of each state from the mean of all Southern states. We surmise that a wide variety of factors made each state differ from the others in the number of persons who voted for president in 1964: registration laws and practices, remnants of discrimination against blacks, interest in the races for Senate and House, level of party competition in the state, how the media treated the campaigns, the weather on election day. *One* of these factors appears to be associated with the residents' income. We have measured this by calculating the regression slope. Each additional $100 of median income boosts turnout by 1.3%.

After we remove the effect of income, which is reflected in the regression slope, the effect of all these other variables is represented by the dashed lines in the right-hand diagram. Expressed in algebra, this is $Y - Y_c$ for each state. These values are known as *residuals.* Looking at them thoughtfully may give some clues as to what other variables are important. Mississippi (Miss), Alabama (Al), and Virginia (Va) are some distance below the line, while Arkansas (Ar), Tennessee (Tenn), Kentucky (Ky), and North Carolina (NC) are above it. Is there something in the political culture of the first group that differs from that of the second? Have certain states traditionally had lower turnouts? Is the proportion of blacks relevant? One place to turn in search of hypotheses is the literature on Southern politics.

If we find a second variable that correlates with turnout, we may use the technique of *multiple regression* (which hasn't been treated yet) to further account for the phenomenon and further reduce the residuals. We might then introduce a third or fourth variable. We would still be left with some "unexplained variance," for we are unlikely to imagine all the factors causing turnout and even less likely to be able to measure them with the necessary precision. What we are doing here is analogous to the proportional reduction in error which was expressed in Chapter 13 when we calculated *tau* or *gamma.* The information provided by the independent variable partially accounted for or explained the variation in the dependent variable. There it was done in terms of right-minus-wrong guesses. Now at the interval level we have done the same, but with much more precision.

Interpreting the Regression

One problem, which may already have been troubling you, is that income does not itself "explain" turnout. Median state income is itself a product of other factors, such as level of education, urbanization, access to communication media, and the state's natural resources. It serves as an "index" of these qualities. This will be discussed later.

Another, somewhat stickier, point is that the 12 dots in Figure 17.4 are not a sample; they are the *universe* of Southern states, as defined, in 1964. As long as our interest is exclusively historical, simply describing what those states did in that year, this does not constitute a problem. Most students of political behavior, however, seek generalizations. We want to express a relationship between variables, in this case income and turnout, and this relationship is one that we expect will hold for the future. If this is our purpose, we may wish to consider these observations as a sample of the universe of all similar observations that could be made. The universe would include, at the very least, the prediction made from the regression line as to the expected vote of a Southern state with, say, a $2,600 median income, although none of these states has that particular figure. If we consider these points a sample, then we must make some statistical calculations to allow for random error, and we must also face the fact that 1964 was, to say the least, a rather biased sample of all the past, present, and future observations of these variables in the Southern states. Even though the analogy to a random sample is dubious, we can use the standard deviation as the best available measure of the accuracy of the regression as a predictive device.

We may use the standard deviation of a regression $S(Y_c)$ as a measure of the unexplained variation. It may be plotted on the graph by measuring vertically 1 standard deviation above and below the regression line and drawing lines parallel to it. If the distribution is normal[2] (which happens *not* to be the case with these data), two-thirds of the points will fall within 1 standard deviation of the line. (See Figure 17.5.)

Again the point must be stressed: regression or any other technique only abstracts some aspect of a complex relationship and combines a larger number of values into one formula to express it as a kind of average. Any conclusions about "causality" and any extrapolations or projections from the observed data to other universes are the responsibility of the researcher. He or she must steer a judicious course between the Scylla of mechanical application and too literal interpretation of measures, which lead to dubious conclusions, and the Charybdis represented by the statistical purist's ability to demonstrate that almost *any* application of statistical technique takes liberty with one underlying assumption or another. If carried too far, this caution leaves the researcher with the original mass of undigested data, about which no conclusions can be drawn.

[2] The definition of a normal distribution and some additional refinements—for example, that these parallel straight lines are actually an approximation of curves—will be found in the statistics books.

FIGURE 17.5

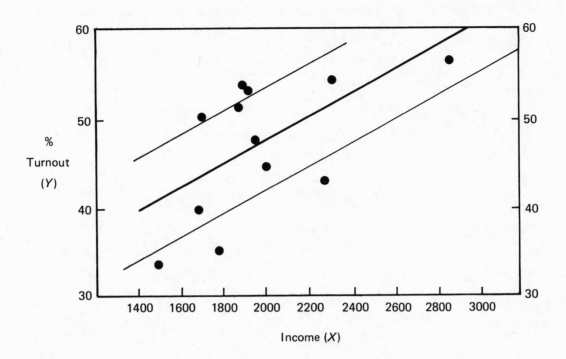

Income (X)

EXERCISE 21 : Is the Single-Member-District System Biased?

A problem of significance to the functioning of representative democracy is the relationship of the votes a party receives at an election to the number of seats it wins in Congress. Robert A. Dahl plotted the regression for the percentage of seats won by the Democrats in the House of Representatives from 1928 to 1954, with X = their percentage of the total vote in the United States for candidates for the House and Y = their percentage of seats in the House. He found Y_c = $2.5X - 70$ expressed the relationship.[3] Interpret this: for every voting increase of 1% in the population, the party won about _____% more seats in the House.[4]

But the political system changes. The once-safe Democratic seats in the South are now competitive. Incumbents of either party are less likely to be defeated. Yet Democrats have controlled the House since 1954. It is time to re-examine Dahl's findings. Here are the figures on the Democratic percentage of the two-party vote for Congress since World War II.

Year	Dem. % of 2-party Vote X	Dem. % of House Seats Y	Year	Dem. % of 2-party Vote	Dem. % of House Seats
1978	54.5*	63.5	1960	55.0	60.0
1976	56.2	67.1	1958	56.1	65.0
1974	57.6	66.6	1956	51.0	53.7
1972	51.7	54.9	1954	52.5	53.5
1970	54.2	58.5	1952	49.9	48.8
1968	50.9	55.8	1950	50.3	54.0
1966	51.3	57.0	1948	53.7	60.5
1964	57.5	67.7	1946	45.7	43.3
1962	52.7	59.5			

*Estimated from unofficial returns.

[3] This, of course, is the same as $Y_c = -70 + 2.5X$.

[4] The relationship between seats and votes in the British Parliament was first expressed as the "cube law"—when the vote divides in the ratio $a:b$ the seats divide $a^3:b^3$. See D. E. Butler, *The Electoral System in Britain* (London: Oxford University Press, 1952), and James G. March, "Parliamentary Representation as a Function of Election Results," *Public Opinion Quarterly,* 21 (1957), 521–542. Dahl's *A Preface to Democratic Theory* (Chicago: University of Chicago Press, 1956), pp. 147–149, gives regressions and graphs for the House and Senate up to 1954. More recent analyses of the problem include Edward R. Tufte, "The Relationship between Seats and Votes in Two-Party Systems," *American Political Science Review,* 67 (1973), 540–554, and Richard G. Niemi and John Degan, Jr., "A Theory of Political Districting," *ibid.,* 72 (1978), 1304–1323.

1. Plot these points on a sheet of graph paper. Is linear regression an appropriate technique for summarizing the tendency? _____

2. Calculate the regression coefficient. Y_c =   + X.

3. Plot the regression line on your graph.

4. Now plot the line that would express the relationship if each party got exactly the same proportion of seats as its proportion of the vote.

5. Suppose the Democrats were to get slightly fewer votes than the Republicans in the next election, say 49.5%. According to your regression, what proportion of the seats would they get? _____

6. Write a brief paragraph summarizing your findings and a second paragraph speculating on the reason for them.

The Uses of Regression

Simple bivariate regression is one of the most versatile research tools. Knowing when to use it involves more than an understanding of the technique itself; it depends upon the genius of the researcher. Recognizing when some hoary formulation does not correspond to one's intuitive sense of the reality of politics, then discovering or collecting data that bear upon the problem, then choosing a research technique that appropriately summarizes these data—all these steps reveal the difference between the research *artist* and the research *mechanic.* As we list some of the various ways that regression has been employed, you should consider other uses that might be made of the technique.

One of the current uses of regression is in election night forecasts. The process and assumptions are substantially the same as those in the Maine example. As the first precinct returns come in from the early closing towns on the East Coast, they are fed into a computer that has been programed with the data from past years. The program contains the regression of those precincts as predictors of their states and of the nation as a whole, and even the relation between their percentage for the Democratic party candidate and the percentage he has won in the Western states. The computer estimates from these regression slopes how each state will go, even before the polls have closed in the West, and then totals their electoral vote for a prediction of who will win the election. In simple form, the vote of a New Jersey precinct becomes X in the formula; the United States vote or the California vote, or whatever is being predicted, becomes the Y variable. The regression equation is computed for a series of recent elections. On election night, the early returns from this precinct are substituted in the formula, and Y_c predicts the outcome of the election. Of course, many precincts are in fact incorporated into the formula, which becomes rather complex. The more sophisticated models are not based on geography alone, but select a sample of early return precincts to represent religion, ethnic, and income characteristics as well.[5] So far, election night predictions have been quite accurate, demonstrating that "as your precinct goes, so goes the nation."

Such predictions as these, though they demonstrate empirically some political relationships within the nation, do not of themselves advance our understanding of political behavior. The important questions are the theoretical ones: *why* do such phenomena occur? We know that the basic assumption on which they are based is that people in all areas react comparably to the same elements of the campaign. If the nation should divide sharply on an East-West issue, the early election night predictions would be quite erroneous.

[5] See Robert A. Skedgell, "How Computers Pick an Election Winner," *Trans-Action* (November, 1966), 42–46, and Richard F. Link, "Election Night on Television," in *Statistics: A Guide to the Unknown,* Judith M. Tanur, ed. (San Francisco: Holden-Day, 1972), pp. 137–145.

Regression is employed to state the relations between demographic and political variables, for which there are numerous measures in the census and election returns. Income, level of education, percentage of the labor force employed in manufacturing, number of homes with telephones or television sets, foreign-born and non-white population, turnout, percentage voting Democratic and Republican for various offices, governmental expenditure for welfare and other purposes have been collected for the states, cities, and/or counties of the United States. You will find such figures in *Statistical Abstract of the United States, County and City Data Book, Historical Statistics of the United States,* and other Census Bureau publications. What are the relationships between these variables? Can you postdict the John F. Kennedy vote or the Al Smith vote from figures on the proportion of Catholics in a city, county, or state? Do states that elect Democrats to office spend more on welfare? Historians of the American party system and political scientists interested in historical analysis have made sophisticated use of regression to study the shifts of voting behavior in critical election periods. An example is Walter Dean Burnham, *Critical Elections and the Mainsprings of American Politics* (New York: Norton, 1970).

Time series regression has been a useful device to economists for generations, and some of the earliest quantitative studies of political behavior addressed themselves to fluctuation in the vote with changes in business conditions and farm prices.[6] Public officials, particularly school administrators, rely heavily on projections of future populations when planning expansion, and these estimates are based upon more or less sophisticated regressions.

Of course, regression is one of the fundamental techniques upon which both economic theory and calculations of estimates for the purpose of taxation, budgeting, and monetary policy are based. To give just one example, to know that the variation in GNP is more closely related to changes in the supply of money than to char ges in government spending has important consequences for policy-makers. (An official of the Office of Management and Budget recently quipped that his is the only office where 0.1 normally means $100,000,000.)[7]

In Chapter 4 we used the Banks-Textor data to examine relationships at the nominal and ordinal levels. Some of these variables, and a number of others, may be measured more precisely at the interval level. Regression may be used to seek patterns in comparative government. We might assume that nations that have elected Social Democrats to office for a number of years would have lower rates of unemployment than those with Conservative governments. But is this true? If so, do they have higher rates of inflation?[8]

[6]For a list of these studies, see V. O. Key, Jr., *A Primer of Statistics for Political Scientists* (New York: Crowell, 1954).

[7]Leonall C. Andersen, "Statistics for Public Financial Policy," in Tanur, pp. 321–325.

[8]See Edward R. Tufte, *Political Control of the Economy* (Princeton, N.J.: Princeton University Press, 1978), Ch. 4.

You may use regression for any of three purposes. The first is _description:_ it provides an economical way of summing up the relation between two variables. The second is _prediction:_ it may be used for estimating the value of one variable if we know the other. The third is _hypothesis testing:_ the direction and slope of the _b_ coefficients tell us for the interval level roughly what the sign and value of _phi, tau,_ etc., tell us for the nominal and ordinal levels.

Calculators, Computers, and Statistics Books

The arithmetic required to calculate regression slopes was somewhat daunting until advances in technology produced the computer and the pocket calculator. Many colleges have available computers with statistical packages which include regression. For less than $50 you can buy a statistical version of the pocket calculator, which has a built-in program for producing the mean, standard deviation, regression slopes and intercepts, and the correlation coefficient. All you do is punch in the raw data. Even if you don't have one of these, a calculator with several memories and a square root key will perform the computations without too much trouble.

Whatever hardware you use for your regression, it is essential to plot the points on a graph, preferably in advance. If they form a curve, or a blob, or if one or two points are some distance from the rest, you cannot put much confidence in the technique of _linear_ regression.

Every introductory statistics book deals with interval measures. Most of them start with measures of central tendency and dispersion, and then go on to analysis of variance, which is treated in some detail because it is essential for a theoretical knowledge of interval measures. Analysis of variance has not been treated here, since it is not often used in political research. It is indispensable in comparing _groups_ of students or subjects who have been measured on some interval continuum; hence, it is widely used in psychological and educational research.

We have omitted most of the theoretical underpinnings of regression, as well as many of the qualifications and assumptions involved, on the principle that it is best to learn what a technique _can_ do before becoming entangled in what it _cannot_ do. To follow up with more detailed descriptions, V. O. Key, Jr., _A Primer of Statistics for Political Scientists_ (New York: Crowell, 1954), which has recently been reissued in paperback, is the simplest. For political applications, G. David Garson, _Handbook of Political Science Methods_ (Boston: Holbrook, 1971), is a brief summary. Dennis J. Palumbo, _Statistics in Political and Behavioral Science_ (New York: Appleton-Century-Crofts, 1969) is a more thorough treatment and H. M. Blalock, _Social Statistics,_ 2nd ed. (New York: McGraw-Hill, 1972), is even more detailed. Blalock believes that regression is a more useful technique for social analysis than many statisticians have realized.

Jacob and Patricia Cohen, *Applied Multiple Regression/Correlation Analysis for the Behavioral Sciences* (New York: Halsted Press/Wiley, 1975), is written for those with a minimal background in statistics.

Though these will help, reading on your own is not a very satisfactory way of learning statistics, and you will be better off to start with an introductory course and master the fundamentals with the help of an instructor who can answer your questions.

Appendix: Calculations

All the computations for the example on p. 274 are set forth here. You may ignore them unless you need a model to copy in working a problem. $S(Y)$ and $S(Y_c)$ are calculated by short-cut formulae for desk calculators.

State	X Income (rounded)	Y Percentage Turnout	XY	X²	Y²
Maryland	$2830	57.0	161,310	8,008,900	3,249.00
Virginia	2270	43.1	97,837	5,152,900	1,857.61
N. Carolina	1920	53.2	102,144	3,686,400	2,830.24
S. Carolina	1690	40.1	67,769	2,856,100	1,608.01
Georgia	2000	44.9	89,800	4,000,000	2,016.01
Mississippi	1490	33.7	50,213	2,220,100	1,135.69
Kentucky	1890	54.1	102,249	3,572,100	2,926.81
Tennessee	1880	51.7	97,196	3,534,400	2,672.89
Alabama	1780	36.2	64,436	3,168,400	1,310.44
Florida	2290	54.5	124,805	5,244,100	2,970.25
Arkansas	1710	50.4	86,184	2,924,100	2,540.16
Louisiana	1940	47.9	92,926	3,763,600	2,294.41
	$23,690	566.8	1,136,869	48,131,100	27,411.52
	ΣX	ΣY	ΣXY	ΣX^2	ΣY^2

$$b = \frac{N\Sigma XY - (\Sigma X)(\Sigma Y)}{N\Sigma X^2 - (\Sigma X)^2}$$

$$b = \frac{(12 \times 1,136,869) - (23,690 \times 566.8)}{(12 \times 48,131,100) - 23,690^2}$$

$$b = \frac{13,642,428 - 13,427,492}{577,573,200 - 561,216,100} = \frac{214,936}{16,357,100}$$

$$b = .01314$$

$$a = \frac{\Sigma Y - b\Sigma X}{N}$$

$$a = \frac{566.8 - (.013140226 \times 23{,}690)}{12} = \frac{566.8 - 311.3}{12}$$

$$a = \frac{255.5}{12} = 21.3$$

$$\bar{Y} = \frac{\Sigma Y}{N} = \frac{566.8}{12} = 47.23$$

$$S(\bar{Y}) = \sqrt{\frac{\Sigma Y^2}{N} - \left(\frac{\Sigma Y}{N}\right)^2} = \sqrt{\frac{27{,}411.52}{12} - \left(\frac{566.8}{12}\right)^2}$$

$$= \sqrt{2284.29 - (47.23)^2} = \sqrt{2284.29 - 2230.67}$$

$$= \sqrt{53.62} = 7.32$$

$$S(Y_c) = \sqrt{\frac{\Sigma Y^2 - (a\Sigma Y + b\Sigma XY)}{N}}$$

$$= \sqrt{\frac{27{,}411.52 - (21.3 \times 566.8) + (.01314 \times 1{,}136{,}869)}{12}}$$

$$= \sqrt{\frac{27{,}411.52 - (12{,}072.84 + 14{,}938.46)}{12}}$$

$$= \sqrt{\frac{27{,}411.52 - 27{,}011.30}{12}} = \sqrt{\frac{400.22}{12}}$$

$$= \sqrt{33.35} = 5.78$$

18/**Multiple Regression**

*Because the world is in truth statistical
and not particular—a truth we find hard
to accept, each individual's view being
inescapably particular—the result of
excessive concentration on individual cases
tends to be a spreading irrationality.*
MARTIN MAYER

The bivariate regression formula reveals the relationship between a single independent variable and the dependent variable. But we often wish to fathom a situation in which we suspect the presence of a bundle of causal or related factors underlying a political or social condition. Here we are beyond the capacity of the pocket calculator and must resort to the computer. It is not difficult for anyone with access to a computer that mounts one of the statistical packages to put in five or six independent variables and grind out multiple regression and correlation coefficients. Understanding what the output means—and more important, what it seems to mean but doesn't—requires more sophistication.

In this chapter and the next two, we look into these techniques to describe what social scientists can do and are doing with such multivariate techniques. This should help you to read and understand journal articles and books that use them. You may also want to collect data and run them through the statistical package on your campus computer. This will give you an even better understanding. But unless you have completed a statistics course explaining the measures, their derivations, interrelations, assumptions, and qualifications, you cannot know whether your conclusions are trustworthy or deceptive.

From Bivariate to Multiple Regression

You have already done multivariate analysis at the nominal/ordinal level of measurement (Chapter 14). You "held constant" a "control" variable while looking at the relationship between the independent and dependent variables for each value of the control. Then you could decide whether that relationship was real or spurious or some form of interaction among the variables. The process was clumsy, and would have been even clumsier if you had tried to manipulate four or five variables.

In Chapters 16 and 17 we have been working at the interval/ratio level with two variables. The extra precision with which they are measured gives us a good deal more information on each case. Now we shall take advantage of this extra precision to control on several variables. The controlling will be done mathematically by a process that will not be explained here.

However, we can push our visual model of regression a few steps further to give an intuitive understanding of multiple regression, using the Southern states turnout problem from the last chapter. Suppose, having found only a moderately good path of dots on our regression of income and voting, we decide to examine the effect of education on the same dependent variable. Look at Figure 16.1 on p. 262 and imagine that you are told that it is really an optical illusion. This is not a dozen dots drawn on a flat plane but instead is 12 points embedded in a clear plastic block, a block that extends backward, underneath, and away from the page. Having always looked at the block from the same side, you were not aware that there was this third dimension. Now you turn the block around and look at it from the right-hand side. You discover that the points cluster not about a line but about a plane, tipped up at an angle. If you now measure the vertical distances of the points from the plane, you discover that the total (squared) distance is considerably less than their distance from the apparent regression line which you had been working with. Assume that the dimension extending back from the page measures median school years attended. By introducing this second independent variable, we can account for additional variance among the states in their level of voting turnout. Now we have three regression slopes. There is the original relationship between income and turnout, perceived by looking at the block as a page in a book. There is the second viewpoint, from the right-hand side of the block, which shows the relation of education to turnout, the latter still being measured in the vertical dimension. And, looking down from the top, we would view education and income, the two independent variables, and would observe the relationship between them.

This last relationship is a bother, not a help. If a state's level of income and its level of education are related to each other—as they must be—then we don't know which of them is affecting turnout directly and which of them is operating through the other. We would like to remove the influence of education in order to appraise the influence of income by itself, and then to control for income and appraise the influence of education alone. That is what multiple regression, somewhat miraculously, accomplishes.

We call income X_1 and education X_2 and get a new regression equation that is not much different from the old one:

$$Y_c = a + b_1 X_1 + b_2 X_2$$

The values for a and b_1 are not the same as we got for our bivariate equation. The new b_1 tells us what the effect of income is when we control for education. And b_2 tells us the effect of education when controlling for income. In other respects the formula has the same uses. If we know the average income and average educational level for a state, we can estimate Y_c—the expected turnout. And the additional information should give us a better estimate, since we have substituted our regression plane for the regression line, and the residual differences between points and the plane will be smaller than the differences between the points and the earlier regression line. Since each b value indicates the effect of that variable with all the others held constant, they are called *partial* regression coefficients.

Though our capacity for visual analogy boggles at the fourth dimension, mathematics does not, and we may construct multiple regression formulae having any number of variables. When we start using multivariate techniques, the rigorous statement of hypotheses derived from theory, the designation in advance of independent and dependent variables, and other methodological demands are often relaxed. A hypothesis specifying the relative influence of half a dozen independent variables, or even one neatly distinguishing independent from dependent variables, is difficult to come by in the present state of theory. Multivariate research tends to be more inductive and exploratory than deductive and theoretically explicit. Often the symbol Y is replaced with an X, and the variables designated $X_1, X_2, \ldots X_n$ to indicate that *any* variable may be considered dependent. A series of equations is derived, with each variable rotated into the dependent position. Sometimes an e or E term is added at the end to represent "error" or unexplained variance, acknowledging the presence of other variables not investigated and random effects not susceptible to control. Thus you may see: $X_4 = a + b_1 X_1 + b_2 X_2 + b_3 X_3 + E$.

Example : Development and Democracy

Let us examine a study by Philips Cutright, using multiple regression to analyze the problem of what demographic and ecological factors are related to the development of democracy. The author first defines "political development" operationally by forming an index consisting of the amount of party competition in parliament and the free election of chief executives. Nations exhibiting these qualities (which we would roughly equate with "democracy") over a period of time were considered "developed" on an interval scale that ranged from 0 for undeveloped to 66 for the most developed nations. All nations except African ones were included.[1] Since the research sought to account for political development, this was the dependent or Y variable.

The independent variables were:

X_1: a communications index based upon the size and circulation of newspapers, the volume of mail, and the number of telephones per capita.

X_2: an urbanization index based upon the proportion of the people living in cities over 100,000.

X_3: an agriculture index based upon the proportion of the labor force engaged in farming.

X_4: an education index based on the literacy rate and the number of students in institutions of higher learning.

The equation combining these variables turned out to be:

$$Y_c = (-21.46) + (.300X_1) + (.376X_2) + (-.221X_3) + (.282X_4)$$

Thus to estimate the level of political development of a nation, one multiplies the communication index value by .3, the urbanization index by .376, the agriculture index by $-.221$ (note that the more agricultural a country is, the less developed it is), the education index by .282, and then subtracts 21.46 (the a value). Nations such as Jordan, Pakistan, Laos, Cambodia, Portugal, and Spain have Y values in the low 30s. The Philippines, Ecuador, Greece, and Austria fall near the mean of 51. The United States, Canada, Sweden, Chile, and Switzerland are at the top of the scale with Y values of or near 66.

The regression model posits a simple relationship between four independent variables and one dependent variable. In a characteristic process of building upon an initial exploratory research effort, other researchers further refined the concept of "political development," added a time dimension, and began to put the data into more elaborate "causal" models to disentangle the relationships among the independent variables.[2]

[1] Philips Cutright, "National Political Development, Its Measurement and Social Correlates," in *Politics and Social Life: An Introduction to Political Behavior*, Nelson W. Polsby, ed. (Boston: Houghton Mifflin, 1963), pp. 569–582. African nations were omitted because they were too recently formed to provide adequate statistics.

[2] See Donald J. McCrone and Charles F. Cnudde, "Toward a Communications Theory of Democratic Political Development: A Causal Model," *American Political Science Review*, 61 (1967), 72–79; Deane E. Neubauer, "Some Conditions of Democracy," *ibid.*, 1002–1009; Gilbert R. Winham, "Political Development and Lerner's Theory: Further Test of a Causal Model," *ibid.*, 64 (1970), 810–818.

Cutright's regression shows more than the relation of economic variables to political development. By observing the difference between the Y and Y_c values, one may discover which nations are more or less developed politically than they ought to be according to the equation which expresses the relationship for all states. For example, Spain and Portugal are less politically developed than their economic development would lead one to expect, while India and Chile are more developed politically.

Examining these differences between Y and Y_c, called *residuals,* leads us to construct better models. By noting different characteristics of the cases that have positive residual values and those that have negative ones, we are led to discover important variables not in the equation which may account for some of the remaining unexplained variance. For example, one would ask what Spain and Portugal might have in common that is just the opposite of some common characteristic of India and Chile. In this way regression is used to "hold constant" *all* the independent variables in the equation to search for new explanatory factors not contemplated in the original study.

Dummy Variables

A qualitative variable that can be measured only as a nominal dichotomy may also be incorporated into the regression formula by giving it a value of 1 if the characteristic is present and 0 if it is not. This is called a "dummy variable." For example, if Cutright had wanted to take account of geography, he could have given European nations a value of 1 and all others 0. In our turnout example, we could have given states that once exacted a poll tax the value of 1, others 0. A polytomy is somewhat more trouble. The presence or absence of each quality must be treated as a separate variable. For example, Cutright would have had to introduce another variable with Asian nations as 1, others (including Europe) as 0, then a third with South American nations as 1, all others as 0, and so on.

Strictly speaking, ordinal variables should not be used in regression because their measurement intervals are uneven. However, this rule is not always followed.

Beta Weights and Significance Tests

The b coefficients are useful in calculating a Y_c value, but they have one drawback. Since they are related to the original values (percentages, dollars, years of education, etc.), they cannot be compared with one another to determine which variable has the most effect. This problem can be overcome by multiplying b by the ratio of the standard deviations of the independent and dependent variables to give a "standardized regression coefficient," otherwise known as a *beta* coefficient or *beta* weight. $B = b(Si/Sd)$

This is equivalent to dividing the original values by their respective standard deviations, putting them in terms of a "unitless measure." Then the relative impact of each independent variable in an equation may be compared with the effect of all the others.

Significance tests for the relationship of each independent variable to the dependent variable utilize the t statistic (see Chapter 15). Another test, the F statistic used in analysis of variance, tells us whether the relationship of all the variables in the regression equation is significant. The computer obligingly calculates these for us. There are tables to use in getting the probabilities associated with these values. A rough rule of thumb is that if you have 10 or more cases (and you shouldn't do regression with fewer), a minimum t value of 2 or an F value of 5 indicates significance at .05 or better.

While it is possible to put a large number of independent variables into a regression equation, there are mathematical reasons for distrusting more than about half a dozen. If the independent variables are highly correlated with one another, the regression is also questionable. There is a technique called "stepwise" regression which tries out a larger number of variables in various combinations and rejects those that do not have an independent effect at a significant level.

The equations we have treated are all based on the assumption of *linearity*, that the scatter plots show the points clustering about a line rather than a curve. There are curvilinear models, e.g., logarithmic ($Log\ Y = a + bX$), quadratic ($Y = a + bX^2$), multiplicative ($Y = aX^b$), and interactive ($Y = a + b_1X_1 + b_2X_2 + b_3X_1X_2$).[3]

Example : Money in Congressional Elections

Gary Jacobson used multiple regression most effectively in assessing the effect of campaign contributions upon congressional elections.[4] His model hypothesized that money spent by a challenger had a different effect from money spent by an incumbent, who has the advantages of financial and communication resources that go with the job. His basic equation is:

[3] Several alternative models for explaining the George Wallace vote in 1968 are explored in Walter Dean Burnham and John Sprague, "Additive and Multiplicative Models of the Voting Universe: The Case of Pennsylvania: 1960–1968," *American Political Science Review,* 64 (1970), 417–490.

[4] Gary C. Jacobson, "The Effects of Campaign Spending in Congressional Elections," *American Political Science Review,* 72 (1978), 469–491.

$$CV = a + b_1 CE + b_2 IE + b_3 P + b_4 CPS + e$$

(The Y_c, X_1, X_2, etc., that appear in the algebraic expression are often replaced by two- to six-letter terms, since these are the mnemonic devices used to describe variables in a computer program.)

CV stands for the challenger's percentage of the two-party vote, and is the dependent variable in this equation.

CE is the challenger's campaign expenditures in thousands of dollars.

IE is the incumbent's expenditures, also in thousands of dollars.

P is a dummy variable indicating the challenger's party affiliation: 1 if a Democrat, 0 if a Republican.

CPS is the strength of the challenger's party in the district, approximated by the percentage of the vote his or her party's candidate won in the last previous election for that seat.

Here is the regression for the 1974 election:

$$CV = 15.6 + .121CE - .028IE + 9.78P + .351CPS$$

Let's examine each term of this equation:

$a = 15.6$ This is the base percentage to be added to each regression estimate of the challenger's percentage of the vote. It has no important meaning and is usually ignored.

$.121CE$ For each $1,000 spent, the average challenger gets 0.121% more votes. Thus a challenger spending $100,000 on a campaign would be expected to improve his or her vote percentage by about 12%, other things being equal.

$-.028IE$ We would expect this b value to be negative because money spent by the incumbent should reduce the challenger's vote. In this instance, the incumbent's $1,000 outlay shaves only 28/100ths of a percentage point off the average challenger's vote. Thus an incumbent spending $100,000 would expect to improve his or her percentage by only 3%. The incumbent's dollar is only a fourth as effective as a challenger's.

$9.78P$ A Democrat challenging a Republican gets nearly 10% added to his or her expected vote; a Republican challenging a Democrat gets nothing ($9.78 \times 0 = 0$). Coming after Watergate, 1974 was a good year for Democrats; we would expect quite a different coefficient for other elections.

$.351CPS$ This variable measures the relative strength of the two parties in the district. For each percentage point of the vote won by the candidate of the challenger's party in the last election, the 1974 challenger gets one-third of a point.

Using these values, let us estimate how a Democratic challenger spending $150,000 would do in a race with a Republican incumbent spending $100,000 in a district where the last Democratic candidate got 40% of the vote.

$$CV = 15.6 + .121(150) - .028(100) + 9.78(1) + .351(40)$$
$$CV = 15.6 + 18.15 - 2.8 + 9.78 + 14.04$$
$$CV = 54.77\% \text{ of the vote won by the challenger.}$$

The equation postdicted 29 out of the 39 victories by challengers over incumbents in 1974. At present, the formula could not be used to predict the success of future challengers for several reasons. Final spending totals are not known until after the election, nor is the overall swing from one party to the other. Moreover, accurate information about campaign spending has been available only since the 1971 electoral reforms. The formulae for the two elections Jacobson studied were quite different. However, as data accumulate, it may become possible to estimate the swing factor, P, from pre-election polls, estimate candidates' total spending from early reports, and make a moderately good guess as to the outcome of particular races.

Now let us examine the *beta* weights: $\beta_1 = .48; \beta_2 = -.11; \beta_3 = .42; \beta_4 = .28$.

These *betas* tell us the relative importance of each of the factors, which the *b* values could not, since they were expressed in dollars, parties, and votes, which are not comparable. It appears that the challenger's spending was the most important element, and party affiliation was not far behind. The party balance in the district was next, and the incumbent's expenditure had the least important effect on the election. Calculation of *t* tests showed that all the variables had a significant effect.

These are only a few of Jacobson's findings. He added other variables, such as the length of tenure of the incumbent and his or her power in Congress. Using a more complicated regression model, he examined the proposition that it is the potential ability of the challenger to win the seat that enables him or her to raise campaign funds—thus in effect reversing the independent and dependent variables. He concludes that policies, including public funding, that make it easier for challengers to raise money will make elections more competitive, whereas overall limits on spending will lessen competition.

Multiple regression has been used to estimate crop yields and to analyze the performance of stock portfolios. One researcher used it to ascertain what makes a movie a box-office success (not top stars and previous Oscar winners but good directors and supporting actors).[5] National Football League coaches subscribe to computer analyses that incorporate each week's results into a

[5] *Washington Post,* Mar. 6, 1977, L1.

new regression. Statistician Bud Goode concludes from his long-term output that running the ball is more successful than passing it, and that interceptions are disastrous but fumbles aren't too important.[6]

[6]*Sports Illustrated*, Sept. 4, 1978, 34–35.

19/Correlation

*They have endeavored to separate the knowledge of nature
from the colors of rhetoric, the devices of fancy or the de-
lightful deceit of fables. . . .They have striven to preserve
it from being over-pressed by a confused heap of vain and
useless particulars, or from being straitened and bounded
too much by general doctrines.*
THOMAS SPRAT'S
description of the Royal Society, 1667

Most people have heard the term "correlation" and used or misused it many times before they
ever encounter the concept of regression. Yet regression is the more direct and often more meaningful technique upon which correlation of interval data is dependent.

The bivariate regression slope measures the relationship between two variables, but it has
several defects. First, there are always two possible regression equations, Y on X and X on Y. Second, the slope value makes sense only in terms of the units in which the data are measured. A
change in unit, say from feet to inches or from the number of seats in Congress held by Democrats
to the percentage of seats, will change the b value. Finally, we have to turn to the standard deviation to know whether the path of the dots is a narrow one, and reliable, or broad and unreliable.
But this, too, is expressed in the original data units and in its raw form is non-comparable with
other regressions.

Correlation remedies these defects by producing a single measure that has the quality now
familiar to you of varying between +1 for perfect positive association, down through 0 for no
association, to −1 for perfect negative association. The product-moment or Pearsonian coefficient
of correlation, symbolized by r, is named after Karl Pearson, who developed it in following up
Galton's work on genetics. It uses the same intermediate calculations, ΣX, ΣX^2, ΣXY, ΣY, and
ΣY^2 that we have already used in regression. It combines these in a fashion that expresses each

variable in terms of its own standard deviation. Thus it is a somewhat generalized version of the *beta* weight.

What Correlation Means

At all levels of measurement we have treated coefficients that vary from +1 when the two variables are perfectly correlated to 0 when they are entirely independent, and then to −1 when one increased precisely as the other decreased. But there are more meaningful interpretations of the Pearsonian coefficient of correlation, r, as a measure of our ability to account for political, social, and psychological phenomena. This is best seen by returning to our guessing games (pp. 274–278). For example, if we did not know the percentage turnout in the Southern states in the earlier example, we would guess the mean. If we made this guess for each state, our total error could be assessed as the sum of the squared distances from the mean of each state's actual turnout percentage, Y. This, of course, is $\Sigma(Y - \bar{Y})^2$. However, if we have taken account of the effect of income on turnout and calculated the regression formula, we can make better guesses. Instead of the mean, we compute Y_c and that is our guess. The measure of our error here is the residuals, the distances of the points from the regression line, so we can express our total error as $\Sigma(Y - Y_c)^2$. This, of course, is a smaller sum, since we have improved our guesses. The *proportionate reduction in error* in our guesses is expressed by the *coefficient of determination*:

$$r^2 = \frac{\Sigma(Y - \bar{Y})^2 - \Sigma(Y - Y_c)^2}{\Sigma(Y - \bar{Y})^2}$$

(This formula is not used in calculating it, since there are more convenient ones.) We can take the square root to get the correlation coefficient, r, a more familiar but much less useful statistic.

This definition of correlation is of more theoretical than practical importance, since not many of us make a practice of guessing turnout percentages and other Y values, with or without the help of means and regression slopes. But its implications are worth pursuing a little further.

For a visual analogy of correlation to regression, think of any of the previous regression scattergrams as being compressed in its longer dimension and stretched in its shorter one, as though the page were printed on rubber, until it is reduced from a rectangle to a square. The regression line now runs from the lower left to the upper right corner of the square (if positive). The means of the two variables become horizontal and vertical lines meeting in the exact center of the square. The unit of measurement along the sides is now s, the standard deviation, instead of the original measurement unit. The points have now been pushed and pulled into a cluster around the diagonal. If the cluster is tight along the diagonal, shaped like a cigar, the correlation is high, if it is football-shaped, the correlation is moderate, and if it is circular there is no correlation at all ($r = 0$). If the regression is negative, the correlation will be also, and the points will run along the upper left to the lower right diagonal.

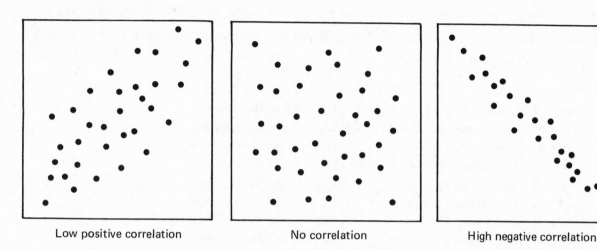

| Low positive correlation | No correlation | High negative correlation |

That is one way to think about the correlation coefficient. Another way—as we have seen—is that it measures the proportionate reduction in the unexplained variance that we achieve when we go from predictions based on the *mean* to predictions based on the *regression line*. If all the points fell on the regression line (and the correlation diagonal), the independent variable would account for *all* the variation of the dependent variable about its mean, and r would be either $+1$ or -1. If the points were so unsystematically scattered that the regression line had no slope at all, and coincided with the mean, then we would have accounted for none of the variation by introducing the independent variable. There would be no relationship and r would be zero. Knowing the value of X would be no help in estimating the value of Y.

With r as an index of association applicable to any pair of variables, we may ascertain from a single statistic whether the variables are related, how closely they are related, and (from the sign) whether positively or negatively. Though one must perform most of the calculations necessary for the regression before computing the correlation coefficient, studies often report only correlations, not regressions. One explanation for this is that social science is still asking what variables are associated with what other variables. Until we can establish that there *is* a relationship, and that it is fairly strong, there is no point in trying to state it more precisely in a regression formula. The correlation coefficient, then, measures the *strength* of a relationship; it does at the interval level what d_{yx} and *gamma* do at the ordinal level. (But note that in the interest of confusing the beginner statisticians have arranged for nominal and ordinal coefficients to be positive when most of the cases fall in a line sloping *downward* from left to right, whereas the regression line and interval level correlation coefficients are positive when the pattern slopes *upward*.)

Through r varies from $+1$ to -1, we should not assume that a coefficient of .50 means that the X variable accounts for half the variance in the Y variable. Instead, this is measured by r^2, the *coefficient of determination,* a discouraging fact which you are obliged to remember if you are to make much sense of articles using correlation. If you will complete the following table you will see how discouraging it can be:

An r of .90 accounts for $r^2 = .9^2 = .81$, i.e., 81% of the variance
An r of .80 accounts for $r^2 = .8^2 = .64$, i.e., 64% of the variance
An r of .70 accounts for $r^2 = 7 = 49$, i.e.,   of the variance
An r of .60 accounts for $r^2 = 6 = 36$, i.e.,   of the variance
An r of .50 accounts for $r^2 = 5 = 25$, i.e.,   of the variance
An r of .40 accounts for $r^2 = 4 = 16$, i.e.,   of the variance
An r of .30 accounts for $r^2 = 3 = 9$, i.e.,   of the variance
An r of .20 accounts for $r^2 = 2 = 4$, i.e.,   of the variance

Thus a bivariate correlation of less than .30 indicates that the independent variable does not have much effect.

There are many versions of the basic formula for the product-moment correlation, of which perhaps the handiest for the pocket calculator is:

$$r = \frac{N\Sigma XY - \Sigma X \Sigma Y}{\sqrt{[N\Sigma X^2 - (\Sigma X)^2]\,[N\Sigma Y^2 - (\Sigma Y)^2]}}$$

The correlation for the example on pp. 274–278 is worked out in the appendix to this chapter. It turns out to be .61. From this we know that variation in income "accounts for" about 37% of the variation in turnout in these Southern states.

Significance of the Correlation

The correlation coefficient r measures the amount of relationship between two variables, and r^2 tells us how much we may improve our guess as to the value of any case on the dependent variable if we know its value on the independent variable. Earlier we calculated *chi square* to estimate the confidence we might have in nominal and ordinal measures of association, since a strong relationship based on too few cases might still fall short of the required level of significance. Now we calculate the significance of *r* separately. But this turns out to be very simple, just a matter of considering the number of cases. Here is a conservative table:

If N is 10, then r must be at least .64 to be significant at $p < .05$

15	.52
20	.45
25	.40
30	.37
35	.34
40	.32
60	.26
100	.20

Since one hardly ever calculates a regression without its corresponding coefficient of correlation, this tables serves as a significance table for regression as well.

A look at the table makes it clear that most of the examples and exercises in this book (which are based on small Ns to ease your problems of comprehension and calculation) deal with correlations which are not statistically significant at .05. The correlation of .61 in our turnout example was based on 12 cases. Is it significant at $p < .05$? _____

Once again it is necessary to repeat the caveat that correlation does not "explain" in a causal sense; the direction of causality is a theoretical assumption. One must be particularly sensitive to the possibility of spurious correlation when dealing with time series in the United States in recent decades. *Everything has been going up.* Population increases. Costs go up along with wages. There are more telephones, cars, miles of highways and accidents. Crime rates have been increasing, and so have divorce rates and the Dow-Jones industrials. Most people go to school and for more years, and they drink more liquor. More people distrust the government and the government spends more money. Each of these trends may or may not be causally related to the others. But each of them is likely to show a correlation with all the others in a regression over time, largely because we have been in a situation of change and expansion.

As we learned earlier, the *variance,* i.e., the standard deviation squared, is a measure of the difference between high and low values of any variable, for instance, the turnout in Southern states. In explaining *why* some turnouts are high and some low, the regression with income has in effect reduced this variance to the residuals around the line of regression. The remaining variance, measured by the residuals, is *unexplained,* i.e., is attributable to some other factors. In multiple regression we add these other factors to the equation—education, political culture, percentage non-white, and so on. The multiple regression equation becomes $Y_c = a + b_1 X_1 + b_2 X_2 + b_3 X_3 \ldots + b_n X_n$. Each new variable that is correlated with Y "explains" more and more, and thus reduces the residual variance. Thus:

$$R^2 = \frac{\text{total variance} - \text{unexplained variance}}{\text{total variance}}$$

This is the same as the bivariate formula, but we now write it with a capital R, the *multiple correlation coefficient*. R^2 now measures how much we can explain about the behavior of Variable Y. It is a measure of our knowledge and understanding of the phenomenon.

Ideally we would like to explain *all* the variance, but we never can in social science. There are always some factors we can't measure, and some inaccuracies in measuring those we can, so the residual error, or unexplained variance, remains with us.

Another deceptive effect that shows up when running correlations on data for geographical units such as counties or states is the "ecological fallacy," discussed on p. 140. Robinson found that the percentage of foreign-born persons in an area correlated +.62 with the percentage who were literate. But if one looked at whether *individual* immigrants could read, he found the correlation reversed, −.12. The explanation, of course, is that the foreign-born constituted a small proportion of the population that had settled in areas of the country where the native-born citizens tended to be literate.[1] Thus correlation of census aggregates may point to tendencies, but we should try to check them with individual survey data before having complete confidence in them.

Multiple Correlation

In the Cutright study (p. 295) the simple correlation of communications with political development was $r = .80$, indicating that communications accounted for $r^2 = 64\%$ of the variance. Simple rs of .64 with urbanization, −.56 with agriculture, and .62 with education account for 41%, 31%, and 38% of the variance, respectively. Adding them up, the four variables together have accounted for 174% of the variance in the dependent variable. This is about three-fourths more variation than there is! This is called "overdetermination" and stems from the fact that independent variables, being themselves correlated with one another, tend to measure the same thing over and over. The multiple correlation coefficient, however, is $R = .85$, indicating that all four vari-

[1]W. S. Robinson, "Ecological Correlation and the Behavior of Individuals," *American Sociological Review,* 15 (1950); 351−357, pointed out the fallacy. W. Phillips Shively, " 'Ecological' Inference: The Use of Aggregate Data to Study Individuals," *American Political Science Review,* 63 (1969), 1183−1196, shows that it is sometimes possible to estimate the inaccuracy or reduce it.

ables together account for $R^2 = 72\%$ of the variance, leaving the remainder unexplained by these factors.

Partial Correlation

In Chapter 16 we examined the problems of multivariate analysis with nominal and ordinal level variables. One of the serious limits in holding one variable constant with these data was sample size. Whenever we broke the original table down into partial tables to control for a third variable, we saw the sample sizes diminish at least by half. Percentage differences that had been statistically significant in the original table were no longer significant in the partials, even when the association remained just as strong, because of the reduced N. At the interval level we have more information available: we know not just whether a characteristic is present or absent but the *degree* to which it is possessed by the person or geographical unit represented by the case. This additional information substitutes, as it were, for additional cases, enabling us to control more effectively. How this is possible is demonstrated in the following contrived tables:

	Nominal level				*Interval level*			
	2 and under	*3 or more*			1	2	3	4
2 and under	10	10		1	0	0	0	5
				2	0	10	5	0
3 or more	10	10		3	0	5	10	0
				4	5	0	0	0

The two tables contain the same data, but the greater precision in the second table reveals a rather strong association ($r = .67$) which is obscured when the two variables are reduced to dichotomies. This gain in information is why Pearsonian coefficients of correlation are more powerful analytical tools than Q, *phi*, d_{yx}, or *gamma*. We take advantage of this efficiency in controlling for a third variable in partial correlation.

Bivariate correlation, as treated at the beginning of this chapter, produces "simple" or "zero-order" coefficients. "First-order" partial correlation coefficients are those in which one variable is held constant while the relationship of two others is examined.

If you have a dependent variable X_1 and two independent variables, X_2 and X_3, and have already calculated the simple or bivariate r between each pair of variables, then you can calculate the partial correlations. Suppose you want to find the relationship between X_1 and X_2 with X_3 held constant. A dot is used to set off the controlled variable, and the formula is:

$$r_{12.3} = \frac{r_{12} - (r_{13})(r_{23})}{\sqrt{1 - r_{13}^2} \; \sqrt{1 - r_{23}^2}}$$

This is not too difficult to manage on a pocket calculator. But when you get to second-order partials, manipulating four variables, you need a computer.

(For significance of first-order partials revise the table on p. 309 to read: for 10 cases, .67; for 15 cases, .54; for 20 cases, .46; for 25 cases, .41; with larger samples, no change.)

"Causal modelling" and "path analysis" are names for techniques based upon partial correlation or regression using *beta* weights. They are used to test hypotheses about relationships between three or more variables. For example Muller examined three variables:

> *Political efficacy:* the belief that government officials are responsive to citizen pressures.
> *Political involvement:* the tendency of respondents to follow governmental affairs and personalities in the media and understand them.
> *Ability to influence government:* the degree to which respondents said they would try, and succeed, in influencing government policies.

Two models were examined:

(1) That political efficacy led to political involvement, and this in turn led to belief in the ability to influence government, thus:

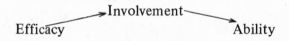

(2) That political efficacy led *directly* to belief in ability to influence government, in addition to the two-step effect just described:

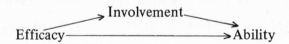

Analysis of data on five nations demonstrated that the first model was characteristic of Italy and Mexico, the second of the United States, Great Britain, and West Germany.[2]

---

[2]Edward N. Muller, "Cross-National Dimensions of Political Competence," *American Political Science Review*, 64 (1970), 792–809. Data are from Gabriel A. Almond and Sidney Verba, *The Civic Culture* (Princeton, N.J.: Princeton University Press, 1963).

Factor Analysis

Multiple and partial correlation and multiple regression are not adequate for another problem—that in which we have dozens of variables, many of them known to be highly correlated with one another, and need somehow to simplify the pattern. Psychologists encountered such problems in the 1930s when they constructed tests with large numbers of items or batteries of items, each of which could be said to measure some intellectual, emotional, manual, or sensory variable. How does one define the traits which clusters of tightly intercorrelated items measure?

To grasp what is involved, we diagram variables as lines intersecting at the center. A high correlation is represented by a small acute angle, as in the left-hand diagram below. Absence of correlation is represented by two lines at 90-degree angles from one another, as in the right-hand diagram:

When several measurements correlate with one another, we assume they are measuring the same underlying quality. If we found six variables in the following constellation, we would conclude that each cluster of three essentially measures two different, uncorrelated qualities. Such clusters of variables are known as "factors."

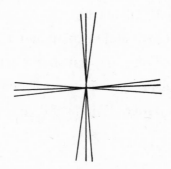

It is not possible to think of a third factor that is not correlated with either of these two so long as we are confined to a plane, but once again we may imagine another cluster thrust through the page at right angles to both of these. And, as we have done before, we can at least imagine a fourth or fifth dimension. Thus we could break down a matrix of hundreds of variables into a few factors. The correlation between a single variable and the composite value of all the variables in a factor is spoken of as a factor "loading."

The use of factor analysis is demonstrated by a study of the American states by John Crittenden, seeking to discover whether the concepts of *modernization* and *development* which have been applied to the nations of the world are also applicable to the American states.[3] He selected thirty-three statistical indicators having to do with development and subjected them to a factor analysis. Instead of a clear-cut, single "development" factor emerging, the variables clustered into four major factors. The first was comprised of these variables: high salaries for state executives, large population, ethnic diversity, many city dwellers and commuters, many lawyers and physicians, high newspaper circulation, a high proportion of employment and spending by local, rather than state, governments, and a low fertility rate among women. New York, California, Illinois, and New Jersey were highest on this factor. He labelled it "metro-urbanism." The second factor to emerge included a combination of variables that would hardly have been predicted or shown to cluster together by any other technique. It consisted of high voting turnout, many telephones and TV sets, competition between political parties, high income and education, good housing and automobiles, a heavy proportion of taxes raised by local rather than state governments, and Republican strength. Connecticut, Iowa, Kansas, Massachusetts, and Nebraska were high on this factor, which was labelled "integrative message exchange." The third factor was clearly composed of variables related to population increase and in-migration, with Nevada, Arizona, New Mexico, and Florida high. The fourth factor consisted of high taxing and spending levels per capita, with a group of states having little else in common ranking highest on it: New York, Wyoming, Louisiana, and North Dakota. In the American context, he concluded that development is not a single dimension. The various political characteristics measured go with particular economic indicators, rather than grouping together in a single political dimension.

Factor analysis requires a great deal of computation, which is now invariably done by computer. Interpreting it requires considerable statistical sophistication, in the absence of which you should not try to use the technique. To learn more about it, see R. J. Rummel, *Applied Factor Analysis* (Evanston, Ill.: Northwestern University Press, 1970).

---

[3] John Crittenden, "Dimensions of Modernization in the American States," *American Political Science Review,* 61 (1967), 989–1001.

Appendix: Calculations

$$r = \frac{N\Sigma XY - \Sigma X\Sigma Y}{\sqrt{[N\Sigma X^2 - (\Sigma X)^2]\ [N\Sigma Y^2 - (\Sigma Y)^2]}}$$

$$= \frac{(12 \times 1{,}136{,}869) - (23{,}690 \times 566.8)}{\sqrt{[(12 \times 48{,}131{,}100) - 23{,}690^2]\ [(12 \times 27{,}411.5) - 566.8^2]}}$$

$$= \frac{13{,}642{,}428 - 13{,}427{,}492}{\sqrt{(577{,}573{,}200 - 561{,}216{,}100)(328{,}938.24 - 321{,}262.24)}}$$

$$= \frac{214{,}936}{\sqrt{16{,}357{,}100 \times 7{,}676}} = \frac{214{,}936}{\sqrt{125{,}557{,}099{,}600}}$$

$$= \frac{214{,}936}{354{,}340} = .61$$

20 / The Application of Research Methods

*Those who have handled sciences have been either men
of experiment or men of dogmas. The men of experiment
are like the ant, they only collect and use; the reasoners
resemble spiders, who make cobwebs out of their own
substance. But the bee takes a middle course; it gathers
its material from the flowers of the garden and of the
field but transforms and digests it by a power of its own.*
SIR FRANCIS BACON

The article that follows, Jack L. Walker's "The Diffusion of Innovation Among the American States," operationally defined a familiar concept and used it to draw conclusions about the way federalism operates in the United States.

Use the outline below to mark in the margins of the article the skeleton of his research method.

1. The theoretical background of the study in what others have found about policy outcomes at the state level, regionalism, decision-making processes, and so on. From what disciplines does he draw his theory?

2. Locate (a) his conceptual definition of the dependent variable and (b) the operational definition. (c) Note where he explicitly avoids a value judgment. Is this appropriate?

3. For independent variables, note the use of data collected and operationally defined by others: (a) the Census, (b) other political scientists.

4. In Table 2 identify the independent variables and the dependent variable. How would you classify "time"?

5. In Table 4 identify the dependent variable, the independent variables and the control variables. The first column consists of zero-order partials, the next four of first-order partials. If Col. 1 values are designated by r_{ij}, Col. 2 by $r_{ij.k}$, Col. 3 by $r_{ij.l}$, how would you designate the values in the last column?

6. Note that factor analysis seeks to identify clusters of cases which are correlated on the same variables. The variables in this instance are the innovative policies; hence states

which are similar will show up with high loadings on the same factor. The higher the loading of a state, the more similar it is to other states in the same cluster in its innovation pattern. One then looks to see if the cluster is a regional one. Do the data support the hypothesis of regional emulation which he states?

7. What further propositions about innovation, emulation, regionalism, or the effect of government structure on decision-making does this article suggest to you? Formulate one hypothesis and suggest how data could be collected to test it.

8. If there were some policy innovation on which you placed a high value that could be implemented only through state action, on which states would you concentrate your efforts?

9. The 10 states that had revised their automobile insurance laws by 1972 were Connecticut and New Jersey ("no fault"), Maryland and Virginia (mandatory coverage), and Massachusetts, Florida, Delaware, Oregon, South Dakota, and Minnesota (other changes). Reduce Table 1 to an ordinal variable and test the proposition that states that have been innovative in the past would be in this group.

THE DIFFUSION OF INNOVATIONS AMONG
THE AMERICAN STATES*

JACK L. WALKER
University of Michigan

We are now in the midst of a notable revival of interest in the politics of the American states. During the last decade many studies have been conducted of the social, political and economic determinants of state policy outcomes.[1] Several of these writers have argued that the relative wealth of a state, its degree of industrialization, and other measures of social and economic development are more important in explaining its level of expenditures than such political factors as the form of legislative apportionment, the amount of party competition, or the degree of voter participation.[2] It has been claimed that

such factors as the level of personal income or the size of the urban population are responsible *both* for the degree of participation and party competition in a state, *and* the nature of the system's policy outputs. By making this argument these writers have called into question the concepts of representation and theories of party and group conflict which, in one form or another, are the foundations for much of American political science.[3]

There is a growing awareness, however, that levels of expenditure alone are not an adequate measure of public policy outcomes. Sharkansky has shown, for example, that levels of expenditure and levels of actual service are seldom correlated; presumably, some states are able to reach given service levels with much less expenditure than others.[4] Besides establishing the appropriate level of expenditure for a program, policy makers must also decide about the program's relative scope, provisions for appeal from administrative orders, eligibility requirements, the composition of regulatory boards and commissions, and many other matters which have little to do with money. Before we can evaluate the relative importance of structural and political factors as determinants of policy, therefore, we need to investigate decisions outside the budgetary process. In order to advance that object this study will focus on one of the most fundamental policy decisions of all: whether to initiate a program in the first place.

States have traditionally been judged according to the relative speed with which they have

* Thanks are due to the Committee on Governmental and Legal Processes of the Social Science Research Council, the Carnegie Corporation, the Michigan Legislative Intern Program, and the Rackham Faculty Research Fund of the University of Michigan for grants which made this study possible; to Mrs. Adarsh Trehan, Doyle Buckwalter, Michael Traugott, Mrs. Jennifer Drew Campbell, and Terry Bender who assisted in the collection and analysis of the data; and to H. Douglas Price, Rufus Browning, Warren Miller, Lawrence Mohr, Robert Friedman, Joel Aberbach, Robert Putnam, Ronald Brunner, Dennis Riley, Gail MacColl, and my wife, Linda Walker, whose criticisms and comments have helped me avoid several errors of inference and judgment.

[1] Beginning with Richard E. Dawson and James A. Robinson, "Inter-Party Competition, Economic Variables, and Welfare Policies in the American States," *Journal of Politics* (May, 1963), 265–289, there have been numerous articles and books on the subject. The most recent summary is: John H. Fenton and Donald W. Chamberlayne, "The Literature Dealing with the Relationships Between Political Processes, Socio-economic Conditions and Public Policies in the American States: A Bibliographical Essay," *Polity* (Spring, 1969), 388–394.

[2] For examples see: Herbert Jacob, "The Consequences of Malapportionment: A Note of Caution," *Social Forces* (1964), 260–266; the chapters by Robert Salisbury, Robert Friedman, Thomas Dye, and Dawson and Robinson in: Herbert Jacob and Kenneth Vines (eds.), *Politics in the American States: A Comparative Analysis* (Boston, 1965); Richard I. Hofferbert, "The Relation Between Public Policy and Some Structural and Environmental Variables in the American States," this REVIEW (March, 1966), 73–82; and Thomas

Dye, *Politics, Economics and the Public: Policy Outcomes in the American States* (Chicago, 1966).

[3] For an evaluation of the significance of this literature and its implications for political science see: Robert Salisbury, "The Analysis of Public Policy: A Search for Theories and Roles," in Austin Ranney (ed.), *Political Science and Public Policy* (Chicago, 1968), pp. 151–178.

[4] Ira Sharkansky, "Government Expenditures and Public Services in the American States," this REVIEW (1967), 1066–1077. Sharkansky also identifies important political variables in his: "Economic and Political Correlates of State Government Expenditures: General Tendencies and Deviant Cases," *Midwest Journal of Political Science* (1967), 173–192.

Source: Jack L. Walker, "The Diffusion of Innovations among the American States," *American Political Science Review*, 63 (September 1969), 880–899. Reprinted with the permission of the publisher and author.

accepted new ideas. Wisconsin, because of its leadership during the Progressive period and its early adoption of the direct primary, the legislative reference bureau, and workmen's compensation, gained a reputation as a pioneering state which it has never lost. Reputations of this kind are usually based only on random impressions and they may be inaccurate or misleading, but if it is true that some states change more readily than others a study of the way states adopt new ideas might lead to some important insights into the whole process of political change and development.

This essay is primarily an exercise in theory building. My aim is to develop propositions which might be used as guides to the study of the diffusion of innovations and which might also apply to budgeting and other forms of decision making.[5] Limitations in the data I have collected do not allow empirical testing of all the explanations I propose; the currently untestable propositions are presented in the hope that they may help in preparing the ground for future research. The study begins with an effort to devise a measure of the relative speed with which states adopt new programs. Once a measure of this phenomenon is created efforts are made to discover its principal demographic and political correlates. The article concludes with an effort to devise an explanation for the adoption of innovations based on insights gathered from studies of decision making, reference group theory, and the diffusion of innovations. The major questions being investigated are: (1) why do some states act as pioneers by adopting new

programs more readily than others, and once innovations have been adopted by a few pioneers, (2) how do these new forms of service or regulation spread among the American states?

I. DEFINITIONS AND DISTINCTIONS

Several terms have already been used here which have ambiguous meanings and it is important to make clear just how they are to be defined. The most important, and potentially misleading, is the term "innovation." An innovation will be defined simply as a program or policy which is new to the states adopting it, no matter how old the program may be or how many other states may have adopted it. Even though bureaucratic innovations or new departures by regulatory commissions or courts may be mentioned in the course of the discussion, the data used to measure the relative speed of adoption of innovations consists exclusively of legislative actions, simply because the data was readily available only in that form.

We are studying the relative speed and the spatial patterns of *adoption* of new programs, not their invention or creation. Invention, or bringing into being workable, relevant solutions to pressing problems, is an important activity and has been the subject of fascinating research.[6] We will concentrate on the way in which organizations select from proposed solutions the one which seems most suited to their needs, and how the organizations come to hear about these new ideas in the first place.[7] We are not trying to specify the circumstances under which new ideas or programs will be conceived or developed; we are studying instead the conditions under which state decision makers are most likely to adopt a new program.

The object of this analysis is the process of diffusion of ideas for new services or programs. Sometimes new legislation is virtually copied from other states. The California fair trade law, adopted in 1931, "was followed either verbatim or with minor variations by twenty states; in fact, ten states copied two serious typographical errors in the original California law."[8] No as-

[5] There is a well established body of research on the diffusion of innovations from which I have drawn many insights. For general reviews of this literature see: Everett M. Rogers, *Diffusion of Innovations* (New York, 1962), Elihu Katz, Martin L. Levin, and Herbert Hamilton, "Traditions of Research in the Diffusion of Innovations," *American Sociological Review* (1963), 237–252. For early attempts to study the American states from this perspective see: Ada J. Davis, "The Evolution of the Institution of Mothers' Pensions in the United States," *American Journal of Sociology* (1930), 573–582; Edgar C. McVoy, "Patterns of Diffusion in the United States," *American Sociological Review* (1940), 219–227; and E. H. Sutherland, "The Diffusion of Sexual Psychopath Laws," *American Journal of Sociology* (1950–51), 144–156. Also see: Torsten Hagerstrand, *Innovation Diffusion as a Spatial Process* (Chicago, 1967); and Robert Mason and Albert N. Halter, "The Application of a System of Simultaneous Equations to an Innovation Diffusion Model," *Social Forces* (1968), 182–193.

[6] For examples see: Gary A. Steiner (ed.), *The Creative Organization* (Chicago, 1965); and Tom Burns and G. M. Stalker, *The Management of Innovation* (London, 1961).

[7] There is much confusion over this distinction in the literature on diffusion. For an excellent discussion of the problem see: Lawrence B. Mohr, "Determinants of Innovation in Organizations," this REVIEW (1969), 111–126.

[8] Once the mistake was discovered, the Arkansas statute, which reproduced a model prepared by the National Association of Retail Druggists, was

sumption is being made, however, that the programs enacted in each state are always exactly alike or that new legislation is written in exactly the same way by every legislature. It is unlikely that the highway department established in Wisconsin in 1907 had the same organizational format as the one adopted by Wyoming in 1917, or that the council on the performing arts created in New York in 1960 bears an exact resemblance to the one created by Kentucky in 1966. In each case, however, a commitment was made to offer a new service, establish a new principle of regulation, or create an agency which had never existed before. Our concern is the origin and spread of the idea to provide public subsidies for the arts, not the detailed characteristics of institutions created in each state to implement the policy.

No ideological bias was employed in selecting issues for study. The patterns of diffusion for each issue have been treated equally, and no effort was made to develop any method of determining the relative importance or desirability of the programs.[9] Programs are sometimes enacted only to provide symbolic rewards to groups within the population and once created are left with inadequate funds or otherwise disabled.[10] Oklahoma's legislature, for example, emulated other states by creating a state civil rights commission, but once the commission was established, only $2,500 was appropriated for its operation.[11] For the purposes of this study, however, all adoptions are equal. My goal is to provide an explanation of the relative speed of adoption and the patterns of diffusion of innovations; I am not interested in the effectiveness of Oklahoma's civil rights commission, but in where the legislature got the idea to create such a commission and why it acted when it did.

II. THE INNOVATION SCORE

My first aim is to explain why some states

adopt innovations more readily than others. I assume that the pioneering states gain their reputations because of the speed with which they accept new programs. The study must begin, therefore, with an attempt to devise an innovation score that will represent the relative speed with which states adopt innovations.

The innovation score is based on the analysis of eighty-eight different programs (see the Appendix for a list) which were enacted by at least twenty state legislatures prior to 1965, and for which there was reliable information on the dates of adoption. In order to make the collection of programs as comprehensive and representative as possible, I adopted a list of basic issue areas similar to the one employed by the Council of State Governments in its bi-annual reports included in the *Book of the States.* I tried to study six to eight different pieces of legislation in each of these areas: welfare, health, education, conservation, planning, administrative organization, highways, civil rights, corrections and police, labor, taxes, and professional regulation. In the course of my analysis I studied issues ranging from the establishment of highway departments and the enactment of civil rights bills to the creation of state councils on the performing arts and the passage of sexual psychopath laws. Most of the programs were adopted during the twentith century, but sixteen of them diffused primarily during the latter half of the nineteenth century.

Once the eighty-eight lists of dates of adoption were collected they were used to create an innovation score for each state. The first step was to count the total number of years which elapsed between the first and last recorded legislative enactment of a program. Each state then received a number for each list which corresponded to the percentage of time which elapsed between the first adoption and its own acceptance of the program. For example, if the total time elapsing between the first and last adoption of a program was twenty years, and Massachusetts enacted the program ten years after the first adoption, then Massachusetts received a score of .500 on that particular issue. The first state to adopt the program received a score of .000 and the last state received a 1.000. In cases in which all the states have not yet adopted a program, the states without the program were placed last and given a score of 1.000.[12] The in-

copied either verbatim or with minor changes by seventeen states. Ewald T. Grether, *Price Control Under Fair Trade Legislation* (New York, 1937), pp. 19–20.

[9] In later work I will report the results of comparisons of the diffusion patterns of issues from different subject matter areas. Preliminary efforts at such comparisons, however, have not revealed significant variations. There does not seem to be much difference in the diffusion patterns of issues of different types.

[10] For a discussion of this phenomenon see: Murray Edelman, *The Symbolic Uses of Politics* (Urbana, 1964), chapters 2 and 9.

[11] Duane Lockard, *Toward Equal Opportunity* (New York, 1968), p. 23.

[12] The beginning point for the existence of each state was the date upon which it was officially organized as a territory. Using this system, Oklahoma is the last state to come into being, having been organized in 1890. If a program began its diffusion before a state came into existence, that

novation score for each state is simply 1.000 minus the average of the sum of the state's scores on all issues. The larger the innovation score, therefore, the faster the state has been, on the average, in responding to new ideas or policies. The issues may be divided into groups according to subject matter areas or time periods, and separate scores can be created for these smaller groupings of issues by following the same procedure. The results of this scoring procedure, using all eighty-eight issues, are presented in Table 1.

A note of caution should be sounded before the results of this exercise are analyzed. We are endeavoring to measure a highly complex process in which an enormous number of idiosyncratic influences are at work; an official with an unusually keen interest in a particular program, a chance reading of an article or book by a governor's aide, or any number of other circumstances peculiar to any one issue might lead to the rapid adoption of a piece of legislation by a state which is usually reluctant to accept new programs. Mississippi, which has the lowest average score and ranks last among the states in relative speed of adoption, was nonetheless the first state to adopt a general sales tax.

If this reservation is kept in mind, the data in Table I provide a crude outline of the standard or typical pattern of diffusion of new programs or policies among the American states. The states at the top of the list tend to adopt new programs much more rapidly than those at the bottom of the list. Having provided a preliminary measurement of this phenomenon, we must now try to explain it. Why should New York, California and Michigan adopt innovations more rapidly than Mississippi, Wyoming and South Dakota?

III. THE CORRELATES OF INNOVATION

Demographic Factors: After studying the acceptance of technological innovations by both individuals and organizations, several writers have concluded that the decision maker's relative wealth, or the degree to which "free floating" resources are available, are important determinants of the willingness to adopt new techniques or policies.[14] If "slack" resources are available, either in the form of money or a highly skilled, professional staff, the decision maker can afford the luxury of experiment and can more easily risk the possibility of failure.[15] Other studies, especially in the areas of agriculture and medicine, have also shown organizational size to be a strong correlate of innovation.[16] Given these results from prior studies in other fields we might expect to find

[14] Everett M. Rogers, *Diffusion of Innovations* (New York, 1962), pp. 40, 285–292. Also see: S. N. Eisenstadt, *The Political Systems of Empires* (New York, 1963), p. 27, 33–112.

[15] For a discussion of "slack" resources and innovation see: Richard M. Cyert and James G. March, *A Behavioral Theory of the Firm* (Englewood Cliffs, N.J., 1963), pp. 278–279.

[16] Rogers, *op. cit.,* Mohr, *op. cit.;* and also: Edwin Mansfield, "The Speed of Response of Firms to New Techniques," *Quarterly Journal of Economics* (1963), 293–304; Jerald Hage and Michael Aiken, "Program Change and Organizational Prop-

issue was not included in figuring the innovation score for the state.

[13] Alaska and Hawaii were omitted from the analysis because data for their years of adoption were often missing.

TABLE 1. COMPOSITE INNOVATION SCORES FOR THE AMERICAN STATES[13]

New York	.656	New Hampshire	.482	Idaho	.394
Massachusetts	.629	Indiana	.464	Tennessee	.389
California	.604	Louisiana	.459	West Virginia	.386
New Jersey	.585	Maine	.455	Arizona	.384
Michigan	.578	Virginia	.451	Georgia	.381
Connecticut	.568	Utah	.447	Montana	.378
Pennsylvania	.560	North Dakota	.444	Missouri	.377
Oregon	.544	North Carolina	.430	Delaware	.376
Colorado	.538	Kansas	.426	New Mexico	.375
Wisconsin	.532	Nebraska	.425	Oklahoma	.368
Ohio	.528	Kentucky	.419	South Dakota	.363
Minnesota	.525	Vermont	.414	Texas	.362
Illinois	.521	Iowa	.413	South Carolina	.347
Washington	.510	Alabama	.406	Wyoming	.346
Rhode Island	.503	Florida	.397	Nevada	.323
Maryland	.482	Arkansas	.394	Mississippi	.298

that the larger, wealthier states, those with the most developed industrial economies and the largest cities, would have the highest innovation scores. It would seem likely that the great cosmopolitan centers in the country, the places where most of the society's creative resources are concentrated, would be the most adaptive and sympathetic to change, and thus the first to adopt new programs.

In order to test these assumptions several measures of social and economic development were correlated with the innovation score. As we can see in Table 2, there is evidence that the larger, wealthier, more industrialized states adopt new programs somewhat more rapidly than their smaller, less well-developed neighbors. Fairly strong relationships exist between the innovation score and the value added by manufacturing, the average per acre value of farms, the size of the urban population, and the average per capita income. These relationships remain virtually unchanged in all time periods. In fact, the only relationship which changes substantially over time is that between innovation and the percentage of illiterates in the population which declines steadily across the three time periods. This declining relationship and the low correlation between innovation and the median school year completed is caused primarily by the states in the Rocky Mountain region which have the highest rankings on median school years completed and yet are among the slowest to adopt new programs.[17] The median of educa-

erties: A Comparative Analysis," *American Journal of Sociology* (1967), 516–517; and Richard J. Hall, S. Eugene Haas, and Norman J. Johnson, "Organizational Size, Complexity and Formalization," *American Sociological Review* (1967), 903–912.

[17] Regional affects of this kind appear frequently in analyses of data from the American states. In many studies, especially those which involve measures of political participation or party competition, strong relationships appear which are actually only a result of the distinctive nature of the southern states. In order to insure that the correlations in this analysis were not merely a result of the social and political peculiarities of the South, the eleven states of the confederacy were removed from all distributions. Since the Southern states do not cluster at one extreme of the innovation scale, no great changes occurred in correlation coefficients based upon data from the thirty-nine states outside the South. Within the eleven Southern states, however, almost all the relationships were substantially reduced in size. Because only eleven states are involved, this fact is difficult to inter-

tional attainment in the states with the highest innovation scores is pulled down by the presence of a large, poorly educated, lower class, living primarily in the inner cities. The highly industrialized states with large urban concentrations are characterized by great inequality of social status and attainment. It would seem, however, that the elements necessary to foster innovation are present in these states even though they do not have highest average level of educational achievement.

Political Factors: Although students of policy

TABLE 2. CORRELATIONS BETWEEN INNOVATION SCORES AND FIVE SOCIAL AND ECONOMIC VARIABLES, BY TIME PERIODS

Social-Economic Variables	Innovation Scores*			Composite Score
	1870–1899	1900–1929	1930–1966	
Per Cent Population Urban:	.62**	.69	.62	.63
Total Population:	.52	.40	.50	.59
Average Income, Per Capita:	—***	.62	.50	.55
Value Added Per Capita by Manufacturing	.46	.55	.57	.66
Average Value, Per Acre, of Farms:	.70	.52	.52	.54
Per Cent Population Illiterate:	—.58	—.44	—.12	—.23
Median School Years Completed:	—***	—***	.24	.26

* In order to insure that the innovation score and the social and economic variables came from comparable periods, separate innovation scores were calculated for three time periods: 1870–1899, 1900–1929, and 1930–1966. In constructing this table each innovation was placed in the time period during which the first ten states adopted it. Thus, if a program was adopted by only four states during the 1890's, and completed its diffusion during the 1900's, the program is placed in the second time period: 1900–1929, even though its first adoptions took place during the nineteenth century. Social and economic data are taken from the years 1900, 1930, and 1960. The composite score is correlated with social and economic data from 1960.

** The table entries are Pearson product-moment correlations.

*** Measures of these phenomena corresponding with these time periods do not exist.

pret, but will be treated more fully in later work. For an example of this problem discussed in another context see: Raymond Wolfinger and John Osgood Field, "Political Ethos and the Structure of City Government," this REVIEW (1966), 306–326. For a more extensive discussion of the methodological implications see the discussion of "interaction effects" in Hugh Donald Forbes and Edward R. Tufte, "A Note of Caution in Causal Modelling," this REVIEW (1968), pp. 1261–1262; and the communication from Dennis D. Riley and Jack L. Walker, this REVIEW (September, 1969), pp. 880–899.

making have begun to doubt the importance of the political system as an independent determinant of the behavior of decision makers, it seems likely that both the degree of party competition and a state's system of legislative apportionment would affect its readiness to accept change. It would seem that parties which often faced closely contested elections would try to out-do each other by embracing the newest, most progressive programs and this would naturally encourage the rapid adoption of innovations. Lowi argues that new departures in policy are more likely at the beginning of a new administration, especially when a former minority party gains control of the government.[18] If this tendency exists it would also seem likely that state political systems which allow frequent turnover and offer the most opportunities to capture high office would more often develop the circumstances in which new programs might be adopted.[19]

Another prerequisite for the rapid adoption of new programs might be a system of legislative apportionment which fully represented the state's urban areas and which did not grant veto power to groups opposed to change. Such a system might be expected to allow consideration and debate of new policies and programs in all areas. Some recent findings, such as Barber's study of legislators in Connecticut,[20] lead us to speculate that representatives from newly developing urban and suburban areas would be more cosmopolitan, better informed, and more toler-

---

TABLE 3. CORRELATIONS BETWEEN INNOVATION SCORES AND MEASURES OF POLITICAL VARIABLES, BY TIME PERIODS

Political Variables*	Innovation Scores			Composite Score
	1870–1899	1900–1929	1930–1966	
Party Competition for Governorship:	.36	.02	.14	.24
David-Eisenberg Index of Malapportionment:	**	.07	.55	.65

* The Index of party competition used in this table is the per cent of the total vote going to the gubernatorial candidate coming in second, times 2. This yields a scale from 0 to 100. It was created by Richard Hofferbert. The apportionment Index appears in Paul T. David and Ralph Eisenberg, *Devaluation of the Urban and Suburban Vote* (Charlottesville: Bureau of Public Administration, University of Virginia, 1961).

** Measures of this phenomenon corresponding with this time period do not exist.

---

ant of change. If nothing else, urban legislators would probably be more willing to deal with problems of sanitation, planning, transportation, and housing peculiar to large metropolitan areas.

No matter what the composition of the legislator's constituency, however, it would seem that the presence of competent staff, superior clerical facilities, and supporting services would allow him to give serious consideration to a larger number of new proposals. Several studies of the diffusion of technological innovations have demonstrated that the best informed individuals are most likely to pioneer in the use of new techniques or tools,[21] and so the states which provide the most extensive staff and research facilities in their legislatures ought to pioneer in the adoption of new programs.[22]

In Table 3 efforts to test some of these hypotheses in different time periods are displayed. Measures of political variables are usually based on evidence only from contemporary periods because data are seldom available on state and local elections or the operation of legislatures in earlier decades. Measures are available, however, for the degree of party competition and the ex-

---

[18] Theodore Lowi, "Toward Functionalism in Political Science: The Case of Innovation in Party Systems," this REVIEW (1963), 570–583. Evidence which seems to confirm Lowi's theory may be found in: Charles W. Wiggens, "Party Politics in the Iowa Legislature," *Midwest Journal of Political Science* (1967), 60–69; and Frank M. Bryan, "The Metamorphosis of a Rural Legislature," *Polity* (1968), 191–212.

[19] Joseph A. Schlesinger has developed an index of the "general opportunity level" in each state. The index measures the relative number of chances which exist in each state to achieve major political office. See: *Ambition and Politics: Political Careers in the United States* (Chicago, 1966), pp. 37–56.

[20] James D. Barber, *The Lawmakers: Recruitment and Adaptation to Legislative Life* (New Haven, 1965). For testimony from legislators about the importance of reapportionment see: Frank M. Bryan, "Who is Legislating," *National Civic Review* (December, 1967), 627–633; Allan Dines, "A Reapportioned State," *National Civic Review* (February, 1966), 70–74, 99.

[21] Rogers, *op. cit.* Also see: Mansfield, *op. cit.*; James S. Coleman, Elihu Katz, and Herbert Menzel, *Medical Innovation: A Diffusion Study* (Indianapolis, 1966); and John W. Loy, Jr., "Social Psychological Characteristics of Innovators," *American Sociological Review* (1969), 73–82.

[22] For a somewhat different view see: Norman Meller, "Legislative Staff Services: Toxin, Specific, or Placebo for the Legislature's Ills," *The Western Political Quarterly* (June, 1967), 381–389.

tent of legislative malapportionment.[23] As we can see in Table 3 party competitiveness does not seem to be consistently related to the innovation score, at least as it is measured here.[24] Legislative apportionment is not correlated with the innovation score in the 1900–1929 period, but is related in the 1930–1966 period. Since legislatures steadily became less representative of urban populations after 1930, it may be that we have here some empirical evidence of the impact of malapportionment on policy making in the states.

Recent studies of state expenditures have shown that the explanatory effects of political variables could be eliminated if statistical controls for social and economic variables were applied. Therefore, in Table 4 I have presented both the zero-order correlations of the composite innovation score with measures of party competition, turnover in office, legislative apportionment, and legislative professionalism,[25] and

[22] There is one other index in existence which deals with political phenomenon: Rodney Mott's Index of Judicial Prestige. The Mott index measures the degree to which state supreme courts were used as models by the legal profession. It is based on a study of citations in federal Supreme Court decisions and all state supreme court decisions, the number of cases reprinted in standard textbooks, and the opinion of a panel of prominent legal scholars; it covers the period 1900 to 1930. The Mott index and the innovation score from the same time period are correlated at .62. This finding might be interpreted to mean that emulative behavior in the judicial arena is not much different from that in the legislative arena. For details of the Judicial Prestige Index see: Rodney L. Mott, "Judicial Influence," this REVIEW (1936), 295–315.

[24] Data for this table was derived from Richard Hofferbert's collection, "American State Socioeconomic, Electoral, and Policy Data: 1890–1960" which he has graciously allowed me to use.

[23] The sources are: Richard Hofferbert, "Classification of American State Party Systems," Journal of Politics (1964), 550–567; Dennis Riley and Jack L. Walker, "Problems of Measurement and Inference in the Study of the American States" (Paper delivered at the Institute of Public Policy Studies, University of Michigan, 1968); David and Eisenberg, op. cit.; Glendon Shubert and Charles Press, "Measuring Malapportionment," this REVIEW (1964), 302–327, and corrections, 968–970; Schlesinger, op. cit.; and John Grumm, "Structure and Policy in the Legislature," (Paper presented at the Southwestern Social Science Association Meetings, 1967).

TABLE 4. RELATIONSHIPS BETWEEN THE COMPOSITE INNOVATION SCORE AND MEASURES OF LEGISLATIVE APPORTIONMENT AND PARTY COMPETITION

| | | Partials | | | | |
	Zero-Order	Value Added Manufacturing	Per Cent Urban	Total Population	Per Capita Income	Four Factors Combined
Apportionment						
David-Eisenberg Index	.65	.47	.64	.67	.60	.58
Schubert-Press Index	.26	.12	.34	.31	.26	.21
Party Competition						
Hofferbert Index	.54	.35	.34	.50	.26	.12
Riley-Walker Index —Gov.	.40	.33	.22	.47	.09	.17
Riley-Walker Index —Legis.	.31	.24	.17	.34	.04	.07
Turnover in Office						
Schlesinger Index of Opportunity	.53	.40	.39	.32	.34	.24
Legislative Services						
Grumm's Index of Legislative Professionalism	.63	.38	.33	.41	.51	.11

also partial correlations with four social and economic variables controlled. The control variables are value added by manufacturing, per cent urban population, total population size, and per capita personal income, all of which earlier proved to be independently related to the innovation score. In Table 4 the effect of each control variable is displayed separately along with the combined impact of all four. The results tend to corroborate earlier analyses which minimize the independent effects of these political variables on policy outcomes. The Schlesinger index of opportunity, which measures the difference among the states in the average number of times major offices have changed hands, and the Hofferbert index of inter-party competition seem to have some independent impact on innovation, although it is greatly weakened when all four control variables are combined. This finding lends some credence to Lowi's argument that turnover in office fosters change.

Certainly, the most important result depicted in this table is the consistent strength of the correlation between innovation and the David and Eisenberg index of urban representation.[26] Earlier studies, using expenditures as a measure of policy outcomes, have consistently found that apportionment has little importance as an explanatory variable.[27] Our findings indicate that apportionment does make a difference where innovation is concerned. Although the other political factors do not have great independent impact on innovation, the clear implication arising from Tables 3 and 4 is that those states which grant their urban areas full representation in the legislature seem to adopt new

[26] Although much simpler than the Schubert and Press measure, the David and Eisenberg index seems to have more relevance to political outcomes. Thomas Dye had the same experience. See Dye, *op. cit.*, pp. 19–20, 63–69, 112–114, 146–148, 174–177, 236–237, 270–281.

[27] Herbert Jacob, "The Consequences of Malapportionment: A Note of Caution," *Social Forces* (1964), 260–266; Thomas R. Dye, "Malapportionment and Public Policy in the States," *Journal of Politics* (1965), 586–601; Richard I. Hofferbert, "The Relation Between Public Policy and Some Structural and Environmental Variables in the American States," this REVIEW (1966), 73–82; David Brady and Douglas Edmonds; "One Man, One Vote—So What?" *Trans-action* (March, 1967), 41–46. A recent article calls some of the conclusions of this research into question: Alan G. Pulsipher and James L. Weatherby, Jr., "Malapportionment, Party Competition, and the Functional Distribution of Governmental Expenditures," this REVIEW (1968), 1207–1219.

ideas more rapidly, on the average, than states which discriminate against their cities.

Given the results of this correlational analysis, we might conclude that New York, California and Michigan adopt new programs more rapidly than Mississippi, Wyoming, and South Dakota primarily because they are bigger, richer, more urban, more industrial, have more fluidity and turnover in their political systems, and have legislatures which more adequately represent their cities. Although these findings are important, they leave many important questions unanswered. The political system does not react automatically in response to the growth of manufacturing industries or to the increase in the percentage of the population living in cities. Developments of this kind obviously cause problems which public officials might try to solve, but the mere presence of such a stimulant does not cause public officials to act, nor does it determine the form the solution will take, or which state might act first to meet the problem. Our analysis has provided us with evidence that change and experimentation are more readily accepted in the industrialized, urban, cosmopolitan centers of the country, but we have not improved our understanding of the institutions and decision-making processes which cause strong statistical relationships between industrial output and innovation. Also, we have not explained the way innovations spread from the pioneering states to those with lower innovation scores. In order to develop explanations of these processes we must go beyond the search for demographic correlates of innovation and develop generalizations which refer to the behavior of the men who actually make the choices in which we are interested.

IV. POLITICAL SCIENCE AND INNOVATION

In one form or another, interest group theories, based on self-regulating systems of countervailing power, are at the heart of much of the recent research into American politics.[28] Studies of the legislative process in the United States, for example, have been strongly influenced by theories which emphasize the importance of the

[28] Examples of this general approach to policy making are: David B. Truman, *The Governmental Process* (New York, 1960); Edward Banfield, *Political Influence* (New York, 1961); and Richard E. Neustadt, *Presidential Power* (New York, 1960). For an excellent critique of theories which employ concepts of power as a major explanatory variable see: James G. March, "The Power of Power," in David Easton (ed.), *Varieties of Political Theory* (Englewood Cliffs, 1966), pp. 39–70.

group basis of politics. Beginning with the efforts of A. Lawrence Lowell[29] political scientists have worked to discover the basic factions within the legislature and have striven to develop operational definitions of power or influence.[30] Extensive efforts have been made to isolate and measure the various influences which come to bear on the individual legislator and motivate him to join one or another legislative bloc: what is a legislator's most important source of cues; is it a lobbyist with whom he has close connections, his party leaders, members of his constituency, the governor, or members of his own family? What impact on his attitudes does the legislative institution itself have; do its informal rules and traditions affect the legislator's decisions, and if so, in what way?[31] Great emphasis has been placed on the analysis of roll-call votes and several sophisticated research techniques have been developed to pursue this work, ranging from Beyle's cluster bloc analysis and Guttman scaling to the more complex, computerized routines presently in use.[32] But all this machinery is useful only in studying those roll-calls which cause divisions in the house; all unanimous votes, nearly eighty per cent of the total in most legislatures, are ignored. Riker has devised a technique in which he uses the percentage of the total membership which is present for the vote and the closeness of the division to determine the relative significance of roll-call votes in legislatures. The more legislators present and the closer the vote, the more significant the issue involved.[33] The full attention of the researcher is thus focused on the relatively small number of decisions which cause significant disagreements, because it is assumed that these are the most important votes; at least, they are the only ones which will provide clues to "the conflicting forces and pressures at work in the legislative system,"[34] and the discovery of those forces and pressures, according to the group theory of politics, is the principal object of political science.

One of the main purposes in this study is to develop an approach to governmental policy making which will serve as a guide in the analysis of *all* legislative decisions, the unanimous as well as the contested ones, and which will lead as well to a better understanding of decisions made by bureaucrats, political executives and other governmental officials. Rather than focus upon the patterns of conflict among factions within the legislature or the administrative agencies, I will search for the criteria employed by legislators and administrators in deciding whether a proposal is worthy of consideration in the first place. This search rests on the belief that whoever the decision maker may be, whether administrator, lobbyist, party leader, governor or legislator, and however controversial a particular issue may become, a set of general criteria exists in every state which establishes broad guidelines for policy making. Regardless of the interests supporting an innovation, no matter whether the decision system is primarily monolithic or pluralistic, if a proposal for change does not fall within those guidelines its chances for acceptance are slim. Many of the propositions I will develop cannot be verified until they are tested with evidence from individual decision makers;[35] they are presented here only as a first, tentative step toward a more comprehensive theory of governmental policy making.

V. EMULATION AND DECISION MAKING IN THE STATES

We are searching for answers to three major questions: 1) why do certain states consistently adopt new programs more rapidly than other states, 2) are there more or less stable patterns of diffusion of innovations among the American states, and 3) if so, what are they? Our answers to these questions will be founded, in part, on the theories of organizational decision making developed in recent years by writers like Simon, March, Cyert and Lindblom.[36] At the

[29] A. Lawrence Lowell, "The Influence of Party Upon Legislation," *Annual Report of the American Historical Association* (1911), pp. 321–543.

[30] The best example is: Robert Dahl, "The Concept of Power," *Behavioral Science* (1957), pp. 201–215.

[31] For the best general review of the results of research on the legislative process, see: Malcolm E. Jewell and Samuel C. Patterson, *The Legislative Process in the United States* (New York, 1966).

[32] For a discussion of these techniques see: Lee F. Anderson, Meridith W. Watts, Jr. and Allen R. Wilcox, *Legislative Roll-Call Analysis* (Evanston, 1966). Also see Jewell and Patterson, *op. cit.*, pp. 528–550.

[33] William H. Riker, "A Method for Determining the Significance of Roll Calls in Voting Bodies," in John C. Wahlke and Heinz Eulau (eds.), *Legislative Behavior* (Glencoe, 1959), pp. 337–383.

[34] Jewell and Patterson, *op. cit.*, p. 416.

[35] Thanks to a grant from the Carnegie Corporation I have been able to launch a pilot study involving interviews in several states.

[36] I refer to: Herbert Simon, *Administrative Behavior*, Second Edition (New York, 1957); Richard M. Cyert and James C. March, *A Behavioral*

329

heart of these theories is the concept of the decision maker struggling to choose among complex alternatives and constantly receiving much more information concerning his environment than he is able to digest and evaluate. An ordinary decision maker, required to make frequent choices and faced with an inconclusive flood of reports, programs, suggestions and memos, must simplify his task in some way. According to Simon, he does not—cannot—search in every case for the best possible solution to the problems he faces; he has neither the time nor the energy. Instead, he makes decisions by searching until he finds an alternative which he believes is good enough to preserve whatever values are important to him. The limits of rationality imposed by human capacities prevent him from maximizing his benefits in every situation; rather, he "satisfices," or chooses a course of action which seems satisfactory under the circumstances.

The individual in a complex organization, therefore, does not deal directly with all the sources of information potentially available to him, nor does he evaluate every conceivable policy option. In place of the debilitating confusion of reality he creates his own abstract, highly simplified world containing only a few major variables. In order to achieve this manageable simplicity he adopts a set of decision rules or standard criteria for judgment which remain fairly stable over time and which guide him in choosing among sources of information and advice. A decision maker decides both where to look for cues and information and how to choose among alternatives according to his decision rules; these rules also embody the current goals and aspirations of his organization, or the values which the organization is designed to advance and protect. Hence, if we wish to predict the decision maker's behavior, we should try to discover these rules of thumb, or "heuristics" as they are sometimes called, which shape his judgment. His choices could then be explained in terms of the alternatives he considers, his knowledge of each alternative, the sources of his knowledge, and the standard decision rules he applies in cases of this kind.[37]

Taking cues from these theories of human choice and organizational decision making our explanation of the adoption of innovations by the states is based on the assertion that state officials make most of their decisions by analogy. The rule of thumb they employ might be formally stated as follows: *look for an analogy between the situation you are dealing with and some other situation, perhaps in some other state, where the problem has been successfully resolved.*[38]

We are looking to what has been called the "inter-organizational context."[39] or the *horizontal* relationships among the states within the federal system, for the principal influences which regulate the speed of adoption and the patterns of diffusion of innovations. Most of the existing work on intergovernmental relations and federalism concentrates on the question of centralization within the American system of government. In line with the general interest of most political scientists in the factors which affect the access of organized groups and the lines of authority within a political system, many writers are concerned with the virtues of centralization or decentralization and try to determine how much of either exists in the system. They have studied primarily the *vertical* relationships among national, state and local governments, and have usually identified the party system and its demands as the institutional influence most responsible for maintaining the present, decentralized, federal relationships.[40] I want to focus attention on the mutual perceptions and relationships among state governments and to show how

ory of Organizations," in Robert E. L. Faris (ed.), *Handbook of Modern Sociology* (Chicago, 1964), pp. 485–529.

[38] Decision rules of this kind are mentioned in both Taylor, *op. cit.,* pp. 73–74; and Cyert and March, *op. cit.,* especially pp. 34–43.

[39] William M. Evan, "The Organization-Set: Toward a Theory of Inter-Organizational Relations," in James D. Thompson (ed.) *Approaches to Organizational Design* (Pittsburgh, 1966), pp. 173–191.

[40] Some recent examples are: William Anderson, *The Nation and the States, Rivals or Partners?* (Minneapolis, 1955); M. J. C. Vile, *The Structure of American Federalism* (London, 1961); William Riker, *Federalism: Origin, Operation, Significance* (Boston, 1964); Daniel J. Elazar, *American Federalism: A View From the States* (New York, 1966); Morton Grodzins, *The American System* (Chicago, 1966). For a general critique see: A. H. Birch, "Approaches to the Study of Federalism." *Political Studies* (1966), 15–33.

Theory of the Firm (Englewood Cliffs, N.J. 1963); and Charles E. Lindblom, *The Intelligence of Democracy* (New York, 1965).

[37] For a comprehensive review of the literature on decision making see: Donald W. Taylor, "Decision Making and Problem Solving," and Julia Feldman and Herschel E. Kanter, "Organizational Decision Making," in James G. March (ed.) *Handbook of Organizations* (Chicago, 1965), pp. 48–86, 614–649. Also see: W. Richard Scott, "The-

these relationships affect the behavior of state decision makers.[41]

One of the most common arguments used in state legislatures against raising taxes or passing measures designed to regulate business is the fear that such measures might retard industrial development or force marginal plants to leave the state. Lawmakers often are called upon to deal with the problems which arise when one or two states establish extremely permissive standards for the granting of licenses, such as the corporation laws in New Jersey and Delaware, or the divorce laws in Nevada. However, interstate competition does not always drive standards down; it has a positive side as well. State decision makers are constantly looking to each other for guides to action in many areas of policy, such as the organization and management of higher education, or the provision of hospitals and public health facilities. In fact, I am arguing that this process of competition and emulation, or cuetaking, is an important phenomenon which determines in large part the pace and direction of social and political change in the American states.[42]

[41] This is not the first study to discover the important role of emulation and competition in the development of public policy. Richard Hofferbert in: "Ecological Development and Policy Change in the American States," *Midwest Journal of Political Science* (1966), p. 485; and Ira Sharkansky in: "Regionalism, Economic Status and the Public Policies of American States," *Southwestern Social Science Quarterly* (1968) both mention the influence of other states in the calculations of state decision makers. Several earlier students of local government complained that sparsely populated, arid Western states had blindly copied from the heavily populated Eastern states forms of local government which were inappropriately suited for the conditions prevailing in the Great Plains. See: A. Bristol Goodman, "Westward Movement of Local Government," *The Journal of Land and Public Utility Economics* (1944), pp. 20–34; Herman Walker, Jr. and Peter L. Hansen, "Local Government and Rainfall," this Review (1946), 1113–1123. Robert L. Crain has recently used emulation as a principal explanatory variable in his study of the spread of water fluoridation programs among American cities: "Fluoridation: The Diffusion of an Innovation Among Cities," *Social Forces* (1966), 467–476; as did Thomas M. Scott in his: "The Diffusion of Urban Governmental Forms as a Case of Social Learning," *The Journal of Politics* (1968), 1091–1108.

[42] This set of hypotheses is consistent with more general theories concerning the manner in which human beings formulate judgments and establish

Uncertainty and the fear of unanticipated consequences have always been formidable barriers to reform. Proponents of new programs have always had to combat the arguments of those who predict dire consequences if some innovation is adopted. Even though American history is full of cases where the opponents of change have later had to admit that the dangers they feared never materialized, inertia and the unwillingness to take risks have prevented a more rapid rate of change.

Inertia can more easily be overcome, however, if the proponent of change can point to the successful implementation of his program in some other similar setting. If a legislator introduces a bill which would require the licensing of probation officers, for example, and can point to its successful operation in a neighboring state, his chances of gaining acceptance are markedly increased. As Harsanyi has asserted:

. . . it is not an overstatement to say that a very considerable part of the social values of most societies is based on sheer ignorance. . . . One of the reasons why other persons' example is so important in encouraging changes in people's values and behavior lies in the fact that it tends to dispel some groundless fears about the dismal consequences that such changes might entail. Another reason is of course that people can more easily face the possible hostility of the supporters of the old values if they are not alone in making the change.[43]

In fact, once a program has been adopted by a large number of states it may become recognized as a legitimate state responsibility, something which all states ought to have. When this happens it becomes extremely difficult for state decision makers to resist even the weakest kinds of demands to institute the program for fear of arousing public suspicions about their good intentions; once a program has gained the stamp of legitimacy, it has a momentum of its own. As Lockard found in studying the passage of Fair Employment Practices laws the actions of other states are sometimes key factors in prompting

expectations in all areas of life. See: Leon Festinger, "A Theory of Social Comparison Processes," *Human Relations* (1954), 117–140; and Robert Merton, *Social Theory and Social Structure* (Rev. Ed.; Glencoe, 1957), pp. 225–420.

[43] John C. Harsanyi, "Rational Choice Models v. Functionalistic and Conformistic Models of Political Behavior," (Paper delivered at American Political Science Association Meetings, 1967), p. 17.

reluctant politicians to accept controversial programs.

Pressure mounted in New Jersey during 1944 and 1945 for some stronger policy, and when New York passed its FEP law certain key politicians in New Jersey decided to act. Governor Walter E. Edge concluded, apparently reluctantly, that he had to commit himself to such a law. "As the session drew to a close," Edge wrote in his autobiography, "minority racial and religious groups pressed for adoption of an antidiscrimination program. While it was a subject which I would have preferred to give greater study, politically it could not be postponed because New York had passed a similar measure and delay would be construed as a mere political expedient."[44]

For similar reasons there have been numerous efforts to enact a program of homesteading in Hawaii as a way of disposing of its arable public lands even though the circumstances there are quite different from other states where homesteading was successfully introduced.[45] And in Connecticut one of the most powerful arguments in favor of introducing the direct primary system during the 1950's was simply that all the other states had adopted one.[46]

The Connecticut case neatly illustrates some of the generalizations we are developing. Lockard points out that the leaders of both political parties privately opposed the introduction of a primary system but felt that an endorsement of the idea had to be put into their platforms to avoid having their opponents charge them with "bossism." Demands for the primary came for the most part from small groups in the state's suburban areas which were interested in the issue as "a consequence of the influx of migrants from states with primaries."[47] Speaking as a professional political scientist as well as a legislator, Lockard was well suited to counter the extreme fears expressed by the party leaders who predicted that party organizations would be completely destroyed if primaries were introduced. Lockard reasoned by analogy to the experience in other states both in countering the opponents of change and in shaping his own moderate position:

I expressed my considerable doubts about the

effect of party primaries on party organization. From observations of politics in some of the most thoroughgoing party primary states, [however,] it seemed that the party organizations had been shattered with many undesirable consequences. In my campaign I expressed support only for a limited form of a primary and not one calculated to wreck the party system.[48]

Events like these illustrate the way in which the agenda of controversy in a state is determined, at least in part, by developments in other states, and they also show how experiences and examples from outside the system help to overcome the natural reluctance of any institutional structure to risk the consequences of change. The constituent units of any federal system are under considerable pressure to conform with national and regional standards or accepted administrative procedures. These norms result primarily from the processes of emulation and competition we have described and also from the efforts of nationally organized interest groups. They are affected also by the growth and development of professional organizations and other forms of communication among state administrators, and the natural circulation of active, politically involved citizens among the states, such as the Connecticut suburbanites who began agitating for a primary system in their adopted political home.

VI. REGIONAL REFERENCE GROUPS AND
STANDARDS OF EVALUATION

Nationally accepted standards or norms provide a convenient measure which can be used by interested citizens or political leaders to judge the adequacy of services offered in their own states. But these norms have an ambiguous influence on the performance of state governments. On the one hand, the existence of national standards probably encourages *higher* performance among the *poorer* members of the federation than we could expect if functions and service levels were established independently within each unit of government, solely as a result of internal demands. An example of this tendency was discovered by May in his study of Canadian federalism:

Newfoundland chose for a long time to remain outside the Canadian federation, thus not subjecting itself to the forces of national reorientation, and when, after joining the Dominion, a royal commission reported on its financial position, the commission observed that Newfoundland's public services were very backward in re-

[44] Duane Lockard, *Toward Equal Opportunity* (New York, 1968), pp. 20–21.

[45] Allan Spitz, "The Transplantation of American Democratic Institutions," *Political Science Quarterly* (1967), 386–398.

[46] Duane Lockard, *Connecticut's Challenge Primary: A Study in Legislative Politics* (Eagleton Case #7, New York, 1959).

[47] *Ibid.*, p. 2.

[48] *Ibid.*, p. 22.

lation to those of the other provinces, including even the maritimes. . . .[49]

In the United States, Mississippi, Vermont, and North Dakota are good examples of relatively poor states which are making unusually large efforts to bring their public services into closer approximation of national standards. But, on the other hand, national standards and norms can have a *conservative* impact, especially in the richer, industrial states which are able to provide services somewhat above the national averages with relatively little effort.[50] Hansen complains of this tendency when he points out that:

Some northern states fall considerably below their northern neighboring states in public service standards. . . . Their fiscal problems arise not because they are poor but because their tax levels are low by northern standards. This is notably true for example of a tier of large industrial states—Illinois, Indiana, Ohio and Pennsylvania. . . . These states are not excessively hard pressed by tax burdens relative to the country as a whole.[51]

This statement by Hansen is drawn from an essay in which he expresses disapproval of what he considers the inadequate public services of large industrial states which have relatively low tax burdens. But the statement we have cited contains several ambiguities. For example, Hansen charges that "some northern states fall considerably below their northern neighboring states in public service standards," but then he specifically points as examples to Illinois, Indiana, Ohio, and Pennsylvania, states which border on each other. It is not clear whether we are being asked to compare these states to their neighbors, to other northern states with higher tax burdens, or to "the country as a whole." Within Illinois, however, the states' decision makers are probably comparing their own performance with their counterparts in Indiana, Ohio, Pennsylvania or New Jersey. Officials in Illinois may know of the procedures and performance levels in New York or California, but they are unlikely to think of events in these states as legitimate guides to action.[52]

When examining the public policy of any state, therefore, it is important to discover in which "league" it has chosen to play. For example, Salisbury, in a statement much like Hansen's, reasons by analogy in arguing that Missouri does not provide as much aid for its schools as its potential resources might warrant. He points out that in 1959 the "state ranked 18th in per capita income but 38th in per capita expenditure for local schools."[53] This relatively low level of support seems to result from the correspondingly low aspirations of the officials of the Missouri State Teachers Association who, according to Salisbury, "have chosen to get what they can with a minimum of agitation or conflict rather than attempt broader public campaigns in behalf of larger objectives."[54] The officials of MSTA "are fully conscious of the gap between the Missouri school aid level and that of, say, neighboring Illinois," but they are quick to point out "that by comparison with other neighboring states—Arkansas, Oklahoma, or Nebraska, for example—Missouri's record is much more impressive."[55] It would seem from this example that Missouri's leaders, at least those concerned with public education, are emulating and competing primarily with the states to their south and west, rather than with the Great Lakes states to their north and east, or the Rocky Mountain states, the Deep South or the Far West. The choice of relatively poor states like Arkansas and Oklahoma as the principal, legitimate reference groups establishes an upper limit of aspirations which is considerably below that which might exist if Missouri's accepted basis for comparison were the public services of Illinois, Wisconsin or Michigan.

VI. REGIONAL GROUPINGS AMONG THE STATES

We have come far enough in our analysis to see that our original presentation of the innovation scores in Table 1 as a linear distribution masked some pertinent information. A more useful representation of the data, which would con-

[49] Ronald J. May, *Financial Inequality Between States in a Federal System* (unpublished doctoral dissertation submitted to Nuffield College, Oxford University, 1966), p. 168.

[50] For a somewhat similar argument concerning government spending see: Anthony Downs, "Why the Government Budget is too Small in a Democracy," *World Politics* (July, 1960), 541–563.

[51] Alvin H. Hansen, *The Postwar American Economy: Performance and Problems* (New York, 1964), pp. 30–31.

[52] For evidence of this perspective, see Thomas J. Anton, *The Politics of State Expenditure in Illinois* (Urbana, 1966), p. 263.

[53] Nicholas A. Masters, Robert Salisbury, and Thomas H. Eliot, *State Politics and the Public Schools* (New York, 1964), p. 12.

[54] *Ibid.*, p. 25.

[55] *Ibid.*, p. 21. For a similar discussion of the importance of aspirations in determining the speed with which innovations are adopted see: Rufus P. Browning, "Innovative and Noninnovative Decision Processes in Government Budgeting," in Robert T. Golembiewski (ed.), *Public Budgeting and Finance* (Itasca, Illinois, 1968), pp. 128–145.

form more closely to the actual patterns of diffusion, would have to be in the form of a tree. At the top of the tree would be a set of pioneering states which would be linked together in a national system of emulation and competition. The rest of the states would be sorted out along branches of the tree according to the pioneer, or set of pioneers, from which they take their principal cues. States like New York, Massachusetts, California, and Michigan should be seen as regional pace setters, each of which has a group of followers, usually within their own region of the country, that tend to adopt programs only after the pioneers have led the way. For example, Colorado, which ranks ninth in Table 1, might be seen as the regional leader of the Rocky Mountain states. The rest of the states in that region are found much further down the list: Utah is twenty-second, Idaho is thirty-third, Arizona is thirty-sixth, Montana is thirty-eighth, New Mexico is forty-first, Wyoming is forty-sixth, and Nevada is forty-seventh. All of these states, with the possible exception of Utah which may share in the leadership of the region, might be seen as Colorado's followers who usually pick up new ideas only after the regional pioneer has put them into practice.

If we are right about the general patterns of competition and emulation, we should discover in our data some evidence of the existence of regional clusters among the states. In an effort to find such groupings, a varimax factor analysis was performed, using a matrix of pair-wise comparisons of all state innovation scores on all eighty-eight issues. If states in the same region are adopting programs in a similar order or pattern over time, a factor analysis should uncover several underlying dimensions in the matrix along which all states would be ordered according to their responses to the programs upon which the innovation score is based. The results of the factor analysis are presented in Table 5.

As we can see, the regional groupings we expected to find do exist, although the patterns are not as neat and clear as we might have hoped. To produce each factor I recorded all loadings which were over .400. The five factors which result bring the states into generally recognizable, contiguous groupings. The states with the largest loadings in each region are not necessarily those with the highest innovation scores. Instead, they are states like Connecticut, Florida, or New Mexico whose innovation scores are closer to the average for their regions. The presence of Nebraska, Iowa and South Dakota on Factor 1, which otherwise identifies Southern states, may indicate that more than one regional cluster is being identified on that factor.

There are several ambiguities in the data. For example, New York, Pennsylvania, West Virginia, Arkansas, and Illinois are loading on more than one factor. The easiest explanation of this may be that the states actually have connections with more than one region. This is especially true of New York, the state with the highest innovation score, which displays fairly strong connections in this analysis with the New England. Mid-Atlantic, and Great Lakes states. I believe that this finding reflects the fact that New York actually serves as a model for states in all three areas. Certainly New York is formally involved in interstate compacts with all three regions, and, if nothing else, enjoys a perfect geographical position from which to carry on relations over such a large area. If the findings concerning New York seem explainable, those concerning California do not. I cannot explain why California loads on Factor V, especially since many of its neighbors load on Factor III. These ambiguous findings concerning New York and California might be merely a reflection of ambiguity in the data. Factor analysis will identify regional groupings in the data only if the regions respond to new programs as a unit, adopting some new ideas with haste and lagging behind on others. Since New York and California consistently lead the country in the adoption of new programs, they may not be members of the cohesive regional group or "league" of states, a fact which may prevent their neat categorization through factor analysis.

There is no accounting at all in this analysis for the behavior of three states: Arizona, Colorado, and Kansas. Both Colorado and Arizona load at the .300 level on Factor III, the one which includes most of the rest of the Rocky Mountain states. Colorado and Nevada both load strongly (.577 and .485 respectively) on a separate factor which was not reported since no other state scored higher than .300 on the factor and its contribution score was only 1.7. The same is true for Kansas which was the only state loading strongly (at .658) on a factor whose contribution score was only 1.9.

VII. SPECIALIZED COMMUNICATIONS AMONG THE STATES

Our analysis has provided evidence that a continuum exists along which states are distributed from those which are usually quick to accept innovations to those which are typically reluctant to do so; we also know something about the correlates of innovation and have evidence of regional groupings among the states; but it is not always easy to identify a regional pioneer or to know exactly which states make up each

TABLE 5—(*Continued*)

Factor Loading	State
	FACTOR I (South)
.756	Florida
.711	Tennessee
.663	Alabama
.661	Virginia
.656	Georgia
.630	Mississippi
.621	Delaware
.600	North Carolina
.590	South Carolina
.576	Arkansas
.543	Texas
.517	Nebraska
.464	West Virginia
.460	Louisiana
.459	Iowa
.454	South Dakota
.433	Nevada

7.8   Total Factor Contribution

Factor Loading	State
	FACTOR II (New England)
.795	Connecticut
.766	Massachusetts
.758	New Hampshire
.659	Rhode Island
.536	New York
.512	Vermont
.434	Maine
.404	Pennsylvania

4.1   Total Factor Contribution

Factor Loading	State
	FACTOR III (Mountains and Northwest)
.791	New Mexico
.719	Idaho
.702	Montana
.694	Utah
.638	Washington
.620	North Dakota
.610	Wyoming
.569	Oklahoma
.516	Louisiana
.503	South Dakota
.432	Oregon
.419	Maryland
.410	Arkansas
.407	West Virginia

6.7   Total Factor Contribution

Factor Loading	State
	FACTOR IV (Mid-Atlantic and Great Lakes)
.795	New Jersey
.637	Wisconsin
.605	New York
.577	Minnesota
.536	Illinois
.516	Pennsylvania
.451	Indiana

4.0   Total Factor Contribution

Factor Loading	State
	FACTOR V (Border, Great Lakes and California)
.698	California
.610	Missouri
.584	Kentucky
.577	Michigan
.548	Ohio
.515	Nebraska
.458	Illinois

4.1   Total Factor Contribution

"league" or sub-system of cue-taking and information exchange. Some states seem to have connections with more than one region and may regularly receive cues from states in both groupings. As the American political system has developed, an increasing number of specialized communication systems have been created which cut across traditional regional lines and bring officials from many different regions into contact with each other and with federal and local officials, journalists, academic experts, and administrative consultants.

Several organizations now exist, such as the Council of State Governments, the Federal Commission on Intergovernmental Relations, and the recently established Citizen's Conference on State Legislatures, whose primary function is to improve communications among the states. Most important of these specialized communications networks are the professional associations of state officials, such as the National Association of State Budget Officers, or the National Association of State Conservation Officers. Associations of this kind were first created late in the nineteenth century and more seem to be forming each year. There were only five formed prior to 1900, but by 1930 there were approximately thirty-one, and by 1966 there were at least eighty-six in existence.[56]

[56] Unpublished memo from the Council of State Governments, Chicago, Illinois.

These groups serve two general purposes: first, they are sources of information and policy cues. By organizing conferences or publishing newsletters they bring together officials from all over the country and facilitate the exchange of ideas and knowledge among them, thus increasing the officials' awareness of the latest developments in their field. Secondly, these associations serve as "occupational contact networks" which expedite the interstate movement or transfer of personnel. Through the efforts of these groups officials become aware of desirable job openings in other states and are able to create professional reputations that extend beyond the borders of their own states.[57]

By rapidly spreading knowledge of new programs among state officials and by facilitating the movement of individuals to jobs in other states, professional associations encourage the development of national standards for the proper administration and control of the services of state government. Just as in other sectors of American life such as the business, the military and the academic world, as individuals increase their mobility, their role perceptions are likely to change; they are likely to adopt a more cosmopolitan perspective and to cultivate their reputations within a national professional community rather than merely within their own state or agency.[58]

Since general awareness of new developments is achieved much more quickly now than ever before, we would expect that the time which elapses from the first adoption of an innovation by a pioneering state to its complete diffusion throughout all the states would be greatly reduced. Certainly, several recent innovations, such as educational television or state councils on the performing arts, have diffused rapidly. In Table 6 we have measured the average speed of diffusion in years for three periods of time: 1870–1899, 1900–1929, and 1930–1966. The results shown in the first column of this table make it very plain that the speed of diffusion has been constantly increasing as time has

TABLE 6. AVERAGE ELAPSED TIME OF DIFFUSION IN YEARS FOR INNOVATIONS IN THREE TIME PERIODS

Time Periods	For All Adoptions	First Twenty Adoptions
1870–1899:	52.3	22.9
1900–1929:	39.6	20.0
1930–1966:	25.6	18.4

passed. This measurement, however, is somewhat misleading. The second column of the table indicates the average number of years it took the first twenty states to adopt the programs in each time period. The same trend toward increased speed of diffusion is evident here, but the differences among the three time periods are much smaller.[59] This evidence suggests that the pioneering states, those with high innovation scores, adopted new programs about as quickly in the early part of this century, prior to the development of many specialized communication links, as they did in the 1960's. The total elapsed time of diffusion, however, has decreased primarily because the laggard states, those with low innovation scores, are now reacting more quickly to pick up new programs adopted by the pioneers. This development results partly from the efforts of the federal government to stimulate state action through grants-in-aid, and partly from the increasing professional development in state government. Both these tendencies seem to have had a larger impact on the behavior of the more parochial states than the more cosmopolitan, pioneering states.

VIII. THE PERSISTENCE OF REGIONALISM

Improved communications and greatly increased contacts of all kinds among state officials seem to be accelerating the process of diffusion, but this does not necessarily mean that the regional clusters or "leagues" of states

[57] For a discussion of the role of professional organizations in determining career lines see: Fred E. Katz, "Occupational Contact Networks," *Social Forces* (1958), 52–58. Also see: Jack Ladinsky, "Occupational Determinants of Geographic Mobility Among Professional Workers," *American Sociological Review* (1967), 253–264.

[58] Merton, *op. cit.* Also see: Alvin W. Gouldner, "Cosmopolitans and Locals: Toward an Analysis of Latent Social Roles," *Administrative Science Quarterly* (1957), 281–306; and Harold L. Wilensky, *Intellectuals in Labor Unions* (Glencoe, 1956).

[59] A small portion of the difference between the two columns in Table 6 is an artifact of measurement. Since not all the programs in this analysis have been adopted by all forty-eight states, laggard states sometimes remain. As time passes and programs receive widespread acceptance these laggard states slowly fall into line and adopt the programs. Since the programs in the first two time periods have been around longer, they have more likely completed their spread among the states and thus, given our scoring procedure, are also more likely to have a longer period of diffusion.

to which we have referred have been destroyed.[60] In order to investigate this question the innovation scores in the time periods from 1870 to 1929 were combined, and two matrices of innovation scores of almost equal size were created, one for 1870-1929 and the other for 1930-1966.[61] Within each of these matrices each state's set of innovation scores (issue by issue) was correlated with the set of innovation scores for each other state. A varimax factor analysis was performed on each matrix, just as was done earlier to produce Table 5.

The results of this analysis are presented in Table 7. The factors derived from 1870-1929 are presented in the left column of the table and those from 1930-1966 are presented in the right column. The factors from each time period are arranged with the highest loadings first and the rest following in descending order. As we can see, the factors from the two time periods are not completely comparable. Some states change their relative rankings on the two factors, and some appear on a factor during only one of the time periods. The state of Georgia, for example, is found at the bottom of Factor 1 during 1870-1929 and moves all the way to the top of the same factor during 1930-1966. Some regional groupings, such as New England, seem to be disintegrating, while others, such as the Middle Atlantic states, seem to be more clearly defined in the later period. The factors for the later period include more states, on the average, and have slightly higher contribution scores, but they are not quite as distinct as those in the early period and include more inappropriate loadings. These data do not contain evidence of any large scale erosion of regionalism in the United States, but a drift away from clearly defined clusters of states is apparent.

During the last thirty years many new professional associations have been formed and

more inter-state and federal agencies have begun facilitating communications and encouraging national uniformity. The diffusion process is operating much faster today than ever before, especially among those states which have traditionally lagged behind in adopting new ideas. The older, established modes of communication and evaluation, based on traditional ties of region and common culture, are persisting, but there are indications in these data that the system is slowly changing. Decision makers in the states seem to be adopting a broader, national focus based on new lines of communication which extend beyond regional boundaries.

IX. CONCLUSIONS

This essay began as an effort to explain why some states adopt innovations more rapidly than others, but in order to explain this aspect of American federalism, we have had to make a more extensive investigation of the complex system of social choice by which we are governed. The approach to policy making which has emerged from our investigation is founded on the perceptions and attitudes of individual state decision makers. Of course, as I have already mentioned, the theory cannot be fully elaborated or put to a test until data can be gathered directly from legislators, bureaucrats, governors, and other officials in several states, on a comparative basis. Enough evidence has been presented already, however, to make apparent the major theoretical and practical implications of this approach.

The theory presented here directs our attention to the rules for decision employed by policy makers, rather than their formal group affiliations or their relative power or authority, and thus enables us to offer useful explanations of all policy decisions, not merely those which generate controversy. Emphasis is placed on those factors which lead to the establishment of parameters or guidelines for decision, not on the groups or interests supporting one policy over another. In Figure 1 the outlines of the diffusion process are depicted as it operates in a single state. There are undoubtedly many other influences on the level of agitation for change than the ones presented here, and many other secondary effects stemming from the enactment of new programs; this simple diagram is only meant to summarize the fundamental process operating in most cases of diffusion. Relationships are characterized by plus and minus signs but no effort has been made to estimate their relative importance in the system.

The process we have been describing is extremely complex; many influences shape deci-

---

[60] The best recent analysis of long-term changes in the American political system is: Donald Stokes, "Parties and the Nationalization of Electoral Forces," in William N. Chambers and William D. Burnham (eds.), *The American Party Systems: Stages of Political Development* (New York, 1967), pp. 182-202. Also see: Norval D. Glenn and J. L. Simmons, "Are Regional Cultural Differences Diminishing?" *Public Opinion Quarterly* (1967), 196-205; and Ira Sharkansky, "Economic Development, Regionalism and State Political Systems," *Midwest Journal of Political Science* (1968), 41-61.

[61] When the data are combined in this manner the 1870-1929 matrix contains 42 issues and the 1930-1966 matrix contains 46 issues.

FACTOR I (South)

1870–1929		1930–1966	
Factor Loading	State	Factor Loading	State
.762	Tennessee	.793	Georgia
.748	Mississippi	.759	Virginia
.745	Florida	.649	Delaware
.705	North Carolina	.629	Tennessee
.662	West Virginia	.623	Florida
.646	Kentucky	.593	Texas
.521	Louisiana	.570	North Carolina
*.499	Arizona	*.541	Utah
.465	Delaware	.524	Alabama
.426	Virginia	.494	Maryland
.425	South Carolina	*.493	Nebraska
*.424	Iowa	.493	South Carolina
.404	Georgia	*.451	Arizona
		*.432	Montana
5.7	Total Factor Contribution	*.426	Kansas
		*.415	Iowa
		*.415	Maine
		.413	Louisiana
		*.410	New Hampshire
		7.1	Total Factor Contribution

FACTORS II AND III (New England—Mid-Atlantic—Great Lakes)

.851	Connecticut	.800	Connecticut
.814	New Hampshire	.702	Massachusetts
.707	Vermont	.629	New Hampshire
.705	Massachusetts	*.564	Colorado
.670	Rhode Island	*.498	Oregon
.576	Maine	.467	Rhode Island
.509	Delaware		
.487	New York	1.7	Total Factor Contribution
.467	Pennsylvania		
.467	Virginia		
.405	Maryland		
*.405	Alabama		
5.3	Total Factor Contribution		
.808	Kansas	.778	New York
.694	Indiana	.686	Pennsylvania
.643	Wisconsin	.684	New Jersey
.622	Illinois	.666	Wisconsin
.601	Minnesota	.537	Illinois
*.448	Texas	.491	Michigan
		.486	Indiana
4.5	Total Factor Contribution	.474	Minnesota
		.448	Maryland
		4.8	Total Factor Contribution

FACTOR IV (Plains and Mountains)

.769	North Dakota	.710	North Dakota
.762	New Mexico	.683	New Mexico
.722	Montana	.682	Kansas
.709	Utah	.641	Wyoming

* States which are loading on inappropriate factors are marked with an asterisk.

TABLE 7—(Continued)

FACTOR I (South)

1870–1929		1930–1966	
Factor Loading	State	Factor Loading	State
.665	Idaho	.633	Oklahoma
.639	Washington	.598	Washington
.567	South Dakota	.572	Oregon
*.494	Maine	.557	Utah
		*.494	Alabama
4.7	Total Factor Contribution	.462	Idaho
		*.457	Vermont
		.439	West Virginia
.751	Arizona	*.416	Wisconsin
.588	Nevada	.410	Montana
.578	Wyoming	*.406	Mississippi
*.469	Arkansas		
		6.5	Total Factor Contribution
2.5	Total Factor Contribution		
.730	Oregon		
.611	California		
.645	Colorado		
*.433	Maryland		
2.9	Total Factor Contribution		

FACTOR V (Mid-America)

.885	Missouri	.726	Missouri
.767	Nebraska	.614	Mississippi
*.639	Michigan	*.600	South Carolina
.419	Ohio	.589	Idaho
*.400	California	.573	Arkansas
		.530	Tennessee
3.4	Total Factor Contribution	.432	Illinois
		.426	West Virginia
		*.409	South Dakota
		*.409	Montana
		4.5	Total Factor Contribution

sions to adopt innovations and no two ideas diffuse in exactly the same way. In all cases, however, the likelihood of a state adopting a new program is higher if other states have already adopted the idea. The likelihood becomes higher still if the innovation has been adopted by a state viewed by key decision makers as a point of legitimate comparison. Decison makers are likely to adopt new programs, therefore, when they become convinced that their state is relatively deprived, or that some need exists to which other states in their "league" have already responded.

Before states may respond to new programs adopted in other states their political leaders must be aware of these developments, so interstate communications are an important factor in the process of diffusion. We have mentioned that many specialized systems of communication among the states have grown up during the last thirty years, mainly through the creation of

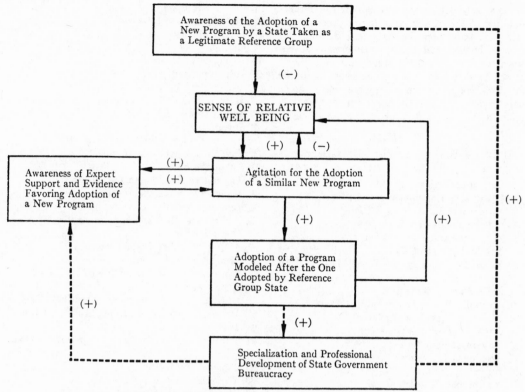

FIGURE 1. Factors Affecting the Adoption of Innovations.*

* Secondary effects depicted by broken lines.

professional associations among state administrators. These new information networks are spreading into all the states, but even today the isolation of some state capitols from the major cosmopolitan centers of the country is a major obstacle to the adoption of new ideas.[62]

Emerging from this study is the picture of a national system of emulation and competition. The states are grouped into regions based on both geographical contiguity and their place in the specialized set of communication channels through which flow new ideas, information and policy cues. Through this nationwide system of communications a set of norms or national standards for proper administration are established. This system links together the centers of re-

search and generation of new ideas, national associations of professional administrators, interest groups, and voluntary associations of all kinds into an increasingly complex network which connects the pioneering states with the more parochial ones. Because of the limitations of the data presently available to us we can only outline each regional grouping of states, and we cannot yet construct an elaborate theory of the interactions among professional associations, federal officials, private interest groups, and political leaders in setting the agenda of politics within a state. Normative questions arise, which cannot be considered here, concerning the responsiveness of this system and the degree to which it is subject to the control of democratic, representative institutions.[63] Much more investigation will

[62] See Alan L. Clem's description of the isolation of Pierre, the capitol of South Dakota, in his: *Prairie State Politics: Popular Democracy in South Dakota* (Washington, 1967), p. 137; and Norton E. Long's emphasis on the importance of information sources in his: "After the Voting is Over," *Midwest Journal of Political Science* (1962), 183–200. For a general review of communications theory and its application to politics see: Richard R. Fagen, *Politics and Communication* (Boston, 1966), especially pp. 34–69, 88–106. Also see: Karl

W. Deutsch, *The Nerves of Government*, Second Edition, (New York, 1966), especially pp. 145–256.

[63] Questions of this kind have been raised already in: Daniel P. Moynihan, "The Professionalization of Reform," *The Public Interest* (1965), 6–16; Theodore J. Lowi, "The Public Philosophy: Interest Group Liberalism," this REVIEW (1967), 5–24; and Philip Green, "Science, Government, and the Case of RAND: A Singular Pluralism," *World Politics* (1968), 301–326.

be necessary before we can gain a full understanding of this system and its function as a device for controlling the pace and direction of policy development in the American states. Once we know more, it might be possible to prescribe with confidence some changes in the decision-making system, or the creation of some new governmental institutions, which might accelerate or redirect the process of innovation.

APPENDIX

NOTE: Following are the eighty-eight programs upon which the innovation score is based.

1. Accountants Licensing
2. Advertising Commissions
3. Agricultural Experiment Stations
4. Aid for Roads and Highways
5. Aid to the Blind (Social Security)
6. Aid to Dependent Children (Social Security)
7. Aid to Permanently and Totally Disabled (Social Security)
8. Air Pollution Control
9. Alcoholic Beverage Control
10. Alcoholic Treatment Agencies
11. Anti-Age Discrimination
12. Anti-Injunction Laws
13. Architects Licensing
14. Australian Ballot
15. Automobile Registration
16. Automobile Safety Compact
17. Beauticians Licensing
18. Board of Health
19. Budgeting Standards
20. Child Labor Standards
21. Chiropractors Licensing
22. Cigaret Tax
23. Committee on the Aged
24. Compulsory School Attendance
25. Conservation of Oil and Gas
26. Controlled Access Highways
27. Council on the Arts
28. Court Administrators
29. Debt Limitations
30. Dentists Licensing
31. Direct Primary
32. Education Agencies
33. Education Television
34. Engineers Licensing
35. Equal Pay for Females
36. Fair Housing—Private
37. Fair Housing—Public Housing
38. Fair Housing—Urban Renewal Areas
39. Fair Trade Laws
40. Fish Agency
41. Forest Agency
42. Gasoline Tax
43. Geological Survey
44. Highway Agency
45. Home Rule—Cities
46. Human Relations Commissions
47. Initiative and Referendum
48. Integrated Bar
49. Junior College—Enabling Legislation
50. Juveniles Supervision Compact
51. Labor Agencies
52. Legislative Pre-Planning Agencies
53. Legislative Research Agencies
54. Library Extension System
55. Mental Health Standards Committee
56. Merit System
57. Migratory Labor Committee
58. Minimum Wage Law
59. Normal Schools—Enabling Act
60. Nurses Licensing
61. Old Age Assistance (Social Security)
62. Parking Agencies—Enabling Act for Cities
63. Park System
64. Parolees and Probationers Supervision Company
65. Pharmacists Licensing
66. Planning Board—State Level
67. Development Agency
68. Police or Highway Patrol
69. Probation Law
70. Public Housing—Enabling Legislation
71. Real Estate Brokers—Licensing
72. Reciprocal Support Law
73. Retainers Agreement
74. Retirement System for State Employees
75. Right to Work Law
76. School for the Deaf
77. Seasonal Agricultural Labor Standards
78. Slaughter House Inspection
79. Soil Conservation Districts—Enabling Legislation
80. Superintendent of Public Instruction
81. Tax Commission
82. Teacher Certification—Elementary
83. Teacher Certification—Secondary
84. Urban Renewal—Enabling Legislation
85. Utility Regulation Commission
86. Welfare Agency
87. Workmens' Compensation
88. Zoning in Cities—Enabling Legislation

21 / Where We Stand

*Too much attention to epistemology induces
hallucinations of negativism.*
V. O. KEY, JR.

The topics and terms that make up an elementary understanding of the kinds of political data, the operations one may perform upon them, and the rationale for research have been presented in approximately their order of difficulty for the beginner. Now we undertake to fit them together into a more logical outline:

I. Empirical *theory* is a framework for the systematic formulation of what we know (or think we know) about political behavior.

II. A. The *data* of politics consist largely of observations of:

1. *Persons* and their characteristics, including the opinions and attitudes they express

2. *Institutions,* particularly governmental ones

3. Patterned actions or *processes*

4. The *situations* or circumstances in which persons interact with one another, including the environment of time and place

B. The principal sources of political data are:

1. Either complete *censuses* or sample *surveys* of:

a. Mass *publics*

b. Governing *elites* (such as courts or legislatures)

2. The recorded output of institutional *processes* (e.g., roll calls, elections, administrative records, court decisions)

3. Descriptions of governmental *institutions* (organization charts, by-laws, etc.)

4. Evaluations of policies, projects, and programs

III. A. Most of these data are susceptible to *measurement* and therefore may be treated as *variables.*

    B. Relevant *levels* of measurement are:

        1. Cardinal

          a. Ratio

          b. Interval

        2. Ordinal or rank

        3. Nominal (dichotomous or polytomous)

    C. A large number of cases distributed along a single variable may be reduced by summary *statistics* to single figures, which are more comprehensible, particularly for comparative analysis. Among these univariate statistics are:

        1. Proportions or *percentages*

        2. *Averages* (mean, median, and mode)

        3. Measures of dispersion of values about their mean, especially *standard deviation, variance,* and *coefficient of variation*

IV. Some behavioral variables involve attitudes or tendencies that may not be adequately measured by a single questionnaire item or observation. *Guttman* (cumulative) *scaling* provides an empirical method of establishing these underlying dimensions by combining a number of nominal items into an ordinal scale. The criterion of *reproducibility* indicates whether items with different cutting points fall on a single dimension, i.e., are *unidimensional.* The technique is used with questionnaire items, legislative and judicial records, and data on population aggregates or governmental units.

V. A. *Theory,* when expressed in terms of measurable variables, ordinarily postulates that there will be a particular *relationship* between two or more variables under certain circumstances.

    B. 1. *Inductive* reasoning begins with an observation and proceeds to a generalization—a statement of theoretical relationship between variables, sometimes called a *model*

        2. *Deductive* reasoning proceeds from existing theory to a *hypothesis*—a limited statement of an observed relationship which is derived from the more generalized model or abstract theory

C. Theory in the social sciences does not have the unity, precision, scope, or constancy of theory in the physical sciences, so that alternative bodies of propositions about relationships between variables may be widely accepted at the same period.

D. When anyone—student, professor, columnist, or politician—based upon an understanding of the governmental process, contends that certain actions are more probable than other actions in specified situations, that is a *theoretical deduction*. One who then makes observations to check the accuracy of this proposition is a researcher engaged in testing a hypothesis.

VI. A. *Hypothesis testing* breaks down generalizations into simple propositions which can be verified by empirical observation. The process consists of:

    1. Deducing from theory some statement of postulated relationships between *conceptual* variables

    2. *Operationalizing* the concepts by formulating definitions which:

        a. Are approximate equivalents of the concepts, and

        b. Will enable different observers to assign each datum to the same category with a minimum of disagreement

    3. Collecting the data

    4. Comparing the actual with the hypothetical distribution of the data to confirm or reject the hypothesis

    5. Concluding that the data support, disconfirm, or require revision of the theory from which the hypothesis was derived

B. The researcher's values suggest which hypotheses are worth testing, but beyond that point one tries to prevent them from influencing the research. Quantification and measurement make it easier to achieve this goal.

VII. Measures of *association* and *correlation* are summary statistics that compactly express the degree of relationship between two variables. With some measures this is also the proportionate improvement in guessing the value of a case on the dependent variable if one knows its value on the independent variable, over guessing without this knowledge. Measures treated were:

A. Nominal level:

    1. D (percentage difference), Somers' d_{yx} (its equivalent), Yule's Q and the *phi* coefficient, all used with dichotomies

    2. Cramér's V, used with polytomies

B. Ordinal level:

    1. *Gamma,* d_{yx}, *tau*-b, and *tau*-c, used with grouped data

    2. R_s (Spearman's rank difference coefficient), used with individual data

C. Interval or higher level:

    1. Regression

    2. The Pearsonian coefficient of correlation *r*

VIII. A. *Tests of significance* tell whether samples are sufficiently large to be representative of the universe from which they were drawn. There are dozens of them, of which only three were treated here:

    1. The Table of Significant Differences for percentage comparisons

    2. *Chi square* for nominal or ordinal tables of any size

    3. Student's *t* for comparing means

B. A test of significance indicates the probability that a relationship could have occurred due to chance alone. In general, this is more likely if the sample is small. We seek to reject the *null hypothesis* that a discovered difference between percentages is so small that, given the sample size, it could easily be attributed to chance.

C. The minimum level of confidence normally required in social science research is that the relationship found could not have been caused by chance more often than one time in 20 ($p < .05$).

D. Significance tests assume a *universe* or *population* of persons or events, which is *randomly* sampled. In surveying human populations that are widely dispersed, such as electorates, only an approximation of randomness is possible.

E. A large number of cases leads to a higher confidence in the conclusions. But the availability of large samples does not always correspond with the importance of a finding. There are occasions when statistical significance at $p = .05$ is too rigorous a standard, and others when it is not rigorous enough.

F. When dealing with aggregates rather than samples, significance tests may be thought of as measuring *stability,* which is greater with large numbers.

IX. *Multivariate* techniques explain the relationships among three or more variables.

A. At the nominal level one selects a *control* variable and makes a separate table for each value on this variable, thus *holding constant* its effect. Each of these *partial* tables indicates a relationship between the independent and dependent variables.

B. Comparing the partial tables with the original table may produce these possible results:

    1. I ———→ D   in which the control variable does not alter the original values appreciably, and is thus ruled out as a cause of the apparent relationship.
         C

2. I → (C) →D   in which the control variable substantially alters the size and/or direction of the relation so that the partial tables diverge from one another. Thus one cannot express the relation of *I* to *D* without *specification* of their relation to *C*.

3a. in which an apparent relation between *I* and *D* (nearly) disappears in *both* partials. *C* is prior in time to both, so the relation is "spurious."

3b. which appears the same as 3a. in the disappearance of the relation in both tables. But because of time order *C* cannot be considered causal of both *I* and *D*. (3a. and 3b. differ from 2. in that the association in both partials diminishes, whereas in 2. one partial increases.)

C. At the interval level there are a number of multivariate techniques:

1. Just as bivariate regression enables one to predict the value of *Y* from *X*, so *multiple regression* permits one to predict the value of a dependent variable from the composite effects of any number of independent variables, $X_1, X_2 \ldots X_n$.

2. As simple correlation expresses the amount of relationship between two variables, the coefficient of *multiple correlation R* summarizes the total relationship between a number of independent variables and one dependent variable.

3. The *coefficients of determination, r^2 and R^2*, rather than the correlation coefficients themselves, measure the amount of variability explained.

4. *Partial* correlation, $r_{id.c}$, expresses the relation of the independent variable to the dependent variable when the control variable is held constant.

5. *Beta* weights permit one to determine which independent variables have the greatest impact.

D. Ideally, one should control on every possible variable before considering a hypothesis confirmed. But some control variables cannot be operationalized, and controlling on others does not occur to the researcher due to gaps in the theory.

E. Correlation and regression are often used inductively with data aggregated by political subdivisions or annual series published by federal agencies. The significance test of confidence in a hypothesis is not as appropriate for this sort of exploratory data manipulation as with a hypothesis the researcher has deduced and operationalized. One must be more alert for spurious correlations and ecological fallacies, and conscious of the pitfalls in data which have been collected for purposes other than those of the researcher.

X. Research may take the form of:

A. Controlled experiments in the laboratory, where subjects (including humans) are divided into groups and exposed to different treatments, stimuli, or conditions. Their responses are carefully measured, using significance tests.

B. Social surveys in which a cross-section of the population is interviewed in person or by phone and the responses of each category are compared. Much larger samples are required, and significance tests are used if feasible.

C. Aggregate data analysis, using records usually collected for another purpose. The data often refer to populations, not samples. There are unresolved questions about the relevance of significance tests on population data.

D. Quasi-experiments in which aggregate data are subjected to a number of tests of validity in addition to statistical significance.

XI. The ultimate purpose of political and social analysis is improving the human condition, and this depends upon an understanding of *causation*. But an examination of research methodology reveals that, while we may improve our inferences about it and avoid certain fallacies, we can never finally *prove* causation.

Technological Developments and Research Methods

In the 1920s the pioneers Rice, Bogardus, and Merriam worked with pencil and paper, 3 × 5 cards, tally sheets, slide rules, and hand-cranked adding machines. In the 1930s and 1940s Lazarsfeld, Cantril, Newcomb, and Key were aided by the key-punch and counter-sorter in tabulating the data they recorded on punch cards. They ran their statistics on motor-driven desk calculators. The work of Almond, Lipset, Pool, and Campbell and his associates in the 1960s made use of electronic computers and magnetic tapes which compiled huge masses of data in accessible form. Foundation and government grants made it possible to collect ever larger bodies of survey data; at the same time governmental agencies at the national, state, and local levels were improving their record-keeping processes and generating steady flows of statistics that were useful to economists, sociologists, and political scientists. The Interuniversity Consortium for Political and Social Research circulates the raw data from major quantitative studies to universities and colleges for secondary analysis. These include the Center for Political Studies' presidential election surveys, which provide data covering the quarter century since 1952. Commercial poll data go back to the 1930s. Historians make use of this material in studying changes in the population over time.

The orientation of the researcher and his strategy of data processing have changed in the process. The pioneers sometimes relied on data of dubious quality, lacking the staff and facilities to gather better information. Testing hypotheses and computing measures of correlation or significance were tedious processes. One compelling incentive to scientific parsimony—to a spare and rigorous theoretical scheme with carefully specified hypotheses—was the cost in time and effort of collecting, tabulating, and analyzing data.

In favor of the more primitive techniques, it may be observed that they "kept us close to our data." As we watched the punch card that represented an interview we had conducted slide the length of the sorter and drop into a pocket, we got the sense that the opinions of some individuals were being quite literally sorted into one class or another. When we copied the raw numbers from the counting register and took them over to the desk to percentage them, we retained the feeling for the material. As we reached the end of each tedious calculation, we felt a tingle of excitement from knowing how our hypothesis had fared in the test.

Now the researcher simply specifies a list of variables to be cross-tabulated, and the computer does the rest. The tables, bivariate and multivariate, are spewed out, percentaged in both directions, with measures of association and tests of significance already calculated. Only when one undertakes an original study and sets up the data specifications is it necessary to think in terms of hypothesis testing.

Behavioralism

The approach to politics described here—the use of quantitative measurement of variables—was one aspect of a broader movement called "behavioralism." David Easton has culled and synthesized a number of statements indicating what distinguishes the behavioral approach to politics from other approaches:

1. Regularities: There are discoverable uniformities in political behavior. These can be expressed in generalizations or theories with explanatory and predictive value.
2. Verification: The validity of such generalizations must be testable, in principle, by reference to relevant behavior.
3. Techniques: Means for acquiring and interpreting data cannot be taken for granted. They are problematic and need to be examined self-consciously, refined and validated so that rigorous means can be found for observing, recording, and analyzing behavior.
4. Quantification: Precision in the recording of data and the statement of findings requires measurement and quantification, not for their own sake, but only where possible, relevant, and meaningful in the light of other objectives.
5. Values: Ethical evaluation and empirical explanation involve two different kinds of propositions that, for the sake of clarity, should be kept analytically distinct. However, a

student of political behavior is not prohibited from asserting propositions of either kind separately or in combination as long as he does not mistake one for the other.

6. Systematization: Research ought to be systematic; that is to say, theory and research are to be seen as closely intertwined parts of a coherent and orderly body of knowledge. Research untutored by theory may prove trivial, and theory unsupported by data, futile.

7. Pure science: The application of knowledge is as much a part of the scientific enterprise as theoretical understanding, but the understanding and explanation of political behavior logically precede and provide the basis for efforts to utilize political knowledge in the solution of urgent practical problems of society.

8. Integration: Because the social sciences deal with the whole human situation, political research can ignore the findings of other disciplines only at the peril of weakening the validity and undermining the generality of its own results. Recognition of this interrelationship will help bring political science back to its status of earlier centuries and return it to the main fold of the social sciences.[1]

Politics, Government, and Research

The appropriate relationship between behavioral research and policy-making is easy to state. Research will not reveal what ought to be done, but, given a goal determined by the values of the policy-maker or the people he or she represents, then research should indicate the factors (inputs or independent variables) to be worked upon in order to achieve the ends (altered outputs or dependent variables) desired, and to do it with the minimum of undesired alteration of other variables (costs or "side effects").

Some research is well done, and some poorly, but social research appears to be indispensable to the operation of a complex society. Candidates for office find survey research on voter reactions worth its high cost; congressmen use (and sometimes misuse) surveys to understand constituencies embracing 400,000 persons; the Federal Reserve Board plumbs buying and saving intentions; the Department of Agriculture studies the organization of the farm economy; agencies attacking the problems of employment, poverty, and mental health rely heavily on social scientists; the armed forces have examined the dynamics of leadership in military organizations; the State Department evaluates domestic and foreign attitude surveys; educators study the relation of student to teacher and school to community; political scientists seek to understand the correlates of distrust, alienation, violence, and terror—all for purposes you might or might not approve. It is

[1]David Easton, "The Current Meaning of 'Behavioralism'," in *Contemporary Political Analysis,* James C. Charlesworth, ed. (New York: The Free Press, 1967), pp. 16−17.

clear that social and political research can provide answers to important questions dealing with the means to some given end. It is equally clear that other problems—for example, the human dynamics that lead to international conflict and imperil all living organisms on the globe—though researchable in principle are not yet well enough understood to make research results unmistakably relevant to policy decisions.

Governmental bodies have become increasingly dependent upon research in recent years. Social indicators describing crime, health, living costs, education, employment, and income are analyzed to assess the *need* for government action. Data from quasi-experiments and social surveys may be used to appraise the *feasibility* of proposed solutions. Evaluation research tests the *effectiveness* of ongoing programs to indicate whether they should be continued—and often reveals that they are not living up to the expectations of legislators who authorized them.

This applied research utilizes the techniques developed over the years by scholars, and it is appraised according to standards set by academic statisticians and methodologists. Basic and applied research depend upon essentially the same paradigm.

Envoi

The research model that has been presented here is the product of some of the best minds in our tradition: Aristotle, Bacon, Hume, Mill, Galton, Pearson, Lazarsfeld, Simon, and others. Yet like all learning and all science it remains a tentative and provisional explanation of what researchers do. You may have noted discrepancies between prescription and practice, and you should have many unanswered questions. Some of these will be resolved if you study methodology and statistics more deeply. Others remain for the next generation to attack, so that we will have a more realistic paradigm for explaining the logical processes by which we seek to understand political reality.

The limited objective of the measures, prescriptions, and exercises presented here is to give you a better comprehension of the journal literature of the social sciences and some primitive tools for conducting research into whatever aspect of human behavior interests you. Perhaps, being alerted to the problems of inference and evidence and the potential offered by the more sophisticated techniques which we have only touched upon, you may be inspired to seek the basic theory which will enable you to *know*, rather than merely to *know about*, statistical methods. Thus, when you some day face a policy decision, and someone offers "scientific" evidence supporting a particular course of action, you may avoid the pitfalls that have trapped others: the complacent schoolboy's acceptance of whatever the books say; the naive cynicism of the local "pol," who distrusts whatever is said in books; the finical pedantry of the statistical purist whose data cannot be trusted because they always fall short of assumptions; the incurable romanticism of the speculative theorist, who requires no evidence beyond intuition; and even the compulsive earnestness of the quantitative technician who accepts nothing that cannot be expressed in numbers and everything that can.

Appendix: Four Computer Programs in BASIC

These programs are useful with minicomputers with small storage capacity, especially when the same statistic is to be calculated several times with different inputs. There are slight differences in BASIC language and in sign-on and sign-off procedures, depending on the configuration of your institution's computer. You should learn about this from a staff member before you begin.

Chi Square and **Cramér's** *V*

Prepare your table of observed frequencies in advance. The computer will ask for the number of rows, then the number of columns, then the frequencies in each cell, going across the rows. After each number is entered, hit the Return key.

```
 1 LET A(J,L) = Ø
 2 LET N=Ø
 3 LET C= Ø
 4 FOR J = Ø TO 1Ø
 5 FOR L = Ø TO 1Ø
 6 A(J,L) = Ø
 7 NEXT L
 8 NEXT J
1Ø PRINT "NO. OF ROWS"
2Ø INPUT R
3Ø PRINT "NO. OF COLS"
```

```
 4Ø INPUT K
 5Ø FOR J = 1 TO R
 6Ø FOR L = 1 TO K
 7Ø PRINT "ROW"; J ; "COL" ; L ;
 8Ø INPUT A(J,L)
 82 LET N = N + A(J,L)
 83 LET A(J,K+1) = A(J,K+1) + A(J,L)
 85 LET A(R+1,L) = A(R+1,L) + A(J,L)
 87 LET A(R+1,K+1) = A(R+1,K+1) + A(J,L)
 9Ø NEXT L
1ØØ NEXT J
11Ø FOR J = 1 TO R
12Ø FOR L = 1 TO K
13Ø LET B = A(R+1,L)/A(R+1,K+1)*A(J,K+1)
14Ø LET C = C + (A(J,L)-B)**2/B
15Ø NEXT L
16Ø NEXT J
17Ø PRINT
175 PRINT "CHI SQUARE IS ";C
177 PRINT "D.F. IS ";(R-1)*(K-1)
18Ø IF R > GO TO 19Ø
185 LET K = R
19Ø PRINT
195 PRINT "CRAMER'S V IS "; SQR(C/(K-1)/N)
2ØØ END
```

Gamma d_{yx} and Tau-b or Tau-c

For this program you must prepare your table in advance, including adding up the totals for the row and column marginals and the number of cases (N). The column variable must be the independent variable (otherwise you'll want d_{xy} instead of d_{yx}—you can have either). When the program asks for N, R and C, type in the number of cases, a comma, number of rows, a comma, and the number of columns, then hit Return. Then enter the cell values by row, hitting Return after each number. When all have been entered, the program will ask for row and column marginals, entered the same way. It will decide from the shape of the table whether you want tau-b or tau-c.

```
 2 LET S1 = Ø
 3 LET P1 = Ø
 4 LET P2 = Ø
 5 PRINT "WHAT ARE N, R, AND C?"
 6 INPUT N, R, C
 8 FOR I = 1 TO R
 9 FOR J = 1 TO C
1Ø LET X(I,J) = Ø
11 NEXT J
12 NEXT I
13 PRINT "ENTER VALUES ONE AT A TIME BY ROWS"
14 FOR I = 1 TO R
15 FOR J = 1 TO C
```

```
16 INPUT X(I,J)
17 NEXT J
18 NEXT I
19 FOR L = 1 TO R-1
2Ø FOR K = 1 TO C - 1
21 FOR I = L+ 1 TO R
22 FOR J = K + 1 TO C
23 LET S1 = S1 + X(I,J)
24 NEXT J
25 NEXT I
28 LET S1 = S1 * X(L,K)
30 LET P1 = P1 + S1
32 LET S1 = Ø
33 NEXT K
34 NEXT L
36 FOR K = C TO 2 STEP -1
37 FOR L = 1 TO R - 1
38 FOR J = 1 TO K - 1
4Ø FOR I = L + 1 TO R
42 LET S1 = S1 + X(I,J)
44 NEXT I
45 NEXT J
48 LET S1 = S1 * X(L,K)
49 LET P2 = P2 + S1
5Ø LET S1 = Ø
51 NEXT L
52 NEXT K
53 PRINT "PS IS "; P1; "PD IS "; P2
54 PRINT "GAMMA IS " ; (P1 - P2)/(P1 + P2)
55 LET S2 = Ø
57 PRINT "ENTER ROW MARGINALS ONE AT A TIME"
6Ø FOR I = 1 TO R
62 INPUT M
64 LET S1 = S1 + ((M*(M-1))/2)
65 LET S3 = S3 + (M **2)
66 NEXT I
68 PRINT "DXY IS   ";   (P1-P2)/((N**2 - S3)/2)
7Ø LET S3 = Ø
79 PRINT "ENTER COL MARGINALS ONE AT A TIME"
8Ø FOR I = 1 TO C
81 INPUT M
82 LET S2 = S2 + ((M*(M-1))/2)
83 LET S3 = S3 + (M*M)
84 NEXT I
85 PRINT "DYX IS "; (P1 - P2)/((N**2 - S3)/2)
86 IF R <> C GOTO 91
87 PRINT "TAU-B IS";(P1-P2)/SQR(((N*(N-1)/2)-S1)*((N*(N-1)/2)-S2))
88 GOTO 95
91 IF R > C GOTO 94
92 PRINT "TAU-C IS"; (P1-P2)/(N*N/2*(R-1)/R)
93 GOTO 95
94 PRINT "TAU-C IS"; (P1-P2)/(N*N/2*(C-1)/C)
95 END
```

Bivariate Regression and Correlation

First enter the number of pairs. Then enter each pair of X and Y values on the same line, with a comma between, and Return. The program will print the a and b values, the coefficients of determination r^2 and correlation r. Then it will say "X is" in case you want to calculate the Y_c value for some value of X. When you are tired of this, type RUN to do another regression or BYE to get out of BASIC.

```
  7 S1 = 0
  8 S2 = 0
  9 S3 = 0
 10 S4 = 0
 11 S5 = 0
 12 A = 0
 13 B = 0
 14 R = 0
 15 R2 = 0
 18 PRINT "NUMBER OF POINTS"
 20 INPUT P
 25 PRINT "ENTER X AND Y VALUES IN PAIRS"
 30 FOR J = 1 TO P
 40 INPUT X, Y
 50 S1 = S1 + X
 60 S2 = S2 + Y
 70 S3 = S3 + X*Y
 80 S4 = S4 + X*X
 90 S5 = S5 + Y*Y
100 NEXT J
110 B = (S3 - S1 * S2/P)/(S4 - S1**2/P)
120 A = S2/P - B * S1 / P
130 R2 = (S3 - S1 * S2 / P)**2/(S4 - S1 ** 2/P)/(S5 - S2**2/P)
135 R = SGN(B) * SQR(R2)
137 PRINT "STANDARD DEVIATION = "; SQR ((S5 - (A*S2+B*S3))/P)
140 PRINT "A =  "; A; "B = " ;B; " R2 = ";R2; " R = ";R
141 PRINT "IF X IS "
142 INPUT X
143 PRINT " PREDICTED Y IS " ; A + B *  X
144 GO TO 141
150 END
```

Multiple and Partial Correlation and Regression with Three Variables

The variables are designated X_1, X_2, and X_3 to enable you to keep track of the partials. In this case the *first* variable, X_1, is the *dependent* variable. The program prints out r and r^2, the a value and two b values—but remember that b1 goes with X_2 and b2 with X_3. The standard error of estimate is for the multiple regression. Then it gives the simple (zero-order) correlation between each pair of variables, including the two independent variables. It then gives the partial correlation coefficients, with the number after the asterisk indicating which variable is being held constant.

```
 2 S1 = Ø
 3 S2 = Ø
 4 S3 = Ø
 5 S4 = Ø
 7 S5 = Ø
 8 S6 = Ø
 9 S7 = Ø
1Ø S8 = Ø
11 S9 = Ø
17 PRINT "NUMBER OF CASES"
18 INPUT N
25 PRINT "ENTER VALUES OF X1, X2, X3 (X1 IS DEPENDENT)"
27 FOR I = 1 TO N
29 INPUT Y, X1, X2
31 S4 = S4 + (X1*X1)
33 S5 = S5 + (X2*X2)
35 S6 = S6 + (Y*Y)
38 S7 = S7 + (X1*Y)
4Ø S8 = S8 + (X2*Y)
42 S9 = S9 + (X1*X2)
45 S1 = S1  + X1
48 S2 = S2 + X2
51 S3 = S3 + Y
52 NEXT I
54 S4 = S4 - ((S1/N)*S1)
57 S5 = S5 - ((S2/N)*S2)
6Ø S6 = S6 - ((S3/N)*S3)
62 S7 = S7 - ((S1/N)*S3)
65 S8 = S8 - ((S2/N)*S3)
67 S9 = S9 - ((S1/N)*S2)
7Ø B1 = ((S7*S5)-(S8*S9))/(S4*S5-(S9*S9))
75 B2 = (S7 - (B1*S4))/S9
8Ø A = (S3/N) - (B1 * (S1/N)) - (B2*(S2/N))
85 Q9 = (B1 * S7) + (B2 * S8)
95 E2 = (S6-Q9)/(N-3)
1Ø3 PRINT "R = "; SQR(Q9/S6); "R2"; Q9/S6
1Ø5 PRINT "A = " ; A ; "B1 = " ; B1 ; " B2 = " ; B2
115 PRINT "STANDARD  ERROR OF ESTIMATE = " ; SQR(E2)
118 C1 = S7/SQR(S4*S6)
119 C2 = S8/SQR(S5*S6)
12Ø C3 = S9/SQR(S4*S5)
126 PRINT "R(12) = ";C1;  "R(13) = " ;C2; "R(23) = " ;C3
136 PRINT "R(13.2) =" ; (C2-(C1*C3))/(SQR(1 - (C1*C1))*SQR(1-(C3*C3)))
138 PRINT "R(12.3) =" ; (C1-(C2*C3))/(SQR(1 - (C2*C2))*SQR(1-(C3*C3)))
14Ø PRINT "R(23.1) =" ; (C3-(C1*C2))/(SQR(1 - (C1*C1))*SQR(1-(C2*C2)))
```

Index of Statistics, Concepts, Symbols, and Variables